Biafra Revisited

Biafra Revisited

Herbert Ekwe-Ekwe

AR
African Renaissance

First published in Great Britain and Senegal in 2007 by
African Renaissance
B P 5336
Dakar
Sénégal

African Renaissance
P O Box 2630
Reading
Berkshire RG1 6XT
England

A catalogue record for this book is available from the British Library

ISBN 0-9552050-0-X
      978-0-9552050-0-2

© Herbert Ekwe-Ekwe 2007

All rights reserved. No reproduction, copy or transmission of this publication may be made without written permission from the author.

To
Okwuonicha Femi Nzegwu and Nnamdi Nzegwu Ekwe-Ekwe and Chidi Nzegwu Ekwe-Ekwe
ifu naanya na oga niiru

The conventional wisdom of the Tower of Babel story is that the collapse was a misfortune. That it was the distraction of the weight of many languages that precipitated the tower's failed architecture. That one monolithic language would have expedited the building, and heaven would have been reached. Whose heaven, she wonders? And what kind? Perhaps the achievement of Paradise was premature, a little hasty if no one could take the time to understand other languages, other views, other narratives. Had they, the heaven they imagined might have been found at their feet. Complicated, demanding, yes, but a view of heaven as life; not heaven as post-life.

Toni Morrison, *The Nobel Lecture in Literature*, 1993

Contents

1 Passages from the Igbo genocide to Darfur **1**

2 The antimonies of the Nigerian state: World War II to genocide **18**

3 Three phases of genocide **59**

4 In these times … **115**

Bibliography **143**
Index **151**

1
Passages from the Igbo genocide to Darfur

When is the heinous crime of genocide not genocide? Perhaps, when everyone of the targeted national, racial, religious, or regional population is *not yet* exterminated. Henceforth, genocide appears to be demonstrable only when it can be demonstrated that the population under attack has been totally destroyed ... So, to prove that genocide has occurred, there must be no survivors ...

In the case of the Sudan, according to the report of the February 2005 UN investigating commission on the character of the slaughter of the African population in the Darfur region by the Khartoum-based Arab regime and its Janjaweed militia allies,[1] such an outcome hasn't yet occurred – therefore, there is 'no genocide'; at least not yet. Instead, there have been what the commission categorises, quite curiously, as 'war crimes' and 'crimes against humanity' committed by the regime. For the UN, Khartoum has apparently not yet crossed that 'dreadful' threshold into the realm of completing its designated mission, its 'final solution', in Darfur. Until this happens, the Darfur report acknowledges that 70,000 Darfuri have been killed during the war waged on them by Khartoum while two million others have been forced into exile,[2] many of them in the neighbouring state of Chad. Equally contradictorily, or so it appears, the UN notes that the 'killing of civilians, torture, enforced disappearances, destruction of villages, rape and other forms of sexual violence, pillaging and enforced displacement'[3] are taking place in Darfur. So, even though these appalling crimes have been indisputably and systematically carried out against the Darfuri, *as a people*, by the Sudanese state and its allies, it is extraordinary that the UN does not think that these 'amount to genocide.'[4]

During the recent UN general assembly's commemoratory session on the 60th anniversary of the liberation of the Auschwitz death camp where millions

---

[1] United Nations, *UN News Service*, New York, 1 February 2005.
[2] Other estimates however put the number of Darfuri murdered so far by the Sudanese regime and its allies significantly much higher than the 70,000 UN figure – between 300,000 and 340,000 killed. See, for instance, *BBC*, http://news.bbc.co.uk/1/hi/world/africa/4268733.stm (accessed 26 September 2005).
[3] *UN News Service*, 1 February 2005.
[4] Ibid.

of Jews, Romany and others were annihilated by Germany's campaign of genocide, several commentators speculated whether the UN could have stopped this crime if the organisation had been in existence then. They didn't need to spend too much time speculating on what would have, at best, been reminiscing on the hypothetical. All that was required was to examine the UN record in confronting genocide in the post-1945 world and they would have concluded, without any equivocations, that the organisation's performance was glaringly pathetic and dismally disappointing. The current UN attempt to desperately cover up the genocide, *yes* genocide, in Darfur, would therefore be seen as consistent with this sordid history of inaction, rather than the bizarre exception that it might otherwise seem to be.

Foundation

In 1966, soon after the world commemorated the 21st anniversary of the liberation of Auschwitz and made the customary solemn declaration of 'Never, Never Again', Hausa-Fulani emirs, muslim clerics and intellectuals, military officers, politicians and other public figures in Nigeria defiled that season of reflection, commiseration and hope. They planned and executed the first phase of the Igbo genocide, the foundational genocide in post-conquest Africa.[5] This genocide became the clearing site for the haunting killing fields that would snake across the African geographical landscape in the subsequent 40 years. A total of 100,000 Igbo were massacred across northern Nigeria and elsewhere in the country, with the active support of the central government in Lagos headed by Colonel Yakubu Gowon during the months of May-October 1966. Most were killed in their houses, offices, businesses, schools, colleges and hospitals, as well as those who were attacked at railway stations and on trains, bus stations and buses, airports and in cars, lorries and on foot as they sought to escape the genocide for their homeland in east Nigeria. Thousands of others sustained horrific injuries, several of whom were maimed for life. No known safe passages for the Igbo (victims or would-be victims) for flight or escape to their homeland from north Nigeria or elsewhere in the country were planned by any of the prosecuting forces involved in the genocide throughout the course of this tragedy.

Just as their German counterparts, the perpetrators of the Igbo genocide would claim to be 'very cultured' people: for instance, they read the Koran, Ibn Battuta, Ibn Khaldun, Shakespeare, and other great world literature. Even though they had strenuously opposed the liberation of Nigeria from British occupation, which the Igbo had spearheaded and sustained since the 1940s, the Hausa-Fulani had been assured the supreme political role in post-conquest Ni-

---

[5]Herbert Ekwe-Ekwe, *Conflict and Intervention in Africa: Nigeria, Angola, Zaire* (Basingstoke and London: Macmillan, 1990), pp. 11-12.

geria, thanks to the British-inflected settlement of 'withdrawal' from the country worked out in the second half of the 1950s.[6] As a result, the main thrust of Hausa-Fulani politics always operated on the premise that the Igbo constituted the principal 'obstacle' to the perpetuation of Hausa-Fulani sociopolitical hegemony in Nigeria.[7] Hence, the plan and execution of the genocide.

There was an extensive coverage of the Igbo genocide in the international media throughout the course of its occurrence. The UN, under its then secretary-general, U Thant, never condemned this atrocity unequivocally. U Thant consistently maintained that it was a 'Nigerian internal affair,'[8] a cue seized upon with relish by the Organisation of African Unity, the African regional organisation affiliated to the UN, which continued to trumpet this shameful line throughout the slaughter.[9] No efforts were made by the UN to stop the killings or bring the perpetrators to justice. On the contrary, U Thant repeatedly thwarted several Igbo initiatives, as well as those of others, to table the subject of the carnage formally for discussion at the UN, especially its security council. U Thant's intention throughout this tragedy was to protect the interests of the Nigerian state,[10] even at a time when its leadership had come to power through a violent coup d'état. As for the welfare of the 2 million survivors of these initial massacres who fled to their Igbo homeland, neither the UN nor the Gowon junta played any supportive role in the massive rehabilitation programme that the Igbo themselves embarked upon to integrate the returnees in society between October 1966 and June 1967.

Apparently emboldened by the scant criticism from the UN (and indeed from most of the countries of the world) for its 1966 murderous escapades, the Nigerian state expanded the territorial range of its genocidal campaign on the Igbo by attacking Biafra, Igboland, in 1967. Essentially, this inaugurated the second phase of the genocide which would go on till January 1970. Three million Igbo or a quarter of the nation's total population were slaughtered during the period.[11]

---

[6]Herbert Ekwe-Ekwe, *African Literature in Defence of History: An Essay on Chinua Achebe* (Dakar: African Renaissance, 2001), pp. 126-132.
[7]Ibid., pp. 112-117.
[8]See, for instance, Hugh McCullum, 'Biafra was the beginning,' *AfricaFiles*, at http://www.africafiles.org/article.asp?ID=5549&ThisURL=./atissueforum.asp&URLName=AT+ISSUE+FORUM (accessed 3 December 2005) and Tobe Nnamani, 'Biafra in Retrospect: Still Counting the Losses (1),' *Kwenu*, at http://www.kwenu.com/publications/nnamani/biafra_retrospect1.htm (accessed 3 December 2005).
[9]Ekwe-Ekwe, *Conflict and Intervention in Africa*, pp. 51-58.
[10]McCullum, 'Biafra was the beginning,' and Nnamani, 'Biafra in Retrospect'.
[11]Ekwe-Ekwe, *African Literature in Defence of History*, especially ch. 4.

Not-'Area Boys'

The Nigerian campaign was unabashedly supported defiantly by leading and influential officials of the state including Obafemi Awolowo, the deputy chair of the federal cabinet and finance minister, who consistently declared openly that it was 'justifiable' to starve the Igbo to death as part of the Nigerian military strategy to overrun Biafra.[12] Most Biafran casualties, particularly children and older citizens, were indeed the people who starved to death as a result of the Nigerian strategy. The Awolowoist credo became the guiding principle of the third marine division of the Nigerian army, a notorious death squad that operated in south Biafra at the time, particularly after the Biafran resistance had virtually frozen the Nigerian advances along its north provinces. Most of the officers and men of the squad were recruited largely from the Yoruba in the west Nigeria, Awolowo's homeland. These include General Olusegun Obasanjo, the current Nigerian head of state, who was one of the commanders of the unit and who, in a January 2006 astonishing public statement at Amichi (north Igboland), acknowledged what many students of the Igbo genocide have always suspected – namely, that Nigeria still has a policy to exterminate the Igbo, well beyond the 12 January 1970 so-called *formal* termination of the genocide.[13]

Just as their Hausa-Fulani counterparts, and the Germans who had established the precedent from which these Nigerian state officials now operated most enthusiastically, Awolowo and his associates (civilian and military alike) would have regarded themselves as 'very cultured' – they surely read the Bible, as well as Shakespeare, Milton, Burke, Paine, Hobbes, Rousseau, Achebe, Okigbo, etc., etc. They listened to Dairo, Beethoven, Olaiya, Handel, Benson, Mozart, Bach, Okonta, Ellington, Onyia, Lawson, Ukwu, Osadebe, Mensah, Armstrong, Basie ... Just as in Germany, the Nigerian planners of genocide demonstrated clearly that genocidist 'theorists' and colonels and generals were often calm, well-educated, cold-blooded practitioners, who were more likely to be dressed in *agbada*, *babariga*, 2-piece suits, *aso oke* or lace, rather than raggedly-attired, barely-educated 'miscreants'. They were neither *alimajiri* nor the dishevelled so-called 'area boys' or street boys that abound in Lagos, Ibadan and several other Nigerian towns and cities.

The UN never challenged Awolowo and his collaborators of 'theorists' and field commanders for proselytising the crime of genocide so brazenly. Similar to its callous indifference during the first phase of the Igbo genocide, the UN did not condemn nor intervene to stop the massacres that went on in Biafra for

---

[12]Ibid., p. 118.
[13]*ThisDay* (Lagos), 12 January 2006.

30 months.[14] Furthermore, key countries that belonged to the world organisation including Britain, Nigeria's principal arms supplier, the then Soviet Union, which equipped the Nigerian air force, and the states of the Arab and muslim World (particularly Egypt, Algeria, Syria, Saudi Arabia, Guinea, the Sudan and Chad), actively supported Nigeria, ploughing it with the assorted weapons, troops and finance that it sought to accomplish its goal.[15] British and Soviet experts were on the ground to advise the Nigerians on the use of weapon-systems that their countries had made available for the mission, and Egyptian pilots (reeling from their defeat by Israel in the recently concluded Six-Day War) flew Nigerian combat aircraft and were involved in the savage bombing and straffing of Biafran cities and villages – targeting refugee centres, hospitals, schools, churches, markets, farms, trains, buses, cars, lorries, and communication infrastructure indiscriminately.

Genocide-State

The UN's inability to stop the Igbo genocide was the clearest example to date that the world had learnt little from the Jewish genocide and others of the 1940s. The apparent triumph of genocidist state officials in Nigeria was made possible with the heavyweight support from especially Britain and some of the other major international powers of the day such as the Soviet Union. There was no censure whatsoever from the UN. This made nonsense of the lofty declarations on the *crime of genocide* which the UN itself had enunciated soon after it came into being, following the Jewish genocide. The British government, despite continuously nationwide popular opposition, supported the genocide against the Igbo. Such was the intensity of the British support that even as the slaughtering worsened, Prime Minister Harold Wilson was certainly unperturbed when he informed C. Clyde Ferguson (the US state department special coordinator for relief to Biafra) that he, Wilson, 'would accept a half million dead Biafrans if that was what it took'[16] Nigeria to destroy the Igbo resistance to the genocide. A senior British foreign office official, who echoed Wilson's disposition to the slaughter, was no less chilling in his own characterisation of Britain's strategic goal. Describing the British response to the concerted international humanitarian efforts then to dispatch urgently-needed relief material to the Igbo aimed at breaking the Nigerian comprehensive blockade of Biafra, a crucial plank of Lagos's 'starvation of the Igbo'-extermination strategy, this official noted that his government's position was designed to 'show conspicu-

---

[14]Cf. McCullum, 'Biafra was the beginning'.
[15]Ekwe-Ekwe, *Conflict and Intervention*, especially ch. 2.
[16]Roger Morris, *Uncertain Greatness: Henry Kissinger & American Foreign Policy* (London & New York: Quartet Books, 1977), p. 122.

ous zeal in relief while in fact letting the little buggers starve out.'[17] Pointedly, both views of these very senior British government officials were hardly at variance with those expressed, during the period, by Brigadier Benjamin Adekunle, one of the most notorious field commanders of the Nigerian mission, who insisted:

> I want to prevent even one I[g]bo having even one piece to eat before their capitulation. We shoot at everything that moves, and when our forces march into the centre of I[g]bo territory, we shoot at everything, even at things that do not move.[18]

---

[17]Ibid. For a related insight on British policy towards international relief support to Biafra, based on recently declassified British state papers, see Michael Leapman, 'While the Biafrans starved, the FO moaned about hacks,' *The Independent on Sunday* (London), 3 January 1999.

[18]*The Economist* (London), 24 August 1968 – cited in John Stremlau, *The International Politics of the Nigerian Civil War* (Princeton: Princeton University, 1977), p. 331. It is revealing to observe the similarities in the utter depravity of Adekunle's utterances in this August 1968 press briefing with those of two notorious German government officials involved in the genocide of Africans in southern Africa in the late 19th century/early 20th century. In 1891, Karl Peters, the head of the German occupation regime in east Africa, gave the following haunting description of some of the gruesome massacres his forces had recently carried out in the region: 'I shall show the Vagogo what the Germans are! Plunder the villages, throw fire into the houses, and smash everything that will not burn ... At about three, I marched further south toward the other villages ... [T]orches were thrown into the houses, and axes worked to destroy all that the fire did not achieve. So by half past four, twelve villages had been burned down ... My gun had become so hot from so much firing I could hardly hold it.' (Quoted in Sven Lindqvist, *'Exterminate All the Brutes'* [London: Granta Books, 1997], pp. 50-51.) In October 1904, Lother von Trotha, the general officer commanding the German military forces engaged in the genocide of the Herero people and others in Namibia issued this proclamation, which he unambiguously captioned an 'Extermination Order': 'The Herero people will have to leave the country. Otherwise I shall force them to do so by means of guns ... [E]very Herero, whether found armed or unarmed, with or without cattle, will be shot. I shall not accept any more women and children. I shall drive them back to their people - otherwise I shall order shots to be fired at them. These are my orders to the Herero people.' (Quoted in Horst Drechsler, *'Let Us Die Fighting': The Struggle of the Herero and Nama against German Imperialism, 1884-1915* [London: Zed, 1980], pp. 156-157.) The outcome of Trotha's campaign was cataclysmic. No sectors of the Herero population, nor indeed those of the other nations in the region such as the Nama and the Berg Damara escaped the resultant genocide as the following statistics from Germany's *own* 1911 census figures for the area show. In that year, there were 15,130 Herero, compared with a population figure of 80,000 in 1904, indicating that at least 80 per cent were destroyed in the holocaust. For the Nama, their population in 1911 was 9,781 people compared with 20,000 in 1904, recording a 51 per cent German annihilation score.

Britain supplied Nigeria with the array of weaponry it sought for its mission and the crucial technical advisers it required to help deploy and attend to the maintenance of the arsenal. Crucially, it must not be forgotten that *direct* British involvement in the genocide began, quite pertinaciously, right from the outset. As Olusegun Obasanjo, the current president of Nigeria and himself the commander of an infamous regiment in south Igboland during the second phase of the genocide unambiguously recalls, 'some British officials and university lecturers,' based in north Nigeria, 'actively encouraged if not assisted' in the execution of the 29 July 1966 military coup d'état[19] – a critical feature of the first phase of the genocide during the course of 1966. The principal motive for the British involvement, Obasanjo acknowledges, is that it is 'no secret that to the British the North was more amenable and less radical and refractory than the South'[20] on both the substantive subject of the 60 years of the British conquest and occupation of Nigeria (which had formally ended six years earlier) and on the future relations between the two countries in the evolving post-conquest epoch. The fact that the Igbo nation in the south of the country had spearheaded the termination of British rule in the country (starting from the 1940s) at a time the Hausa-Fulani north *was not averse* to indefinite British occupation, was not lost on British sensitivities and calculations on the eve of the outbreak of the genocide. As a result, Britain worked feverishly to isolate the restive or 'troublesome' Igbo (to quote the words of a one-time British military occupation commander in the country)[21] from leading the post-conquest government before its hesitant 'departure' from the country in 1960, whilst effectively handing over supreme political power to its favoured northern region.[22] The outcome of this arrangement, as Billy Dudley has argued,

---

There were no detailed, broken down, figures for the Berg Damara, but the Germans reckoned that about 30 per cent of them were murdered in the genocide.

[19]Olusegun Obasanjo, *My Command* (Ibadan and London: Heinemann, 1980), p. 146. See also Alexander Madiebo, *The Nigerian Revolution and the Biafran War* (Enugu: Fourth Dimension Publishers, 1980), p. 41

[20]Obasanjo, *My Command*, p. 146.

[21]Elizabeth Isichie, *Junior History of Nigeria* (Lagos and Ibadan: Macmillan Nigeria Publishers, 1981), p. 101.

[22]On this and related issues on the nature and extent of British sociopolitical manoeuvrings on the eve of its 1960 'exit' to ensure that the north region safeguards its vast economic and strategic interests in Nigeria subsequently, see especially the views of Harold Smith, an official of the outgoing British occupation regime in country during the period, who has set up a website (www.libertas.demon.co.uk) dedicated to documenting the 'treason by the British in Nigeria at the time of Independence and up to the present day .'

was that 'though sovereign,' Nigeria 'behaved as if it were still a colonial state.'[23]

Thus, given its vast and entrenched socio-economic and strategic interests in Nigeria and the pivotal role of the north regional religiopolitical establishment in overseeing and safeguarding these, Britain was arguably the only country in the world that could not maintain a 'neutral' position on the politics and the wider ramifications of the Igbo genocide. Yet, few expected that Britain would have been active and directly involved in its execution. After all, right under its watch as the conquering foreign power on the ground, Britain was fully aware of the series of anti-Igbo pogrom and massacre organised in the past by the Hausa-Fulani during the course of its 60 years of occupation of Nigeria. The most notorious occurred in 1945 and 1953. In the aftermath of the 1953 Igbo massacre in the Hausa-Fulani town of Kano, the findings of the occupation regime's special commission of inquiry on the event concluded on a note that gravely anticipated the catastrophic enactment of the more horrendous blood-bath of 16 years later: '[T]he seeds of the trouble which broke out in Kano on May 16 [1953] have their counterparts still in the ground. It could happen again, and only a realisation and acceptance of the underlying causes can remove the danger.'[24] It should be recalled that the Kano killings coincided with the heightened debates among Nigeria politicians on the possible date for the formal termination of the British occupation, leading to the restoration of independence. In contrast to the Igbo and other nations in the south who favoured the year 1956 for both historic events, the north, as was expected, was vehemently opposed to any such dates. Essentially, the north unleashed the Kano massacres to scuttle these debates – which it succeeded in doing, with evident British relief and satisfaction. Given Britain's involvement in the 1966-1970 genocide, it is now evident that research that critically reexamines the occupation regime's *own* role in the 1953 Kano pogrom, and the 1945 massacres of Igbo in Jos and the contiguous plateau tin mining fields of north central Nigeria is urgently required. The 1945 killings coincided with heightened political activity in Nigeria – this time over a countrywide workers' general strike and concerted demands for a *firm* date set for the termination of the occupation. The regime blamed prominent Igbo leaders and political parties and organisations for leading these campaigns.[25] The carefully organised politics of mass killings by the state would subsequently punctuate the pace and trajectory of

---

[23]Billy Dudley, *An Introduction to Nigerian Government and Politics* (London and Basingstoke: Macmillan, 1982), p. 283.
[24]Quoted in Rudolf Ogoo Okonkwo, 'Igbo: The final battle (1),' *Kwenu*, 18 October 2005, at http://ww.kwenu.com/publications/okonkwo/igbo_battle1.htm (accessed 22 November 2005).
[25]Okwudiba Nnoli, *Ethnic Politics in Nigeria* (Enugu: Fourth Dimension Publishers), 1980, p. 222 and pp. 234-235.

socioeconomic development in Nigeria. Did Britain inaugurate this politics of mass killings with its Hausa-Fulani establishment client, as a rearguard strategy to protect its Africa's jewel in the crown – as it contemplated its inevitable withdrawal from Nigeria in the years soon after the end of the Second World War?

The active British involvement in the 1966-1970 Igbo genocide was no doubt a boon to its Nigerian local allies, who now controlled state power. It reinforced their confidence. With the complicity of the world's leading power on the African scene at the time, they believed that they would receive the necessary protection from London to check the expected international opprobrium that would follow. And the Nigerians were right in their calculations as the British government launched a robust political and diplomatic campaign throughout the period to ensure that the Nigerian state received no censure whatsoever in international forums and organisations for its appalling crimes against humanity. In effect, the Nigerian operators, following the 'dress rehearsals' of 1945 and 1953, were now implementing, as state policy, the politics of liquidation of a people that they had since regarded and targeted as 'political opponents'. It is this politics of the genocide-state that has remained the singular hallmark of Nigerian political development since then, with the all too familiar calamitous consequences. All Nigerian heads of state and several key state/quasi-state officials since mid-1966 were activist-operatives in the planning or execution of the varying features and junctures of the Igbo genocide.

Following the astonishing lack of concern exhibited by the United Nations and most of its affiliate bodies, and the success of British diplomacy, most African countries at the time were equally silent in their lack of condemnation of the Igbo genocide. The overwhelming majority indeed considered the genocide a 'Nigerian internal affair'.[26] For those African countries closely allied to Britain, the Soviet Union, and the Arab World, they were often vociferous in their open support for the Nigerian state, with some of them (for example Egypt, Algeria, Sudan and Chad) actually supplying weapons or personnel deployed alongside the perpetrators.[27] Only very few leaders such as Julius Nyerere of Tanzania, Kenneth Kaunda of Zambia, and Félix Houphouët-Boigny of Côte d'Ivoire voiced their criticism of the slaughter of the Igbo, and warned of the deleterious consequences on the future development of Africa if the genocide was not halted and its organisers punished.[28] It is precisely because the perpetrators of the Igbo genocide appeared to have been let off the hook for their crimes, by the rest of Africa and the wider world, that Africa did not have to wait very long before the politics of the Nigerian genocide-state metamorphosed violently beyond the Nigerian frontiers. Leaders elsewhere on the con-

---

[26]Ekwe-Ekwe, *Conflict and Intervention in Africa*, pp. 51-58.
[27]Ibid., p. 57.
[28]Ibid., pp. 53 and 55.

tinent waged their own versions of the liquidation of 'opponents' as ruthlessly and horrifically as they could, *à la* Nigeria, because they expected no sanctions from either their African colleagues or from the rest of the international community. Soon, the killing fields from Igboland expanded almost inexorably across the continent as the following haunting milestones of slaughter during the epoch illustrate: Uganda, Zaïre/Democratic Republic of Congo, Republic of Congo, Ethiopia, Somalia, Rwanda, Burundi, Liberia, Sierra Leone, Guinea-Bissau, southern Guinea, Côte d'Ivoire, Sudan. Twelve million were killed in these 13 countries. Added to the three million Igbo dead, Africa has had the gruesome tally of 15 million people murdered by its genocide-states in the past 40 years.

The Igbo, the Tutsi, the Darfuri and all those other Africans who have been the victims of the genocide-state have been largely left on their own to defend themselves if they can. The indifference of the UN and the rest of the world to the terror of the African genocide-state is hugely palpable. The present UN effort to exonerate the Sudan from its genocide in Darfur by foisting on Africa a pseudo-hierarchical schema of definitions that casts doubt on what this 'crime against humanity' constitutes or approximates to, is itself a crime against humanity. For the United Nations, this represents a shattering crash of the organisation to its lowest ebb of shame yet. That this has occurred when the UN is led by an African secretary-general further underscores the burden of this tragedy. According to the frightening logic of the UN declaration on Darfur, the crime of genocide will hence be ascertained whilst the targeted population has ceased to exist. *Tu fia kwa*!

It cannot be overstated that it is the African genocide-state that is the bane of African social existence currently. It is what constitutes the firestorm of the emergency that threatens the very survival of the African. It is not the 'debt', 'poverty', HIV/Aids/other diseases and the myriad of socio-economic indices often reeled off in many a commentary. Contrary to the understandable sincerity of purpose in former South African President Nelson Mandela's recent call on the West to simultaneously cancel all Africa's 'debt' and invest the sum of US$500 billion in the continent in the next decade,[29] and the British government's own high-powered but essentially gestural political rhetoric on the subject (made during the July 2005 G8 summit in Scotland),[30] Africans do not require financial assistance from the West, or any other source, in their bid to dismantle the genocide-state on their continent. Africa, presently, remains one

---

[29]See *BBC*, http://news.bbc.co.uk/1/hi/business/4238045.stm (accessed 5 February 2005).
[30]On this, see Herbert Ekwe-Ekwe, 'What the world should celebrate,' *openDemocracy*, at http://www.opendemocracy.net/globalization-G8/africa_2662.jsp, 11 July 2005 (accessed 10 December 2005).

of humanity's most endowed continents.[31] It is not poor. It is rich in human and non-human capacity, with the latter incorporating a vast array of mineralogical and agricultural resource base that outstrips the potentials of most other continents of the world.[32] It is pertinent to note that despite all the noisy propaganda of 'Western aid' to Africa, African émigrés in the Americas, Europe, Asia and the Middle East now dispatch more money to Africa annually than all the 'Western aid' to the continent combined. In 2003, according to the World Bank, African émigrés sent to Africa the impressive sum of US$200 billion[33] – invested directly in their home communities. This is 40 times the sum of 'Western aid' in real terms in the same year – i.e. when the pervasive 'overheads' attendant to the latter are accounted for. It is interesting that the source of the information of the *instrumental* role of African émigrés in current external capital transfers to Africa comes from the World Bank. It is this same World Bank, which, in alliance with the International Monetary Fund and the string of African regimes in the past 30 years, contributed to the virtual destruction of the African economy in its so-called 'structural adjustment programme' of the era.[34] One of the consequences of this programme has been the dramatic flight of the African middle classes,[35] who make up a significant proportion of the 12 million-strong Africans who left the continent for overseas in the past 15 years. Thus, Africa's pressing problem in the past 40 years has not been 'poverty', as it is often uncritically portrayed, but how to husband phenomenal resources, human and non-human, for the express benefit of the peoples at a time when the strategic goal for change is to dismantle the architecture of annihilation posed to African existence by its genocide-states.[36]

---

[31]Ekwe-Ekwe, *African Literature in Defence of History*, particularly pp. 141-162.
[32]Ibid., pp. 142-143.
[33]World Bank, 'Migrant Labor Remittances in Africa,' *Africa Regional Working Paper Series, No. 64*, Washington, November 2003, p.12.
[34]Ekwe-Ekwe, *African Literature in Defence of History*, pp. 3-7.
[35]On this particular impact of the 'structural adjustment programme', Ade Ajayi, historian and former vice-chancellor of the University of Lagos, has correctly observed: 'For me, the overall effect of the structural Adjustment Programme ... is twofold. One, it succeeded in destroying the productive sector of the economy, and two ... it saw to the collapse of the middle class ... With the collapse of the middle class, the country lost the values that encouraged individuals to create personal wealth and enjoy it. What has happened is that people no longer want to work for their wealth; society no longer frowns on vices ... ' (See 'Ade Ajayi in conversation with Toluwanimi Olujimi,' The Chinua Achebe Foundation Interview Series, *Kwenu*, 12 December 2005 – accessed 21 December 2005.)
[36]Ekwe-Ekwe, *African Literature in Defence of History*, especially ch. 5.

Arms-Ban

What Africa needs urgently from the West, and indeed from any others genuinely interested in African advancement, is simply to withdraw their support for the continuing existence of the African genocide-state. This state's ontological mission is to kill – and it surely accomplishes this most viciously as the Igbo genocide testifies. This state will lead Africa nowhere but to perdition. The Igbo genocide casts a distinct, enveloping shadow over contemporary Africa's quest to formulate a way forward out of the debilitating quagmire of the genocide state. It was in Nigeria that, barely 10 years after the start of the African restoration of independence, high-profiled institutions of the state unleashed genocide on 12 million of its citizens, slaughtering one-quarter of them in the process. This genocide essentially shattered the efficacy of this state to capitalise on the resources of multinationality and multiculturality in embarking on redevelopment, following 60 years of the British conquest and occupation of these southeast nations of West Africa.

Without British complicity in the Igbo genocide, it was highly unlikely that that genocide would have been embarked upon in its initial phase by the operatives of the Nigerian state with such unrelenting stretch and consequences between May and October 1966. Without the massive arms support that Nigeria received from Britain especially, it was highly improbable that Nigeria would have been in the military position to pursue its second phase of the Igbo genocide – namely, the invasion of Igboland – which resulted in the death of three million people between July 1967 and January 1970. Such was the grotesque blatancy of the British involvement at the time that Foreign Secretary Michael Stewart told his colleagues, during one of the numerous debates on the subject in the British parliament, that his government was probably the only country in the world that could not cease its support for the Nigerian state's mission against the Igbo.[37] It should be stressed that Nigeria did not have an arms manufacturing capacity then to embark on the latter phase of its mission without external support. Forty years on, Nigeria still does not have such an internal military capability. It still relies heavily on Britain, currently the world's leading arms exporter to Africa, for its supplies.[38] One immediate move that Brit-

---

[37]Suzanne Cronje, *The World and Nigeria* (London: Sidgwick and Jackson, 1972), p. 38.
[38]*The Observer* (London), 12 June 2005. British arms sales to Nigeria increased by approximately 1000 per cent between 2000 and 2004, according to *The Observer*'s special report, and these included armoured vehicles and large calibre artillery. In 2004, Britain earned £53m from its arms sales to Nigeria, the same amount it received from its *entire* arms sales to Africa in 1999. For a genocide state that has never been at war with any known external force, such weapons delivered to Nigeria are inevitably used against targeted or designated *internal* enemies – as indeed the Abuja regime has deployed these in operations against the Igbo, the Ijo and other nations in the Niger Delta, and in

ain, which earned the handsome sum of US$1.8 billion in 2004 selling arms to Africa,[39] the West, and the rest of the world can make to support the ongoing efforts by peoples in Nigeria to rid themselves of the genocide-state is to ban all arms sales to Nigeria – and, by extension, to the rest of Africa. This must be comprehensive and not fudged. Nigeria, and the other African genocide-states, requires the political and diplomatic support from abroad and the deadly array of arms ever streaming into its arsenal from Britain and elsewhere to exist and terrorise the people(s) in its territory. This is part of the cardinal and enduring lessons of the Igbo genocide.

An arms ban on such key states as Nigeria, the Sudan, and the Democratic Republic of the Congo,[40] for example, would radically advance the current hectic quest on the ground by peoples across Africa to construct democratic and extensively decentralised new state forms that guarantee and safeguard human rights, equality and freedom for individuals and peoples – alternatives to the extant genocide-state. Africans know very well that there are alternatives to the genocide-state. They have both the vision and the capacity to create these alternatives.

This is the way forward for Africa. As for the West, a ban on all arms to Africa forthwith will enhance these alternative African state constructions tremendously. On this, Dennis McNamara, a special United Nations adviser on internal displacement, has observed, most cogently:

> Guns are at the heart of the problem ... There is one slogan I would like to suggest for 2006: No Arms Sales to Africa. Zero. Not embargo, not a sanction, a voluntary cessation of all arms sales to Africa ... The kids on the streets of Nairobi, Khartoum, Abidjan and Monrovia have guns in their pockets or up their sleeves ... We provide the arms. We the West, we the G8 ...[41]

Tivland in the central regions. Eighteen thousand of the 20,000 people murdered by the state and its allied agents in Nigeria between 1999 and 2006, i.e., the years of the present presidency of Olusegun Obasanjo, are Igbo.

[39]Ibid.

[40]According to a research recently published in the medical journal, *The Lancet*, 38,000 Africans currently die each month in the Democratic Republic of the Congo as a result of the breakdown of the country's health services caused by several years of uninterrupted war. The research concludes that a total of four million have died as a result of this conflict since 1998. See *BBC*, at http://news.bbc.co.uk/1/hi/world/africa/4586832.stm (accessed 7 January 2006).

[41]See 'U.N. adviser: West killing Africa with gun sales,' *CNN*, at http://edition.cnn.com/2006/WORLD/africa/02/02/africa.guns.reut/index.html (accessed 3 February 2006). For the first comprehensively-argued call for a total ban on all arms sales to Africa, see the following: Ekwe-Ekwe, *African Literature in Defence of History*, pp. 134-137; Herbert Ekwe-Ekwe, 'Ban all Arms Export to Africa,' *USAfricaon-*

Such a ban will in no way entail any complicated budgeting for a new fund allocation from the Western taxpayer. Not one dollar nor euro nor pound would be required nor spent. It also does not require 'agonising' G7/G8/Davos Annual World Economics Forum-style gatherings to implement either. Each government simply takes its decision after a cabinet meeting. For Britain, currently the premier arms-exporter to Africa and a key orchestrator of the Igbo genocide, a decision to ban all arms shipment to Africa can be made easily on any Thursday – the day in the week that its cabinet usually meets during the parliamentary session. This decision does not require any legislation from government that would necessarily seek parliamentary approval.

Closure

Governments in contemporary Britain appear to be steadily emerging from that mineshaft of infamy into which the Harold Wilson regime had sunk the country when it played a crucial role in organising and sustaining the 1966-1970 Igbo genocide. British governments, along side other members of the European Union, and the United States, have recently intervened robustly in the Balkans and elsewhere in the world to halt ongoing genocides or pre-empt those being planned. This is highly commendable. That essence of a *shared humanity*, which deserted the British government with such disastrous consequences in Igboland 40 years ago, appears to be crystallising as the core sensibility that shapes British relationship with the rest of the world – particularly beyond the West. In a move that lends further credibility to this observation, Richard Gozney, the chief British representative in Nigeria, recently condemned, without any reservations, the November-December 2005 Nigerian army and police killing of scores of young, unarmed, peaceful Igbo demonstrators, campaigning for the restoration of Biafran independence in several Igbo towns and cities.[42] These murders and several others carried out earlier on in 2005, and in recent years, are a grim reminder to the world that Nigeria has not yet abandoned its endemic mission to murder the Igbo since the devastating genocide that is the focus of this study. Of the 20,000 people murdered by the state and its varied agencies in Nigeria between 1999 and 2006, i.e., the years of the present presi-

---

line.com, at http://www.usafricaonline.com/ekweekwe.africaarms.html (accessed 2 May 2003); Herbert Ekwe-Ekwe, 'Just ban all arms sales to Africa – nothing else required for now,' *Nigeriaworld*, at http://nigeriaworld.com/articles/2005/mar/142.html (accessed 14 March 2005); Herbert Ekwe-Ekwe, 'Ban arms sales to Africa – nothing else required,' *openDemocracy*, at http://www.opendemocracy.net/democracy-africa_democracy/arms_2602.jsp (accessed 18 June 2005) and Herbert Ekwe-Ekwe, 'Reflections on the quest for African renewal: Inclusion and People-Building,' a lecture, whose main theme was the call on the ban of all arms sales to Africa, delivered by the author to faculty and students of the African and African American Studies Program, University of Tennessee, Knoxville, United States, 10 October 2003.
[42]*The Vanguard* (Lagos), 17 December 2005.

dency of Olusegun Obasanjo, approximately 18,000 are Igbo. Gozney's intervention, made in Umuahia, the heart of the Igbo country and scene of a spate of gruesome massacres by the Nigerian military 40 years ago, is therefore of historic significance. If Gozney's predecessor at that post in Nigeria (in 1966) and the government in London at the time had adopted such a forthright and unambiguous condemnation of mass murder by the Nigerian state, instead of orchestrating and sustaining it, the outcome of this study would surely have been totally different from what is presented here.

Britain must now quickly build upon and expand on Gozney's extraordinary intervention. It should seek to effectuate some measure of closure to its sordid anti-Igbo programme of 1966-1970. Indeed, it has no greater opportunity presently to permanently erase these 'scars of Africa' from its 'conscience', to quote the sentiment that Prime Minister Tony Blair has expressed repeatedly in many an occasion since 2001.[43] Britain should now unreservedly apologise to the Igbo for its involvement in the genocide of 1966-1970 that cost the lives of 3.1 million Igbo. It should follow up this apology by paying reparations to the survivors. No other African people have suffered such an extensive holocaust and impoverishment in 100 years. King Leopold II of Belgium's troops had in the 19th century killed three million Africans in the Congo as they ravaged the country in search of cheap/unpaid labour, ivory, diamonds, timber, game, fish and the like – enormous wealth that would soon transform the nascent Belgian kingdom into a modern European country. This was the aftermath of conquest that David Diop, the irrepressible young Senegalese poet, had in mind in his dirge: 'The white man killed my father/My father was strong/The white man raped my mother/My mother was beautiful/ ...'[44] But unlike the one nation-focused target of the Igbo genocide, the Congolese scourge included peoples from several nations that make up contemporary Democratic Republic of Congo, Republic of Congo, Rwanda, Burundi, Central African Republic, Angola and Zambia. Not even Diop, who died in 1960 and did not live long enough to witness the Igbo genocide, would have comprehended the extent to which an *African-led* state, supported by Britain, would go to match or outstrip the grisly records of the Congo. Equally reprehensibly, this African state, which ordered and sustained the genocide against the Igbo, has the unenviable record, not to talk of responsibility, of literally clearing the undergrowth from which the gruesome killing fields that have since littered across Africa expanded catastrophically. Britain must now realise that that

---

[43]See http://news.bbc.co.uk/1/hi/in_depth/uk_politics/2001/conferences_2001/labour/1575135.stm for Prime Minister Blair's October 2001 conference speech to his governing Labour party in Brighton (accessed 18 January 2006).
[44]Quoted in Chinua Achebe, *Morning Yet on Creation Day* (London: Heinemann Educational Books, 1975), p. 80.

Lugardian contraption called Nigeria,[45] which indisputably has served London's economic and strategic interests so profoundly since inception in 1900, as we demonstrate soon, *does not and cannot advance the well-being* of the Igbo and other nations of the south of the country, especially in the Niger Delta. Nigeria *murders* the Igbo; it indeed murders them most brutally as we have so far shown in this study. Presently, the Igbo and other oppressed nations in the south of the country have embarked on imaginative strategies aimed at the peaceful dissolution of Nigeria. This is surely an outcome that will create the condition for advanced socioeconomic progress in this part of southeast west Africa for the first time in nearly a century. Britain must not stand in the way of this historic African initiative, its interests in Nigeria notwithstanding. Britain must now develop new sites of enterprise elsewhere in the world to generate the incredible level of financial returns that its Nigeria project annually accrues to its treasury in London. It is no longer tenable for these gargantuan returns to be appropriated in a genocide-state that has throughout its history sought to annihilate one of its constituent African nations, and devastatingly impoverishes the rest of the population.

Britain, who, with its allies in the Balkans and elsewhere, has admirably been hunting down fugitive genocidist generals and their civilian counterparts to face trial for crimes against humanity at The Hague International Criminal Court, should now surrender to this same court surviving British officials (military, civil servants, politicians, academics, etc, etc) who were involved in the planning and/or the execution of the Igbo genocide. At The Hague court, these Britons must be joined by their surviving genocidist counterparts in Nigeria who include Generals Obasanjo, Rotimi, Akinrinade, Adebayo, Abubakar, Babangida, Buhari, Gowon, Haruna and Danjuma, Brigadiers Adekunle and Are, Captain King, and Messrs Enahoro, Ayida and Aminu, and tried for crimes against humanity. Most of these Nigerian officials have, in the wake of the genocide, run Nigeria as the degraded fiefdom that is shockingly recognisable by the rest of the world.

Britain should now insist that any of its citizens and each and every member of the Nigerian regime who was centrally involved in the murder of 3.1 million Igbo people 40 years ago, and who, in effect, triggered off the chain of mass killings of 12 million other Africans elsewhere in the continent, must be made to account for their action at the International Criminal Court. Not to do so would be to send the wrong signal to Africa – by rewarding genocidist operatives who have the blood of Africans on their hands, and who have, in tandem, pillaged the Nigerian economy whose resources alone could easily have transformed the entire Africa. On the extent of the pillage in question, Nuhu Ribadu, the chair of the current regime's so-called economic and financial

---

[45]Frederick Lugard was the first appointed British governor of occupied Nigeria after the 'amalgamation' of the north and south provinces in 1914.

crime commission, recently informed a traumatised country that kleptocracy was the 'sole guiding principle for running [the] affairs of state,'[46] and that the total sum of US$400 billion was squandered by the regimes of the era[47] – led principally by the following seven genocidist generals who played the commanding role in the Igbo genocide: Yakubu Gowon, Murtala Mohammed, Olusegun Obasanjo, Muhammadu Buhari, Ibrahim Babangida, Abdulsalami Abubakar and Sani Abacha.

---

[46]*ThisDay* (Lagos), 20 January 2006.
[47]*The Vanguard* (Lagos), 18 May 2005. It appears impossible to exaggerate the staggering kleptomaniac proclivities of these regimes. Gary K. Busch offers the following graphic insight of the contemporary Nigerian economy: 'Every day the Nigerian economy loses between 150,000 and 320,000 barrels of oil. These are stolen by "bunkerers", who have small tanker vessels which load the oil in the Delta and tranship [the consignment] to offshore tankers [for onward delivery] to other West African states. Further inland illegal tanker trucks load their stolen oil and refined products and drive these into neighbouring countries for ... sale. At the current price of around $50 per barrel this amounts to a "leakage" of around US$7.5 to US$16 million a day. On a monthly basis this amounts to around US$365 million or US$4.4 billion a year. This illegal trade was pioneered under President Abacha [in the 1990s]... It is widely believed that both the [current] President [Olusegun Obasanjo] and the Vice-President [Atiku Abubakar] ... condone or participate in ... oil bunkering ... which represented almost 300,000 bbl/day in 2003.' (See Gary K. Busch, 'Bí a bá tò sílé, onípò a m? ipò' ['If someone wets the bed, each person should know where he or she slept'], at http://www.ocnus.net/artman/publish/article_21647.shtml - accessed 29 November 2005.)

2

The antimonies of the Nigerian state: World War II to genocide

As Nigeria approached the 1st October 1960 date for the *reestablishment* of independence for its various peoples, after 60 years of British conquest and occupation, its leaders and the three main political parties they represented scarcely shared a commonly defined worldview on the tasks of post-conquest reconstruction of the country. Even a date for the restoration of independence acceptable to these three political strands or tendencies of the liberation movement was problematic enough.

In 1951, the National Council of Nigeria and the Cameroons (NCNC), the pan-African freedom party, which, close to a decade, had been the pivotal force in the country demanding the restoration of independence, had proposed 1956 as the year for this historic event. This was during the party's annual convention held in Kano. Two years later, the Action Group (AG), the Yoruba regionalist party in the west of the country, tabled a motion in the central legislature in Lagos formally designating 1956 as the year for the restoration of independence. This move was endorsed by the NCNC. It was however rejected out of hand by the third party, the Northern Peoples' Congress (NPC), which was established substantially in 1951 by the British occupation to subvert the country's restoration of independence goal. According to Harold Smith, an ex-official of the occupation regime, the NPC was 'largely a creation of the British and hardly a normal political party in the accepted sense. It was funded by the British controlled [local government] Authorities and was quite simply a tool of the British administration.'[1] Correspondingly, this islamo-aristocratic party also served the age-old feudal interests of the Hausa-Fulani socioeconomic establishment in the north region. Thanks to the virtual safeguard of these

---

[1]Harold Smith, 'How the British undermined democracy in Africa,' at http://www.libertas.demon.co.uk/ (accessed 24 December 2005). Peter Smithers, another surviving ex-British occupation official in Nigeria, has recently condemned the British construction of the Nigerian state. Smithers acknowledges: '[I]n retrospect, it is clear that this was a grave mistake which has cost many lives and will probably continue to do so. It should have been better to establish several smaller states in a free trade area.' (See Idowu Ajanaku, 'Ex-colonial officer faults amalgamation of Nigeria,' *The Guardian* [Lagos], 28 April 2005.)

interests by the British, despite the latter's occupation of Nigeria, the NPC was therefore not opposed to indefinite British rule in the country. In keeping to this position, it sought an urgent amendment to the liberation motion in the legislature to read, instead, '[restoration of independence] as soon as practicable.'[2]

Both the AG and the NCNC were outraged by the NPC intention. They attacked the NPC for complicity in prolonging the continuing British occupation of Nigeria. In turn, the NPC published an 8-point programme of action in which it sought a loose sociopolitical relationship with the rest of the country, with the effective secession of the north as the ultimate outcome if implemented.[3] The NPC often threatened secession or 'pakistanisation' (after the muslim Pakistan example in the 1947 partition of British-occupied India) of the north region from Nigeria as a means of extending British rule indefinitely. On the eve of its so-called departure from the country in 1960, the British handed over supreme political power to the NPC and the north as a 'parting gift' for the latter's unalloyed support during the years of occupation. Subsequently, the NPC and the north would threaten secession or 'pakistanisation' whenever it felt that this 'ascribed' dominant political position in Nigeria was challenged from the south, especially the east region that led the pan-Nigerian liberation enterprise. NPC/north spokespersons would variously argue or indeed warn, alluding to the 'Pakistan-antecedent', that, as muslims, they would rather 'have to divide the country' than accept a non-muslim-led political leadership from either east or west Nigeria.[4]

Despite the NPC's secession threats, the NCNC and AG intensified their criticisms of the north's opposition to a firm date for Nigeria liberation. To reinforce their resolve to achieve freedom for the country in 1956, both the NCNC and AG decided to send their party delegations to the north to campaign for this objective directly among the people of the region. In May 1953, the Action Group sent one of such delegations to tour Kano. The NPC, in concert with religious, local government, and business leaders in Kano and the outlying district, responded to the visit by organising a carefully orchestrated attack against Igbo population centres across the city by mobs of Hausa-Fulani youth. Scores of Igbo people were murdered during the attacks that went on uninterruptedly for four days. Hundreds of thousands of pounds worth of Igbo business enterprises, homes, schools and recreational

---

[2]Quoted in Nnoli, *Ethnic Politics in Nigeria*, p. 236.
[3] Ibid.
[4]On this subject, see, for instance, the interview of leading muslim cleric Sheikh Abubakar Gumi in *Quality* magazine (October 1987), quoted in *West Africa* (London), 19 October 1987, p. 2089. For an extended critique of this feature of the north's political calculations, see Herbert Ekwe-Ekwe, 'Religion: Manipulation or Mobilisation?' *West Africa* (London), 7 December 1987, p. 2380.

centres were looted or destroyed during the pogrom. The pattern of these Igbo killings was a tragic replay to those carried out on Igbo immigrants in Jos, another northern town, during the course of the 1945 countrywide strike. But even more ominously, for the future of the Igbo in Nigeria, these Kano attacks were a portent of the widespread genocide of the Igbo that the Hausa-Fulani would embark upon in 1966, which led to the death of 3.1 million Igbo four years later.

The British occupation regime responded to the Kano pogrom, and the other related features of the reestablishment-of-independence-date crisis in the country, by convening a new conference of Nigerian political parties in London. But this conference, which was held in July-August 1953, failed to resolve the contentious date for Nigeria's liberation. As was expected, the British government sided with the NPC's opposition to a designated freedom date, ensuring that the growing cleavage on the subject between the latter and the NCNC/AG remained, if not deepened. Noticeably, the British 'concession' to the NCNC/AG positions at the conference was its acceptance of the implementation of the principle of *limited* self-government to the regional territorial areas only – east Nigeria, west Nigeria; *full restoration* of independence for all of the peoples in Nigeria, including the peoples within the political jurisdictions of the stipulated limited 'self-governing' east and west Nigeria would still have to wait indefinitely. As James Coleman has correctly argued on the outcome of this London meeting, '[I]t was the north that won the day ... they really conceded nothing on the issue of scheduled [countrywide] self-government.'[5]

While Nigerian leaders would return to London in 1957 to continue their deliberations on a date for the restoration of independence, what was certain was that the fundamental contradictions in the overall trajectory of the politics of the termination of the British occupation, which led to the countrywide crisis culminating in the Kano Igbo pogrom, remained unresolved. These contradictions persisted right through to the eventual restoration of independence seven years later, and thereafter became the main source of the multifaceted crisis of the early 1960s, finally leading to the 15 January 1966 military coup. To the exploration of the background character of these contradictions, we now turn.

Notes on the interstices of a crisis: 1945-1956

The course and outcome of the Second World War gave considerable impetus to the anti-British occupation struggle in Nigeria. In 1939, Britain and France declared war on Germany following the latter's invasion of Poland. Just as in the First World War two decades earlier, peoples in

---

[5]James Coleman, *Nigeria* (Berkeley: University of California, 1958), p. 402.

Nigeria, as well as other Africans, soon found themselves fighting in another global war that was not of their own making. Apart from Liberia and Ethiopia, the rest of Africa was under the occupation of *the same* European powers at war with each other, except, ironically, Germany. Germany had lost its hitherto occupied African countries of Tanzania, Namibia, Cameroon and Togo due to its defeat in the First World War by Britain and its allies. But instead of restoring immediate independence to these African states at the Versailles conference terminating the war, Britain and France scandalously incorporated them into their *own* existing conquest empires overseas (Tanzania and southern Cameroon were seized by Britain; northern Cameroon and Togo were taken over by France), whilst Namibia was assigned to the European minority population-ruled South Africa to 'administer' – a euphemism that hardly disguised Namibia's *de facto* status as Pretoria's newly conquered land. In contrast, the defeat of Austro-Hungary and Turkey, Germany's central European allies in this war, resulted in the liberation of several subject nations and peoples, which included the Pole, Czech, Slovak and Greek.

So, for Africa, whose peoples (in Africa itself, the Caribbean and the United States) lost 400,000 soldiers, mostly conscript combatants who fought for the conflicting territorial claims of rival European powers in the 1914-1918 war,[6] the outcome was grim indeed: continuing occupation. The victorious alliance, including crucially Britain and France, two leading European conqueror-states that then occupied most of Africa, continued to maintain the most contemptuous disregard of the human and national rights of African peoples, even though these countries had claimed that they went to war in 1914 to confront Germany's *territorial ambitions* in Europe and elsewhere. As one and half million African descent conscripts worldwide went to fight for these same European World occupying states in 1939, it was even less likely that Africa's *own* independence would be reclaimed in the event of victory against Germany.

I. War and occupation

About 100,000 Nigerians were part of the total number of one million Africans who fought for the anti-German coalition forces during World War II. All accounts record the valiant performances of the African contingents in the principal fronts of the war: western Europe; the gruesome Far East campaigns against Japan, where Africans casualties were in tens of thousands; the battles in north-east Africa in 1940-1941, which led to the liberation of Ethiopia from Italian occupation, and, finally, the preparations

---

[6]Herbert Ekwe-Ekwe, 'Africans and the European Wars of the 20th Century,' *African Peoples Review*, July-December 1995, p. 18.

leading to the coalition's landings in western Europe in 1944, which was decisive in the subsequent defeat of Germany. Indeed, the role of the African-Guyanese governor of Chad, Félix Éboué, was crucial in the anti-German alliance's successes at this theatre. He provided logistics in west/central Africa and his support for the Free French Forces was unequivocal even at a time when influential French men and women, including François Mitterand (who would later become state president for 14 years), were collaborating with the German occupation regime in France.[7] The total number of African descent casualty in the war is estimated at 900,000 killed, and hundreds of thousands wounded.[8]

Besides providing troops, Nigerian territory was used extensively as rear bases and supply lines, particularly for the north African and west European campaigns against Germany and its allies. This was part of the massive expansion of air and seaport facilities in the west African region in 1940-43. The absence of combat activity in Nigeria itself provided another advantage for the anti-German coalition. Britain, which was now the only effective European occupying power in Africa, with the sudden fall of France to the Germans, was able to offset the sharp drop that occurred in the early 1940s in the global production of palm oil, groundnut, tin and rubber due especially to the Japanese overrun and occupation of southeast Asia. It readily stepped up the production of these commodities in occupied Nigeria, Ghana, Sierra Leone and Gambia. In similar vein, increases in the production of sugar and banana were embarked upon in British-occupied Caribbean, home to mainly peoples of African descent, as part of the war effort at the time. Crucially, direct financial support for the British war effort from British-occupied Africa was spectacular – this totalled £446 million by the end of the war in 1945.[9]

Yet, the feverish increase in all these productive activities for the British war effort from across the African World, co-existed with a sharp deterioration of the living conditions of the majority of the peoples in British-occupied Nigeria. Prices of locally produced goods, as well as imports, especially foodstuffs, soared. In Lagos, for instance, prices of assorted meat had increased by at least 90 per cent between 1939 and 1945;[10] prices of pepper and salt had increased by 150 per cent and 400 per cent

---

[7]See, for instance, 'In Memoriam: François Mitterand,' *BBC*, at http://www.pbs.org/newshour/bb/remember/mitterrand_1-8b.html (accessed 11 March 2006).
[8]Ekwe-Ekwe, 'Africans and the European wars of the 20th century,' p. 17.
[9]Walter Rodney, *How Europe Underdeveloped Africa* (Washington, DC: Howard University, 1982), p. 172.
[10]Quoted in Wogu Ananaba, *The Trade Union Movement in Nigeria* (Benin City: Ethiope Publishing Corporation, 1969), p. 27.

respectively, during the same period, while price rise for rice was 92 per cent and milk rose by 86 per cent.[11] By 1943, there was a distinct possibility of a countrywide famine in Nigeria.[12] The general foodstuff situation had been made worse by the occupation regime's enhanced diversion of local humanpower resources from the farms, producing food for domestic consumption, into the military or associated enterprises to support the war effort. The regime had also decreed a wage freeze, the paltry sums that accounted for payment of African workers notwithstanding,[13] until the end of the war, and its resultant effects added to the despair of the times. Workers' mandatory cash payments to the war effort, supervised by regime officials up and down the country, were also another source of the tense situation.

In July 1941, workers embarked on a mass protest, demanding an increase in their living allowances or what they called, quite appositely, a 'war bonus'.[14] The regime's inability to meet this demand to the workers' satisfaction, coupled with the generalised deterioration of the living standards of the people across the country, ultimately became the background of the 1945 countrywide strike – itself, the turning point in the politics of Nigeria's liberation movement as we shall soon show. It is also important to recall that by January 1941, Nnamdi Azikiwe, whose party, the NCNC, would support the 1945 strike, had begun to show disillusionment in the ability of the principal states of the anti-German war coalition to confront the issue of the British occupation of Nigeria. After all, the only basis that leading officials of the NCNC freedom party such as Azikiwe himself (who was secretary) and Herbert Macaulay (the president) could justify Nigerian peoples' support for the anti-German alliance of the era, in which occupier Britain played a central role, was that the outcome of the war in Europe should lead to Nigeria's liberation. Azikiwe had observed, most solemnly, in an editorial he published in his *West African Pilot* in January 1941: 'Day by day as I taste the bitter pills of being a member of a [subjugated] race, I become sceptical and laugh at the effusions of those who proclaim to the world how paradisical is the lot of the [occupied] peoples in the present scheme of thing.'[15]

In May 1945, Britain and its allies won the war. With victory assured, the European powers were now faced with the choice of implementing the Anglo-America Atlantic charter, which was formulated in 1941. A clause in

---

[11]Ibid.
[12]O.N. Njoku, 'Contributions to War Efforts,' in Toyin Falola, ed., *Britain and Nigeria: Exploitation or Development?* (London: Zed Books, 1987), p. 181.
[13]See, for instance, Ananaba, *The Trade Union Movement in Nigeria*, pp. 26-32.
[14]Ibid., p. 26.
[15]Quoted in Njoku, 'Contributions to War Efforts,' p. 181.

the charter unequivocally affirms the 'right of all peoples to choose the form of government under which they will live [and] to see [the] sovereign rights and self government restored to those who have been forcibly deprived of them ...'[16] But *in practice*, Britain felt that this clause did not apply to Africans (and other conquered and occupied peoples in Asia, the Pacific, South America and the Caribbean). Its wartime prime minister, Winston Churchill, had stressed that he 'had not become the King's First Minister in order to preside over the liquidation of the British Empire.'[17] Bernard Bourdillon, the British occupation governor in Nigeria, was equally blunt, even derisive of the demands for the restoration of African independence: 'The British government ... did not anticipate any change in her policy towards Nigeria ... The war ... did not provide opportunities for the acceleration of greater participation in the administration of the country by Nigerians ... [No one] should expect a reward for failure to cut [their] own throat.'[18]

Once again, after a major global war, it was evident that Britain, and indeed other European conqueror states occupying Africa, was not prepared to pull out of the continent. Just as in 1918, after African peoples had lost 400,000 conscript soldiers fighting on behalf of Britain and France, in the latter's conflictive territorial and hegemonic rivalries with Germany and its allies, London and Paris were about to ignore the extraordinary role that African peoples, their countries, and resources had played in defeating Germany during this second time round. It was clear, though, that unlike 1918, the world after 1945 opened up more advantageous possibilities for African peoples to effect their liberation, on their own terms, across Africa

---

[16] A.N. Porter and A.A. Stockwell, *British Imperial Policy and Decolonisation, 1938-51* (Basingstoke and London: Macmillan, 1987), p. 103.

[17] Ibid., p. 25. The French were similarly contemptuous of the liberation of its occupied African states (as well as those in Asia, the Pacific and the Americas), notwithstanding their early capitulation to the German invasion at the outbreak of war. During the 1944 Brazzaville conference of exiled French occupation governors from across the world, which was chaired by General Charles de Gaulle, the French position on the subject was restated emphatically: 'Self-government must be rejected – even in the more distant future.' (Quoted by Hubert Deschambs, 'France in Black Africa and Madagascar between 1920 and 1945,' in L.H. Gann and Peter Duiganan, *Colonialism in Africa, 1870-1960. Vol. Two: The History and Politics of Colonialism 1914-1960* [Cambridge: Cambridge University, 1970], p. 249.) Sixty years on, France's supercilious disposition to African independence and sovereignty continues unabated. For an analysis of the current epoch, see Herbert Ekwe-Ekwe,'The bogey of African-French solidarity,' *USAfricanonline.com*, at http://www.usafricaonline.com/ekweekwe.africafrench.html (accessed 8 October 2003).

[18] Njoku, 'Contributions to War Efforts,' p. 180.

and the Americas, in a manner that would have a tremendous impact on global development. In the meantime, the irony of the immediate post-World War II pan-European superciliousness towards African liberation, given the tragic history of the world of the previous six years, was not lost on the consciousness of the rest of humanity: Britain, France and Belgium, especially, had fought against German cultural supremacism and territorial expansionism for six gruelling years, but emerged from this war apparently oblivious that *their own form* of cultural supremacism was part of the conquest ideology that had been used to legitimise the occupation of Africa and several regions of the Southern World for centuries. The fact that these conqueror states were not willing to withdraw voluntarily from occupied Africa, despite the cataclysm of the war of 1939-45, was highly indicative of the serious limitations that characterised their publicly-declared war-time political aspirations, propaganda, and objectives.

II. Spearhead

The National Council of Nigeria and the Cameroons was formed on 26 August 1944 to spearhead Nigeria's liberation struggle from the British occupation of the country. The background that led to its formation was of utmost symbolism because this was connected with the ongoing Second World War. Earlier on in the month, students at the Lagos King's College had gone on strike as a result of the deterioration of social conditions in the institution. These were caused initially by poor management, but had become exacerbated by the wartime emergencies. In a rash response to the crisis, Arthur Richards, the newly appointed occupation governor of the country (Richards had acquired notoriety in his implacable opposition to African liberation from the European conquest as evident in his previous position as governor of British-occupied Jamaica[19]), ordered the immediate conscription of the students' strike leaders into military service. A number of other students at the college were arrested and prosecuted for their part in the protest including Chukwuemeka Odumegwu-Ojukwu, the 10-year-old first year student, who would in 1966, aged 33, play an historic leadership role in the resistance of the genocide unleashed against the Igbo people by the Nigerian state and its British allies. A few days later, one of the student conscripts died while still in military custody.

The death sent a shock wave across Nigeria. Many people were outraged. Leaders of the Nigerian Union of Students conferred with Azikiwe, the NCNC secretary, newspaper editor and proprietor of the leading newspapers that made up the liberation press. In response, Azikiwe called for a conference of all pro-liberation organisations based in Lagos to discuss the

---

[19]See, for instance, Coleman, *Nigeria*, p. 275.

crisis. The students' union convened such a conference on 26 August 1944, with the historic outcome being the formation of the NCNC. Part of the conference communiqué, released soon after the end of the gathering, stated categorically:

> Believing our country is rightfully entitled to liberty and prosperous life ... and determined to work in unity for the realisation of ultimate goal of self-government ...[20]

Nine months before the end of the war, the NCNC had, in an historic move, *forced to the fore* the very important question of the restoration of the independence of peoples in Nigeria from the British occupation. This was undoubtedly a momentous development in the peoples' consciousness and aspirations, but it was an unacceptable event as far as the occupation regime was concerned, especially coming fast on the heels of the King's College crisis, not to mention the ongoing war against Germany. The NCNC was essentially a 'federal' party, with membership derived from organisational affiliations such as trades' and students' unions, women's organisations, and cultural associations of constituent nations in Nigeria and the southern Cameroons.

III. Shut down

On 22 June 1945, Nigerian workers declared a countrywide strike to back their demands for an increase in wages. Since the 1941 work stoppage, the cost of living had increased by 200 per cent.[21] While European staff of the labour market had been paid a couple of 'allowances' to cope with these skyrocketing costs, the regime refused to make similar payments to Africans.[22] The strike virtually paralysed Nigeria's economic life. It went on for 44 days in the Lagos capital district, but even longer elsewhere in the country – up to 52 days in some places in the regions.[23] The NCNC and the liberation press (particularly the vanguard *West African Pilot*, and *Daily Comet*) supported the strike, underlying the increasingly evident cooperation between the trade unions and the emerging political leadership in working towards the country's liberation. It was the most far-reaching mobilisation of labour in occupied Nigeria and its political implications were not lost on the occupation regime. It was evident that 'Nigerians, when organised,' as James Coleman noted on the impact and significance of the countrywide

---

[20]Ibid., p. 264.
[21]Ibid., p. 258.
[22]Ananaba, *The Trade Union Movement in Nigeria*, pp. 47-48.
[23]Ibid., p. 44.

shutdown, 'had great power, that they could defy the white bureaucracy, that they could virtually control strategic centres throughout the country, and that through force or the threat of force they could compel the government to grant concessions.'[24] While the occupation regime agreed to enter into negotiations with the workers after the strike was called off, it nonetheless sought to destroy the huge 'political dividend' of liberation consciousness that the shutdown had generated across the country. Earlier on, it had proscribed the circulation of the *West African Pilot* and the *Daily Comet*, and accused Nnamdi Azikiwe (editor of both titles) and the Igbo people for engineering the strike.[25] Having exerted its influence on the north not to participate in the strike, the regime's propaganda on alleged Igbo responsibility for the event was an instigator prop to Hausa-Fulani massacres of Igbo immigrants in Jos, which occurred at the time, as we have already stated.

These manoeuvres represented a crude ploy by the occupation regime to destroy an emerging all-embracing Nigerian freedom movement. Parallel to this, the regime also pursued a more sophisticated juridical strategy to ensure that the NCNC's concerted goal for an *all-Nigeria* territorially defined, realisable liberation project remained unachievable. In effect, Britain succeeded in inaugurating what Adewale Ademoyega has appropriately described as the 'tripartition'[26] in Nigerian politics to guarantee the preservation of its enormous economic and strategic interests in the country in the foreseeable future. Besides, the tripartitioning of Nigerian politics was a British device to empower the north, its domestic client, to oversee these interests in the event of its unforeseen departure or termination of its occupation of Nigeria. For the north, this device also doubled as the ascriptive lever of power from its British friends, which it would seek to exercise quite ruthlessly in future to perpetuate hegemonic political control over the rest of the country – a precondition to its eventual acceptance, in 1958, of a 1960 date for the restoration of independence for the peoples in Nigeria.

IV. Tripartitioning

The strategy of the British *tripartitioning* of Nigerian politics began in 1946 with two policy measures enacted by the occupation regime which, in essence, appeared contradictory. First, the regime formally integrated the northern provinces into the main structure of the Nigerian occupation

---

[24]Coleman, *Nigeria*, p. 259.
[25]Nnoli, *Ethnic Politics in Nigeria*, p. 122 and pp. 234-235.
[26]Adewale Ademoyega, *Why We Struck: The Story of the First Nigerian Coup* (Ibadan: Evans Brothers [Nigeria] Publishers, 1981), p. 3.

administration. Until then, the northern and southern provinces were administered separately, despite the so-called 'amalgamation' of both territories in 1914. Secondly, the regime implemented the Richards Constitution (named after Arthur Richards, the new occupation governor), published in 1945, which split Nigeria into three administrative regions (east, west, north), each with seemingly more devolved powers from the centre, especially in the areas of finance and social services. In practice, the constitution was based on the most undemocratic principles. Representatives in each of the four new legislatures had more members appointed (by the regime) than those elected. For instance in the first central legislature in Lagos, 29 of the 49 member-house were appointed, some of whom had become discredited among the people as a result of their collaboration with the occupation.[27] Other appointees were European who represented strategic financial and business interests in the country. Even for those (Nigerians) elected, the process was carried out via an 'electoral college', as universal franchise was non-existent. To qualify for membership of the college, a personal income or property based in Lagos or Calabar, the former capital, had to be worth £100 per annum.[28] Those living elsewhere in the country were 'elected' through local government authorities, a process which was prone to extensive manipulation by British occupation officials on the ground.

As if the tenets of the Richards Constitution were not provocative enough to the sensibilities of the liberation movement, which was now confident of achieving its goal, the regime, at the same time, passed four ordinances that essentially reinforced the goals of the British conquest. One stated emphatically: 'The entire property in and control of all mineral, and mineral oils, in, under, or upon any lands in Nigeria, and of all rivers, streams and water courses throughout Nigeria, is and shall be vested in, the Crown ...'[29] For the liberation movement, both the Richards Constitution and what it quickly termed the 'obnoxious ordinances'[30] provided another opportunity to mobilise the people for the restoration of independence, coming soon after the successes of the countrywide strike. But the split that would soon become pronounced in the movement was evident in the conflicting methods adopted by the dominant sectors, headed by the NCNC, and the minority Nigerian Youth Movement (which was based primarily in western Nigeria) to confront the emergency. Building on its experience during the 1945 strike, the NCNC launched an 8-month countrywide campaign in 1946 to oppose the constitution and the ordinances. Included in the NCNC campaign

---

[27]Coleman, *Nigeria*, pp. 278-280.
[28]Ibid., p. 280.
[29]Ibid., p. 282.
[30]Ibid., p. 284.

leadership was Michael Imoudu, the labour leader, who had become very popular across the country after the strike. Quite significantly, the convergence of the NCNC freedom politics and that of the labour unions represented another decisive phase in the restoration of independence movement. Also included in the NCNC campaign delegation, was the newly formed radical grouping, the Zikist Movement, which aimed to focus its political work particularly among the youth.

The tour was an historic success, attracting huge crowds up and down the country. In one rally in Lagos, 30,000 people attended,[31] and the funeral in Lagos of the party's leader, Herbert Macaulay, who died whilst the delegation was visiting Kano, attracted more than 100,000 people.[32] While this occasion was solemn and dignified, it was nonetheless a political gathering. Azikiwe underlined this in his tribute: '[Macaulay] has left us an imperishable legacy, the struggle for the attainment of social equality, economic security, religious tolerance and political freedom ... Let us perpetuate his ideas of freedom; they can be realised in our lifetime.' The main plank of the NCNC campaign throughout the country was that the Richards Constitution and the 'obnoxious ordinances' were a divide-and-rule strategy by the occupying regime, aimed at simultaneously consolidating British control of the country and ensuring the non-emergence of a *pan*-Nigerian independence movement. It called on the people to reject these proposals and instead work for a unitary state. The response of the people was overwhelmingly enthusiastic. The political impact of the NCNC campaign in the country was '... unprecedented ... Except for the infrequent tours previously made by governors, *it was the first time in the history of Nigeria that large numbers of people were made conscious of Nigerian unity*' (emphasis added).[33] And to build on this success, the NCNC sent a delegation to London in June 1947 to impress on the British government the extent of popular opposition in Nigeria to its Richards Constitution and the 'obnoxious' ordinances.

The National Youth Movement (NYM) on the other hand was more circumspective in its response to these contentious developments. It was very critical of Richards for not consulting the leaders of the liberation movement before implementing the new constitution and enacting its land seizure decrees. The NYM also attacked the property provisions attached to voting rights, in addition to the ratio of elected-appointed members of both the central and regional legislative legislatures. But it found the 'regionalist' perspectives of the proposed constitution attractive, as these reflected the central thesis of Obafemi Awolowo's (NYM leader at the time) conception

---

[31] Ibid., p. 292.
[32] Ibid., p. 291.
[33] Ibid.

of Nigeria's post-conquest future, later articulated in 1947 in his book *Path to Nigerian Freedom*. Essentially, Awolowo had argued for the *regionalisation* of the post-conquest state according to the territorial imperatives of the constituent nations. So, for the NYM, the Richards Constitution represented a 'working basis'[34] for the restoration of independence for the peoples. Awolowo himself was even more confident than most: 'Maybe this new contrivance is, after all, not so defective as the people thought. Its actual working will show.'[35] Such was Awolowo's enthusiasm with the possibilities of the Richards Constitution that he invited Margery Perham, a recently retired ideologue of the occupation regime in Lagos and who would be a key adviser to the British and Nigerian governments during the 1966-1970 Igbo genocide, to write the forward to his *Path to Nigerian Freedom*. In the meantime, the NYM began to attack the expressive features of the NCNC campaigns against the occupation regime's recent anti-liberation manoeuvrings – particularly the NCNC's countrywide tours, and its visit and meetings in London with the British government. As should be expected, the British Government exploited the schism in the restoration-of-independence movement to the fullest. It rejected the demands of the NCNC's visiting delegation (during talks in London in August 1947) to radically alter or withdraw the Richards Constitution, and abrogate the provocative ordinances. Instead, it insisted that the constitution was a basis for a future restoration-of-independence negotiation, and was 'subject to later revision,' but not 'without a period of trial.'[36] Yet, contrary to the glee with which the NYM reacted to the apparent failure of the NCNC-British government London talks, tens of thousands of people welcomed back the delegation to the country in a pro-restoration of independence rally held in Lagos, ending a momentous era in the development of a pan-Nigeria liberation project.

V. What nation-state? Whose nation-state?

In March 1951, Obafemi Awolowo presided over the launching of the Action Group, of which he became leader. This was now Awolowo's opportunity to implement, concretely, his vision of 'regional' nationalism, and predictably his appeal was to members of the Yoruba nation of the west region. Awolowo's immediate task was to expunge NCNC influence in this

---

[34]Ananaba, *The Trade Union Movement in Nigeria*, p. 87.
[35]Obafemi Awolowo, *Path to Nigerian Freedom* (London: Faber and Faber, 1947), p. 119.
[36]Coleman, *Nigeria*, pp. 293-294.

region,[37] especially in the run up to the election planned later in the year for the central and regional legislatures. His long-term goal was to work against a pan-Nigeria unitary constitutional order, which he felt favoured the NCNC political aspirations and those of the Igbo people.[38] Instead, Awolowo's AG would work assiduously for the emergence of a post-conquest Nigeria divided into regional groupings which represented its various constituent nations.[39] Writing on the AG, Okwudiba Nnoli has observed: '[It was] inspired by, founded on, and nourished by ... chauvinism and regional parochialism.'[40] For the first time, a Nigeria-based pro-liberation political grouping, apparently desirous of freeing the peoples from the British occupation, explicitly associated itself with the destiny of one nation, the Yoruba, in the country. It therefore based its appeals for Yoruba support 'explicitly and implicitly on [chauvinist] sentiments, sensibilities, and interests.'[41] Yet, while the AG was steeped in exclusionist and chauvinist politics based on national differences, the Northern Peoples' Congress, which was largely created by the British occupation, was rapped in a racial and religiocultural exclusiveness that bordered on *apartheid*. Its name was exclusivist enough, even though it was formed in October 1951! It was as if the momentous catalogue of the NCNC-led liberationist politics of the previous decade, reviewed above, had been played out elsewhere – outside Nigeria's frontiers! It was also as if the historic debates on 'negritude' and African World liberation that raged among African World intellectuals resident in France and elsewhere in the previous two decades had been organised somewhere else in the solar system![42] But for the NPC leadership, it really appeared that it was immune to the historical and political implications of these events. Or was it?

The NPC's political platform was right from the outset anti-restoration of independence. It was *not opposed* to the indefinite occupation of Nigeria by Britain. There is no record of any other political party in the history of the liberation politics across the African World with such an unenviable heritage. It is often ignored by scholars interested in the comparative politics of the era that while major liberation endeavours would be embarked upon

---

[37]Nnoli, *Ethnic Politics in Nigeria*, p. 154 and Moyiba Amoda, 'Background to the Conflict: A Summary of Nigeria's Political History from 1914 to 1964,' in Joseph Okpaku, ed., *Nigeria: Dilemma of Nationhood* (New York: Third Press, 1972), p. 25.
[38]Nnoli, *Ethnic Politics in Nigeria*, p. 155.
[39]Dudley, *An Introduction to Nigeran Government and Politics*, p. 47 and pp. 309-310.
[40]Nnoli, *Ethnic Politics in Nigeria*, p. 155.
[41]Ibid.
[42]See Herbert Ekwe-Ekwe, 'Senghor (1906-2001),' *The Literary Encyclopedia*, at http://www.litencyc.com/php/speople.php?rec=true&UID=5154&PHPSESSID=2135 2bc3455ccec00131d9f2a1dac48a (accessed 17 February 2006).

by African peoples soon after the Second World War from Guyana in the Americas to Ghana on the African continent, from Trinidad in the Americas to Tanzania in Africa, and from Atlanta in the Americas to Aba in Africa, there was a major political party in Nigeria *which was not opposed to the indefinite European occupation* of this southeast region of west Africa. The NPC worked feverishly between 1951-1957 to oppose the politics of the liberation of Nigeria. It was only prepared to alter this position of opposition in late 1957 after it had been assured, through a series of relentless British political manoeuvrings (see below), that it would head the first post-conquest government. On finally taking office in 1960, the NPC, in varying political permutations of civilian and military regimes, would embark on nearly 40 years of virtually uninterrupted power in which it would convert Nigeria into a sprawling rentier state to subjugate, plunder and degrade crucial human and non-human resources in the east and its Niger Delta particularly, and finally execute the genocide of the Igbo people. The irony of the NPC's role in the history of Nigeria is captured succinctly in Moyiba Amoda's study of the era: 'Of the three Nigerian parties, the AG, the NCNC, and the NPC, the NPC was the least dedicated to a united Nigeria ...'[43]

Membership to the NPC was restricted to the people of the north, predominantly Hausa-Fulani. The party was principally a mid-20th century reincarnation of the aristocratic oligarchy of Fulani religiopolitical supremacy which held power in this part of Africa, prior to the British conquest.[44] Its retrograde ideology of north regional 'separateness', mediated by islam, charted the parameters of its worldview. Soon after it consolidated its position as the premier party in the north, the NPC proclaimed a policy of 'northernisation', its Nigerian version of *apartheid* that the European-settler exclusionist National Party of South Africa had launched only a few years back in 1948. The codification and implementation of 'northernisation' excluded south Nigerians from jobs in the region's public service, as well as a raft of other restrictive and discriminatory measures such as rights to landed property, districts of abode, establishment of businesses, access to local bank credits and allied facilities, access to state schools and hospitals, etc., etc. In contrast, foreigners, especially from the muslim world – Sudanese, Egyptians, Syrians, Pakistanis, Saudis – were readily given employment in the north instead of peoples from south Nigeria. But the most important foreign beneficiaries of employment opportunities based on 'northernisation' discriminatory codes were Britons, including those in the employ of the occupation regime in the south who could not cope with the increasingly vibrant liberationist politics of the time. The north continued to

---

[43]Amoda, 'Background to the Conflict,' p. 34
[44]Ikenna Nzimiro, 'Nigeria in Search of Ideology,' *Nigerian Statesman* (Owerri), 2-12 October 1982. See particularly the 5th October instalment of the series.

offer this haven for a number of British ex-south state officials and other professionals, in addition to British citizens from elsewhere in the world, well beyond 1960 – the year of Nigeria's so-called restoration of independence.

Two political parties, the Northern Elements Progressive Union, and the United Middle Belt Congress, offered what could distinctly be called some institutionalised opposition to the NPC colossus in the north, but not without these parties aligning themselves to the NCNC and the AG respectively. As the regionalisation of politics finally became entrenched in 1954, the NPC would emerge as the more hegemonic in its control of its north 'chunk' of 'tripartitioned' Nigeria than its east or west rivals. But it was precisely the mechanism underlining the control of this 'chunk', thanks to British subterfuge, which ensured that the NPC led both the pre-restoration of independence provisional central government (1954-1959) and the post-restoration of independence central administration until its overthrow by the military in 1966.

The politics unleashed by the Richards Constitution had now exacted a heavy toll on the concept and expectations of an all-Nigeria state, the linchpin of the liberationist politics launched by the NCNC freedom party a decade earlier. In fact by 1954, following the occupation regime's launch of yet another constitution, Macpherson Constitution, it was clear that the chauvinist and exclusivist political platforms of the AG and the NPC had dislodged an all-Nigeria freedom goal from the central corpus of the liberationist discourse of the era. What was now in place in Nigeria were regional quasi-autonomous political entities which exhibited the most unimaginable rivalries and, quite often, conflicts with each other, and whose relationship with the central provisional government in Lagos (which was ultimately run by the British occupation), varied from the ambiguous to undisguised opportunism. In this dispensation, the political control of the central government by any of the main parties became the necessary condition for the consolidation of power in its regional fiefdom, itself a precondition for existence.

As a result, the NCNC curtailed an impressive countrywide political project that had enthused the African liberationist consciousness of the immediate post-World War II Nigerian public, and retreated to the east region with its predominant support from the Igbo. The NCNC retreat began soon after the controversial 1951 elections to the west regional legislature which it won, despite the Action Group's scurrilous anti-Igbo campaign programme. In what was perhaps the most notorious case of electoral gerrrymandering in Africa to date, Obafemi Awolowo, the AG leader, sought to overturn this crushing electoral defeat in his home turf. He chauvinistically appealed to the elected majority Yoruba NCNC parliamentarians to abandon the party of their democratic choice and election, and defect to the AG. A majority of these heeded Awolowo's appalling racist appeal,[45] which ensured that the defeated AG ended up as victors, forcing the victorious NCNC into losers and opposition. Such was the hate generated in these polls that Azikiwe (the NCNC leader) resigned his position as the leader of opposition in the parliament, and instead contested for a seat in his east regional homeland legislature in Enugwu. Nonetheless, Chinua Achebe, the distinguished novelist, has, in a characteristically forthright review of events of the period, chided Azikiwe for 'capitulating' to the reactionary politics of Awolowo and the Action Group: 'Here was a true [Nigerian] nationalist who championed the noble cause of "one Nigeria" to the extent that he contested and won the first general election to the Western House of Assembly. But when ... Awolowo "stole" the government from him in broad daylight he abandoned his principle which dictated that he should stay in the Western House as Leader of the Opposition and give battle to Awolowo.'[46]

The eventual displacement of the all-Nigeria liberation project no doubt suited Britain – after all, this was what it expected to achieve after it published the 'divide-and-rule' Richards Constitution in 1945. Britain never conceptualised a Nigeria that was going to serve the national interests of the constituent African populations since it occupied these African states and peoples in 1900. It had no intention in 1954, nor indeed anytime in the foreseeable future, to abandon this firmly held strategic consideration in response to the liberation challenge posed by the NCNC. The constitution also suited the leaderships of the Northern Peoples' Congress and the Action Group, and their allies, as we shall elaborate soon. But for most peoples in Nigeria, the sociopolitical implications for the future were least promising. Billy Dudley has observed, quite graphically:

> As an employee, he now found that the level of his tax varied with the region in which he resided: he paid the most income tax if he resided in the East and the least if his residence was in the North. And as a farmer growing export crops, he found that the price he got for his produce varied with the region in which the produce was sold. Thus, for example, he got more for his cocoa if he sold it in the East – which grew little cocoa – than if the same cocoa was sold in the West. As a parent, with children of school-going age, he found that if he resided in the West, he did not have to pay fees for his children in

---

[45]See Nnoli, *Ethnic Politics in Nigeria*, p. 155.
[46]Chinua Achebe, *The Trouble with Nigeria* (Enugu: Fourth Dimension Publishers, 1983), p. 58.

primary schools but he had to do so if his place of abode was in the East or in the North.[47]

VI. Regionalisation

The regionalisation of Nigerian politics therefore accentuated the already disarticulated character of the country's conquest socioeconomic existence.[48] There was a deluge of development projects launched by the various regional governments in the field of education, healthcare, housing, agriculture, water supplies, energy and communications. Successes achieved in the dramatic expansion of educational institutions and opportunities were the most outstanding of these projects. In the first six years of regional government (1952-1958), more was achieved in the education of peoples in Nigeria than throughout the previous 50 years of the British conquest.[49] In 1947, the total number of primary school pupils in Nigeria was about 600,000. By 1958, it had shot up to over 2,500,000, an increase of at least 300 per cent.[50] In the same period, increases in post-primary school admissions (secondary and teacher training) were about 750 per cent (just under 10,000 in 1947 to 85,000 in 1958).[51] The east region established the first fully-fledged university in the country at Nsukka in 1960. This was two years before the University College at Ibadan, set up by the British in 1948, acquired autonomous university status when it severed its links with the University of London. By 1963, there was an unprecedented increase in the enrolment of undergraduates as a result of three more universities (two of which were owned by regional governments). In the first three years of post-conquest government, an increase of over 500 per cent in university enrolment was recorded, compared to the 400 per cent increase of admission at the sole Ibadan University College between 1948-1959, the last 11 years of the occupation regime.[52] To emphasise the importance attached to the education venture, most of the undergraduates, and an equally high proportion of post-primary students enjoyed generous financial sponsorships

---

[47]Dudley, *An Introduction to Nigerian Government and Politics*, p. 54.
[48]For a discussion of the disarticulated features of both the conquest and post-conquest socioeconomics of Nigeria, which nonetheless served British and other foreign interests, see Claude Ake, *A Political Economy of Nigeria* (Harlow: Longman Group, 1981), especially chs. 3 and 5.
[49]Segun Osoba, 'The Nigerian Power Elite, 1952-62,' in Peter Gutkind and Peter Waterman, eds., *African Social Studies: A Radical Reader* (London: Heinemann, 1977), p. 375.
[50]Ibid., p. 381.
[51]Ibid.
[52]Ibid., p. 376.

(scholarships, interest-free or low-interest loans and grants) from their regions (of origin) or the central government.

In spite of the strides made by the regional governments in expanding educational opportunities and facilities in the country, education itself remained an elitist project merely grafted on to the implanted occupation framework. There were scarcely any changes in the standard curriculum with its British conquest and occupation assumptions and worldview. The liberatory possibilities in the education process were hardly posed.[53] Continuous duplications of institutions and disciplines across the country were often the norm, and would probably have appeared rational were the three regions sovereign states, which did not have to contend with a *coherent* all-Nigeria educational policy in the final instance. Essentially, the success story of the educational programme during the period 1951-1959 was the immense opportunity it afforded for the recruitment and expansion of an elite, increasingly divorced from the aspirations of the people,[54] but which would play a strategic role in the major socioeconomic crisis that led to the genocide of the Igbo in the subsequent decade. The fact that this elite was pointedly *trilaterised*, with primary allegiance to one of the three regions, or as the case might be, one of the three majority nations in the country (Hausa-Fulani, Igbo, Yoruba) was an early and distinct trophy won by the chief protagonists of regionalisation in Nigeria.

Elsewhere in the regional economies, a number of industrial enterprises (especially the so-called import-substitute manufacturing) were set up, quite often in co-operation with British capital domiciled in Nigeria or from abroad. This was also the time when budding Nigerian entrepreneurs, who in the first place would have provided vital financial support to one of the parties in power, were beginning to build a stake in the evolving socioeconomic relations. Yet these development initiatives were in the main haphazard, bereft of reconstructive strategies that confronted the essence of the occupation's strategy of underdeveloping Nigeria. These early strides of *redevelopment* therefore remained uncoordinated at the regional level, and non-integrative countrywide. The fact, however, was that the regional autonomy of the era provided the varying strata of the emerging Nigerian merchant and bureaucratic elite the first opportunity since the occupation began to construct some power base of their own, albeit at the behest of the British occupation regime. It was this elite which ultimately oversaw the work of the pre-restoration of independence provisional governments in

---

[53] See, for instance, Femi Nzegwu, *Love, Motherhood and the African Heritage: The Legacy of Flora Nwapa* (Dakar: African Renaissance, 2001), pp. 82-86.
[54] Otonti Nduka, 'The rationality of the rich,' in Gutkind and Waterman, eds., *African Social Studies*, pp. 343-350.

Enugwu, Ibadan and Kaduna (as well as the central one in Lagos) between 1951-1959.

VII. Why Britain did not want to leave *and* why it has not yet left

The regionalisation of Nigerian politics coincided with the height of the boom in the overall economy of the Western World, caused by the post-World War II reconstruction programme. In Nigeria, an intensification of both agricultural and mineral export products (especially palm products, cotton, rubber, hides and skins, beniseeds, groundnuts, tin ore and columbite[55]) to meet with an ever-increasing British demand was embarked upon. In 1946, the value of Nigerian exports was £23.7 million.[56] By 1955, it was £129.8, and in 1960, £165.5.[57] There was a distinct growth in Nigeria's Gross Domestic Product during the period, an annual rate of 4.1 per cent in 1950/51-1957/58.[58] Indeed, not since 1916 had Nigeria enjoyed a favourable net-barter terms of trade with Britain as was recorded between 1951-1955, and 1958-1960.[59] But Nigeria was still a British occupied land, with a socioeconomy that existed principally to serve British interests. This was underlined by the fact that the gargantuan sum of £276.8 million, the preponderant chunk of the surpluses that accumulated from this unprecedented boom, was transferred to Britain between 1947-1960.[60] This is not to mention British surpluses enjoyed by the corresponding increases in the value of Nigerian imports from (mainly) Britain at the time: £19.8 million in 1946, £136.1 million in 1955, and £215.9 in 1960.[61]

Britain's more advantageous trade relations with Nigeria were further consolidated in 1955 when Europe slumped into an economic recession. The prices that Europeans were prepared to pay for imports of (primary) agricultural and mineral products abroad fell considerably. This was an instant blow to the Nigerian economy. Even though its export trade that year increased by 7,000 tons in volume, the value fell by £17 million.[62] The result was a further increase in Nigeria's import bills, which continued to rise as the demands made on the economy particularly by the provisional regional

---

[55]Bade Onimode, *Imperialism and Underdevelopment in Nigeria: The Dialectics of Mass Poverty* (London: Zed Books, 1982), pp. 47-55.
[56]R. Olufemi Ekundare, *An Economic History of Nigeria: 1800-1960* (London Methuen, 1973), p. 255.
[57]Ibid.
[58]Onimode, *Imperialism and Underdevelopment in Nigeria*, p. 48.
[59]Ibid.
[60]Ibid., p. 51.
[61]Ekundare, *An Economic History of Nigeria*, p. 226.
[62]Okwudiba Nnoli, 'A Short History of Nigerian Underdevelopment,' in Nnoli, ed., *Path to Nigerian Development* (Dakar: Codesria, 1981), p. 124.

governments' redevelopment programmes already referred to, went on unabated. While a 'buoyant' Nigerian economy with its dominant reliance on the British economy for imports was clearly an advantage for Britain, especially at a time of recession at home, the enormous strain on Nigeria's own accounting was becoming severe. Not only did the country incur deficits in its balance of payments position, it also drew heavily from its external reserves.[63] Such was the situation that Nigeria allocated at least one-fifth of the total investment bill earmarked for the 1955/56-1961/62 development plan to be financed from abroad.[64] While the total investment by leading Western companies (predominately British) in Nigeria stood at about £11.7 million in 1954, the figure for 1959/1960 was £20.5 million. These companies clearly took advantage of a series of 'liberal' measures, which the provisional central and regional governments initiated to attract such investment. These included the Industrial Development Ordinance (1957), the Industrial Development Ordinance (1958), the Customs Duties Ordinance (1958), and the establishment in 1959 of the Investment Company of Nigeria.[65] The statutes in these ordinances stretched from those that empowered the government to pay for part of some imported products required for a manufacturing enterprise, to provisions for extended tax holidays, in the case of new industries, to those which not only guaranteed investors' protection from competitors elsewhere but specified that import duties be waived from some businesses.[66] Added to the generous statutes contained in earlier ordinances on company taxation, and the overall freedom for investors to transfer their profits and dividends back home,[67] Nigeria was indeed a haven for British and other Western investment: 'Such investment inevitably reinforced external control of the production process established during the early [occupation] period and, therefore, the adverse effects on [Nigerian] self-reliance arising from that control, notably the divergence between local resource use and consumption, and the divergence between consumption and local needs.'[68]

Yet, Britain could no longer carry out such control with the totalising impunity of the past; it had to be mediated somewhat locally, and this historical responsibility lay squarely on the 3-party central and regionalised leaderships that emerged after 1951, as we have already shown. The irony, though, was that Britain was tightening its hegemonic grip on the Nigerian economy precisely at the time that these burgeoning Nigerian leaderships

---

[63] Ibid.
[64] Ibid.
[65] Ibid., p. 125.
[66] Ibid.
[67] Ibid.
[68] Ibid.

were supposedly intensifying their political drive to terminate the occupation. Evidently, it was becoming unclear who, or what, was being liberated from the occupation, as the latter relished in its new lease of life of British muscular consolidation. The heavy price that these leaderships had to pay for what was now a derailment of unfettered liberation from British conquest, at least as conceptualised originally by the NCNC freedom party, was probably eased by the increasing involvement of Nigerian entrepreneurs, technocrats, and political operators in various spheres of public life. As can be expected, this development suited Britain's long-term strategy of having a local elite that would ultimately protect its vast interests if, and when, its occupation of the country formally came to an end. With the establishment of marketing boards in the regions to take care of the purchase of the all-important agricultural export crops directly from the producers, the provisional regional governments ensured that the principal buying agents were local appointees, usually supporters of the party in power. Within a decade, most agents were Nigerians.[69]

Parallel to the activity of the marketing boards, this was also an era which witnessed the proliferation of 'public' corporations in the country. Both central and regional provisional governments paid the politically appointed personnel to these corporations (chairperson, directors, secretaries, etc.) bloated salaries and other perks, thus reinforcing the largesse of institutional patronage available. In effect, this was a 'unique opportunity of accumulating investment capital at public expense.'[70] Correspondingly, British businesses began to appoint Nigerians to their boards as honorary directors with the expectations that the latter would use their influence in the party (or government) to the advantage of the British-run enterprises.[71] British banks, which were notorious in the past for denying credit to Nigerians, suddenly began to make loans available to local entrepreneurs. But the linchpin in these manoeuvrings was the 'joint' enterprise, formed between the British business and the budding Nigerian entrepreneurship.[72] The latter became subordinate operators specialising in using their nascent political clout to help the expansion of the enterprise, while the former provided the lucrative financial rewards so much in demand by party and government department bosses.

As was mentioned earlier, the mid-1950s' deficits in Nigerian accounting which were caused by the economic recession in the Western World, and the ever-escalating costs of imports, exerted enormous pressure on the provisional central and regional governments' budgetary estimates. This was

---

[69]Osoba, 'The Nigerian Power Elite, 1952-65,' p. 371.
[70]Ibid., p. 372.
[71]Ibid., p. 374.
[72]Ibid.

more so on the latter where the administrations did not feel that they could afford to alienate electoral constituencies, crucial in maintaining the trilaterised political order, by trying to balance their books. So, regional expenditure commitments continued to rise, despite the fall in revenue either directly from the export trade or from the central government statutory allocations. But to offset the fall in funds available, regional governments resorted to borrowing more money, particularly from overseas. Soon the budgetary crisis intensified, leaving the central government, which guaranteed all external loans, to introduce restrictions on new regional governments' borrowings from abroad.[73] With such important power exercised by the central government, and also considering that the latter's overall financial position was understandably far healthier than the regions during the period, it was clear to each of the three main political parties (and their respective provisional regional governments) that the political control of the central government was, *in the final instance*, crucial in the maintenance and consolidation of their power base in the regions. This would definitely be the case whenever the restoration of independence occurred. It was therefore clear that the political party that controlled the federal government, particularly on the eve of the restoration of independence, would have emerged as the key political grouping of the increasingly contentious tripartitioned Nigeria. Such a party, it must be stressed, also had the task to oversee a future Nigerian economy bereft of the concomitant internal ownership and control that unfettered liberation envisaged, given the architecture of consolidation that Britain had worked so feverishly to construct between 1951 and 1960. Britain, surely, felt that it was in its own interest to decide which of these three Nigerian political parties (the National Council of Nigeria and Cameroons, Action Group, Northern Peoples' Congress) would enable it continue to exercise the expropriation of the bounty of conquest that is *its* Nigeria – well beyond the country's so-called restoration of independence.

Notes on a crisis: 1957-1965

In May 1957, the NCNC, AG and NPC political leaders returned to London to continue their discussion with the British government on the date and the constitutional arrangements for the restoration of independence. This was the first meeting held on the subject in four years – since the July-August 1953 London conference, which had ended in a deadlock over the independence date. In the meantime, the north's position on the issue had shifted. By now, Britain had decided firmly that it was going to hand over political power to its client, the Northern Peoples' Congress and the north. In turn, the NPC

---

[73]Dudley, *An Introduction to Nigerian Government and Politics*, p. 56.

was confident that it would form the first post-conquest Nigerian government and was prepared to accept a date for the restoration of independence that the north had so vociferously opposed for over a decade. This had already been guaranteed in the 1951 constitution in which Britain arbitrarily allocated 50 per cent of seats in the central legislature in Lagos to the north on the unsubstantiated basis that one-half of Nigeria's population lived in this region.[74] Since the beginning of the 1952 regionalisation of politics, the NPC had maintained an overwhelmingly unchallenged political control of the north. This was unlikely to change in the future, hence the party's confidence. Indeed, as a result of the north's spurious numerical dominance over the rest of the federation, the NPC emerged as the leader of the 1954 central provisional government even though the countrywide elections that determined this outcome were held on a very restricted franchise in the north (apart from the fact that women were completely excluded from participating, the rest of the region's population 'voted' through an electoral college). As Harold Smith, previously of the occupation regime, recalls, 'The British loved the North and had arranged for 50% of the votes to be controlled by the Northern Peoples' Congress ... Because of this, independence was to some extent a sham because the results were a foregone conclusion. The North and the British would continue to rule.'[75] So, for the foreseeable future in Nigeria, thanks to Britain's crass dictat, the NPC did not need to campaign or in fact win electoral seats *outside* the north in order to be able to either form the central government solely by itself, or in coalition with either of its two southern rivals. It was with this trump card that the NPC delegation arrived in London in May 1957 to announce that it would *no longer* be opposed to the liberation of Nigeria, which it had consistently done for well over a decade.

Despite their obvious misgivings and outrage over Britain's essential *coup d'état* to impose the NPC and the north on the future destiny of the peoples in Nigeria, both the NCNC and the AG welcomed the NPC *volte-face* on the restoration of independence. The NCNC particularly did not wish to contest this latest entry in the raft of British diktats, clearly meant to frustrate or complicate, even further, the liberation process. Nonetheless, in a desperate, eleventh hour attempt to neutralise the NPC-ascriptive 50 per cent electoral 'veto', both the NCNC and AG demanded the creation of new regions from the existing three. The NPC was, predictably, opposed to this. As for the British government, it agreed, but not without being evidently sardonic – namely, that for new regions to be created, the date for the

---

[74] As Harold Smith graphically puts it, the British allocated the north '50 per cent of [Nigeria's] population without any census.' – see Smith, 'How the British undermined democracy in Africa.'
[75] Ibid.

restoration of independence would be delayed.[76] Quite clearly, none of the delegations wanted such a delay – not even the NPC, especially now that it was armed with a supposedly priceless veto by the British to run Nigeria in perpetuity. The three parties then demanded the restoration of independence as from 1960.

I. Elections and yet another British diktat

As was expected, the Northern Peoples' Congress won the 1959 pre-restoration of independence election to the central legislature in Lagos. As Harold Smith recalls, pointedly, this poll was a 'mockery because the outcome – Northern domination of Nigeria after independence – was assured before a single vote was cast.'[77] The election was conducted on the basis of a new north/south population ratio of about 54:46,[78] which further consolidated the north's bogus numerical majority over the rest of the country. As a result, the north was assigned 174 seats in the 312-member assembly, the east 73, the west 62, and the Lagos capital territory, 3. In the election itself, the NPC won 134 seats, the NCNC 89, the AG 73 and independent candidates 16.[79] All the NPC seats were won in the north, and once again on a restrictive and discriminatory franchise, which excluded women (this time, the NPC's 'concession' to universal adult franchise in its north homeland was that this should affect men only). The AG won 33 of the 62 seats allocated to the west, 27 went to the NCNC, and the remaining two seats were captured by independent candidates. In the east, the NCNC won 58 of the seats, while the remaining 18 seats went to the AG and independents. All the Lagos seats were controlled by the NCNC.

These results underlined the point we made earlier about the electoral 'veto' at the disposal of the NPC: as long as this party maintained its political supremacy in the north, it did not need to campaign for elections nor indeed win any seats elsewhere in the country to emerge as the victorious party in any countrywide elections. In fact by winning just 77 per cent of the total number of seats assigned to the north in these polls, the NPC became victorious countrywide. In contrast, the NCNC had to win about 80 per cent of the seats in the east, 43 per cent in the west, and 100 per cent of those allocated to the Lagos capital electoral district, to achieve the second position across the country. In spite of the NCNC's much more *countrywide* performance at the polls, it ended up with 45 fewer seats than the NPC which did not step out of its north regional electoral base. Yet, these results

---

[76]Coleman, *Nigeria*, pp. 392-393.
[77]Smith, 'How the British undermined democracy in Africa'.
[78]Dudley, *An Introduction to Nigerian Government & Politics*, p. 58.
[79]Ibid., p. 61.

showed that the NPC electoral 'veto' could be scuttled, especially in a situation where this party failed to achieve an absolute majority over the total (electoral) gains of its opponents. Aware of this, the third party, the AG, sent out delegations to the NPC, as well as the NCNC, to negotiate the possibility of forming either an AG-NPC or AG-NCNC coalition government.[80] Apart from these, the other possible coalitions, were of course the NCNC-NPC or an AG-NCNC-NPC all party government. A sole NPC government was a feasibility, albeit a minority and therefore potentially 'unstable'.

The outcomes just sketched represented the varied electoral possibilities of the surprisingly dynamic situation that prevailed in Nigeria soon after the 1959 election, despite the NPC 'veto' that had so much foreshadowed the exercise. But James Robertson, the outgoing British occupation governor, would have none of the 'uncertainties' that might just exclude the much favoured NPC to take power – according to the clearly laid out script of the British diktat. So, before *all* the results from the election were declared, Robertson, who three years before as the British occupation governor in the Sudan institutionalised north Arab sociopolitical hegemony over the African south (on the eve of Sudan's own restoration of independence from British conquest in 1956), invited the NPC to form a government.[81] Robertson's dramatic intervention ensured that the NPC electoral 'veto' survived, and became entrenched in the future political life of the country. More importantly, though, this 'veto' made nonsense of whatever fairness in the political system, which ironically was called the 'Westminster model' by the British and their Nigerian operatives. This fraudulent model was replicated elsewhere in British-occupied Africa. A few years later, after the system's collapse, a range of eurocentric and often racist 'analyses' in universities and elsewhere would proclaim to the world that it failed because Africans could not run such a *democratic* model!

If ever there were any doubts about the *anti-African* essence of the Lugardian project, the frantic British manoeuvrings of the previous six years to impose the Northern Peoples' Congress (the party that it, itself, virtually created in the first place to oppose the liberation of Nigeria) on post-conquest Nigeria laid these firmly to rest. In these moves, aimed centrally to protect its bounties of conquest in these African lands indefinitely, Britain had literally choked off the liberatory possibilities inherent in the restoration of independence for the peoples. Quite unabashedly, Britain had armed the Northern Peoples' Congress with a 'veto' to take over and stay in power at all costs, rigged an election in favour of the Northern Peoples' Congress, falsified the country's population figures in favour of the Northern Peoples'

---

[80]Ibid., p. 62.
[81]Ibid. p. 61.

Congress, and would soon begin secret talks with the Northern Peoples' Congress aimed at offering it a 'defence pact' for *all time* British 'protection'. In effect, Britain had sown a minefield of discord in Nigeria on the eve of its so-called 'departure' from the country. These would explode intermittently in the following five years, and would ignite into a devastating conflagration in 1966 as the world witnessed the beginning of the Igbo genocide in which three million people were murdered.

Quite clearly, the British-formulated sociopolitical 'framework' for the restoration of independence in Nigeria had, right from the outset, foreclosed fair competition – a critical variable for its operation, 'stability' and survivability. There could indeed be no rationality for a non-NPC party in the 'framework' to play the role of the *opposition*, except of course to provide another vital piece of colouring to its 'Westminster' garb; the 'opposition' was doomed to stagnate in its position politically. Except a non-NPC party wanted to destroy the NPC 'veto', and this would, almost invariably, have to be through some form of extra-parliamentary means, the only incentive open to the NCNC and the AG, following the Robertson diktat, was to work out some electoral 'accommodation' with the NPC. The main considerations for such an 'accommodation' were predicated on what had since 1951 been the *leitmotif* of politics in Nigeria: the preservation and consolidation of the sociopolitical character of the regions. Both the NCNC and AG would also wish to have access to federal resources, albeit under their respective regions. The essence of politics on the morrow of the restoration of independence in Nigeria on 1 October 1960 remained the same as those on 29 June 1951: the existence of three nation-states – namely in the east, north and west, and with the paraphernalia of central government apparatus in Lagos continuing to be an arena where these regions had to engage in a panoply of contestation, aimed at acquiring critical resources to run their administrations. The NPC, much more than its rivals, underlined this functional role of Lagos most symbolically. Its party leader, Ahmadu Bello, retained his premiership of the north, whilst its deputy leader, Abubakar Tafawa Balewa, remained in Lagos as prime minister of the central government. In contrast, both NCNC and AG leaders (Azikiwe and Awolowo respectively) had become members of the central legislature, having resigned their premierships and seats in the regional parliament in Enugwu and Ibadan (respectively).

II. Coalition

With the ironclad backing of the occupation regime, the Northern Peoples' Congress embarked on forming Nigeria's first post-conquest government. It decided to form a coalition government with one of the other two parties because it would have been extremely difficult for it to run the country alone as a 'minority' regime. The NPC's choice of coalition partner was once again based on the regional priorities of Nigerian politics. It spurned the Action Group's approaches for a coalition principally because the latter posed a potential threat to the NPC's political control of the north region's southern Benue valley (or the midbelt).[82] The NPC had been particularly incensed by the electoral successes of the local United Middle Belt Congress, an ally of the AG, during the 1959 poll (it won 25 seats or 14.4 per cent of the north's seats in the central legislature). The UMBC received the majority of the vote of the Tiv, the midbelt's principal nation, who had historically resisted Hausa-Fulani territorial expansionism.[83] Instead, the NPC chose the NCNC to form its working coalition. While the latter's electoral ally in the north, the Northern Elements Progressive Union (NEPU), had won eight seats in Kano during the election, the NPC did not really view this outcome as a long-term threat to its electoral hegemony in the region, an optimism that was borne out when NEPU could only manage to win just one seat in the 1961 north regional elections.

As for the NCNC, the electoral coalition with the NPC suited its sociopolitical interests, even if in the short term. Fundamentally, resources from the central government were essential in consolidating the east's ever-expanding industrial, commercial and agricultural enterprises in a region which, thanks to the heightened regionalisation of Nigeria's sociopolitics since 1951, now had the country's fastest growing economy. In a few years, more successes in this arena would catapult the east to Africa's fastest growing economy. The NCNC had quickly circumscribed its envisaged countrywide post-occupation socio-economic reconstruction development to the east region for implementation. This was clearly in response to the success of the occupation regime's final blockade of the party's long cherished all-Nigeria mission. The NCNC economic team, led by Mbonu Ojike, the brilliant African peoples'-centred economist, had earmarked a 20-year plan to transform the east into an advanced industrial and economic power. The results of the first phase of this plan (1954-1964) were indeed staggering. The east had the best schools and the first independent university system in the country, the best humanpower development in the country across a range of fields including, crucially, engineering, medicine, the arts, and middle range technical cadre. The region also had the most integrated infrastructural development in Nigeria and its manufacturing, distributive and extractive enterprises centred in the Enugwu-Nkalagu-Emene conurbation to the north, Onicha to the west, and Ugwuocha/Port Harcourt-

---

[82]Remi Anifowose, *Violence and Politics in Nigeria* (New York and Enugu: Nok Publishers International, 1982), p. 294.
[83]Ibid.

Aba-Calabar to the south, were clearly the hubs of the making of this African industrial revolution of recent history.

Besides hoping for some financial and allied resources to be tapped for the east's active reconstruction programme, the NCNC expected that its membership of the electoral coalition with the NPC would be a boost to the morale of the near 1.5 million east immigrants in the north of Nigeria (who overwhelmingly supported the NCNC) who were increasingly victimised by the NPC's 'northernisation' policy. The NCNC hoped that through the 'goodwill' generated in the coalition, the NPC would modify or scrap some of the discriminatory government policies which had had adverse effects on the immigrants especially in their business operations (particularly the retail trade) and welfare (housing, schools, culture). In the next few years, the fate of these immigrants would more than once play an important part in deciding not just the future of the coalition, but even more importantly, the future of the *entire* country – it was the premeditated massacre of 100,000 of these immigrants by northern Nigerians and their allies between May-October 1966 that inaugurated the first phase of the Igbo genocide, which would expand latter in 1967-1970 in the second phase and the murder of 3 million Igbo.

Furthermore, the coalition provided the NCNC with the opportunity to continue to play some role in countrywide politics, despite the British enforced containment and the strategic dominance of regionalisation. The NCNC was able to deploy a number of the party's key officials (including Azikiwe) as legislators in Lagos, and quite a number (coming from the region with the country's most educated humanpower) were in position as principal personnel in various spheres of central government (Azikiwe himself first became speaker of the senate, the governor-general, and later non-executive president when the country became a republic in 1963). Such a countrywide role tied up with the NCNC's policy in the west region, which remained unchanged: unhindered by the absence of any existing electoral pacts with the AG, the NCNC sought to improve even further on the political gains it made during the 1959 election, if it hoped to retain its place in the Lagos central legislature as the second largest party. As was the case in the past, the NPC's continuing electoral 'veto' in Nigerian politics meant that either the AG or the NCNC must win the majority of the total number of seats allocated to the south regions of the country to determine the party with the second position in parliament in Lagos. While this dispensation meant that the south was the only geographical zone for a more unfettered, 'open' forms of politics in the country, the NCNC-AG quest for this electoral 'second place' became highly prized, underlined by an increasingly acrimonious and capricious contestation. This was evidently the case in the west where the NCNC's challenge of the AG's overall control of a region the latter considered its principal mobilisation base, was still serious.

III. Fall

Within two years, the NPC-NCNC coalition was in serious trouble. Significantly, the crisis began over a sharp disagreement in the coalition over the regional allocation of funds and projects in the country's £670 million 1962-1968 countrywide 'development programme'. The NCNC was highly incensed by the NPC's allocation of about 85 per cent of all planned expenditure to the north, including the establishment in the region of the strategic Kainji hydroelectric dam installation, the extension of the northeast railway to Maiduguri, and the phenomenal expansion and updating of the military bases in the Kaduna area.[84] For the NCNC, it appeared that its *raison d'être* for joining the coalition – access to some critical resources from the central government to fund its east's economic transformation – was already coming unstuck! The NCNC's expectation that the entire iron and steel industry, another major project in the programme, would be located at the Enugwu-Emene-Nkalagu industrial district in the east, was dashed when the NPC insisted that only one-half of the facility would go to the east as the other one-half would be sited in the north.[85] Finally, the NCNC was frustrated over the £1 million it received for its agriculture, an area of the economy it had planned to expand as part of its regional transformation project, while the NPC allocated £2 million to the north's agriculture.[86] Quite clearly, the NPC felt that as the majority party in the coalition, it had to dictate the principles, and the method in which the funding and establishment of 'development' projects in the country had to be carried out. It did not feel obligated to any other political constituency in Nigeria besides the north, which must have felt satisfied with the receipt of seven-eighths of the total funding allocated to the country's first post-conquest 'development programme', despite its sustained opposition to the liberation of Nigeria. For the NCNC, the east's highly minimal 'appropriation' of the 'development' funds (and projects) undermined the party's key reason for joining the coalition (as we have already stated), more so at a time when petroleum oil products (overwhelmingly) from the east were beginning to account for a major source of central government revenue.[87]

Yet, it was the controversy over the 1962 countrywide census, ordered by the coalition, which showed most dramatically the deterioration of the

---

[84] For details of the regional allocation of the major projects in this programme, see Dudley, *An introduction to Nigerian Government and Politics*, p. 63.

[85] Billy Dudley, *Instability and Political Order* (Ibadan: Ibadan University, 1973), p. 70.

[86] Dudley, *An Introduction to Nigerian Government and Politics*, p. 63.

[87] Dudley, *Instability and Political Order*, pp. 67-69.

relations between the NPC, which accepted the results, and the NCNC, which rejected them. This was the first census in the country since the British fraudulent exercise of 1952, which gave the north the bogus numerical superiority over the two south regions. The 1962 result only replicated the outrage of the previous decade. It claimed that there were 22.5 million people in the north, 12.3 million in the east, 10.2 million in the west, and 576,000 people in the Lagos capital territory.[88] The outcome of the work of a team of independent verifiers that was commissioned by the central and all regional governments to check the authenticity of these figures demonstrated how heavily inflated they had been throughout the country. Out of the 174 electoral constituencies in the north, only 99 passed the exercise (76 failed, of which 49 failed completely); in the east, 53 of the 73 constituencies passed the test (20 failed, 5 of which failed in all categories), and of the 62 constituencies in the west, only 28 passed (34 failed, with 13 of those failing in all categories).[89] Apart form the Lagos capital district where no tests were carried out, the outcome of the exercise once again showed that Nigeria's census figures had been rigged as the British had done a decade earlier, with the north still living the lie as the country's most populous region. Furthermore, no one was certain what Nigeria's true population really was. In fact, this is still the case, 42 years later, as these lines are written.

The 1962 census figures, just as those that Britain concocted in 1952, could therefore not be relied upon as the basis for the distribution of seats in the central legislature in Lagos, and consequently the 'legitimisation' of the NPC and the north's hegemonic control of the politics of Nigeria as the British had so entrenched. The census time bomb that British intrigue had laid to further London's interests in the country had not only rendered crucial statistical data for planning purposes in Nigeria meaningless, but was now fuelling political tension in the country very dangerously. With the 1962 results annulled by the coalition at the end, another census held in the country in 1963 similarly ended with rigged figures. Once again the NCNC rejected the results.

The Action Group, in the meantime, had followed with considerable interest the collapsing fortunes of the NPC-NCNC electoral politics. It had tried to 'settle into' the pointedly cosmetic role of official opposition party in a central legislature whose electoral structure had been designed to ensure an NPC party majority in perpetuity. The political barrenness of opposition in such a set-up was gravely illustrated in the 'poor' performance of the west, the AG's main electoral base, in the NPC's allocation of regional projects in the latter's so-called 'development programme'. Apart from the skimpy

---

[88]Ibid., p. 75.
[89]Ibid., p. 76.

allocation of £700,000 to the west's agriculture,[90] and funds designated to maintain existing central government institutions in the region, the NPC did not establish any major project in the west during the period. Besides, pro-AG financiers and entrepreneurs found that their party affiliations often posed a handicap in getting central government contracts, which were readily scooped up by colleagues who were either members of the NPC or NCNC coalition. The impact of the AG's limited access to central government funding, projects and patronage, meant that subsidies essential in ploughing into the west's economy to produce goods and services aimed at sustaining its electoral support, were beginning to dissipate.

To offset the shortfall in revenue, in the medium term, Samuel Akintola, the regional premier, increased school fees.[91] This was a policy which was hardly popular in a region that had enjoyed low or no fees across its education establishment. But Akintola's substantial reduction of taxes and the basic price of cocoa (the region's principal agricultural crop for export)[92] was no doubt a gesture of goodwill to AG entrepreneurs, whose interests elsewhere had not prospered sufficiently as a result of the country's electoral opposition in the central legislature in Lagos. And it was the change of the AG's official status as the 'opposition party' that Akintola envisaged would, in the long term, enable the west to overcome its growing socioeconomic difficulties. Put bluntly, Akintola wanted the AG to abandon its opposition and join the troubled NPC-NCNC coalition, a proposition he intended to present for debate during the party's February 1962 convention in Jos, north Nigeria. This was a political development that would be particularly welcomed by the NPC for obvious reasons (the prime minister himself who was also the NPC deputy leader had indeed shown an early interest in the Akintola proposition[93]). It also had the potential of pushing the AG into a 'favourable' No. 2 position in an enlarged coalition or even in a revised coalition that forced out the disaffected NCNC. But the success of such a major shift in AG policy remained doubtful, because of the worsening personal relationship between its initiator, Akintola, and Obafemi Awolowo, the party leader and chief opposition spokesperson in the central legislature: 'Akintola maintained that Awolowo was tyrannical; that he interfered unduly with major and minor details of running the Western Regional Government, and that he infiltrated the Ministries and the Corporations with his loyal disciples who then refused to cooperate with him [Akintola].

---

[90]Dudley, *An Introduction to Nigerian Government and Politics*, p. 63.
[91]Anifowose, *Violence and Politics in Nigeria*, p. 189.
[92]Ibid.
[93]Ibid., p. 188.

Conversely, Awolowo charged Akintola with initiating a "personality cult" by making major policy decisions without consulting the party Executive.'[94]

At the Jos convention, Akintola's proposal for a change in the AG's future policy was rejected, forcing the premier and his supporters to walk out of the meeting. Obafemi Awolowo used the opportunity afforded by the convention to attack the effects in the west of the Akintola government's social and fiscal programme (especially those that affected taxation and school fees), which he felt was increasing the gap in the material resources of the 'privileged' and 'non-privileged' members of the party.[95] The party declared its intention to work closely with its United Middle Belt Congress ally in the north's Benue valley. This latter declaration was obviously not going to endear the party to the NPC! Most importantly, however, Awolowo succeeded in effecting personnel changes in the AG party's hierarchy with his own factional supporters, thereby increasing the chances of a permanent split in the party. Five months later, the split in the AG was complete. The Awolowo faction removed Akintola from his post as deputy leader and premier of the west, and replaced him with Dauda Adegbenro. Akintola refused to stand down. A parliamentary session in the west legislature (in Ibadan) summoned to formally appoint Adegbenro as premier was marred by violence between members of the two AG factions, leading the central government to suspend the west government and declare a state of emergency in the region which lasted until January 1963.

Akintola resumed his premiership of the west after the emergency, but this time his faction had formed a new party, the United People's Party, with him as leader. The UPP declared its alliance with the NPC, thereby achieving Akintola's original aim for the Action Group (which he had proposed without success in the previous year). However, in order to govern successfully in the west, where the NPC had no legislators and where UPP members were fewer than those of the rump AG, the UPP formed a coalition government with the NCNC (which had all along been the official opposition party in the region). The AG was now in opposition in west Nigeria! – a fate that it had rigged itself out of in 1951 when it initially lost the region's elections to the NCNC. The tempestuous history of a party formed strategically to defend pan-Yoruba political interests precisely ten years before, under the aegies of separatist regionalism, had now gone full circle.

Coming fast on the heels of the AG political débâcle in west Nigeria, Obafemi Awolowo and a number of his top party aides were arrested by police and charged with plotting to overthrow the federal government. After a trial, which lasted for about eight months, most of the defendants,

---

[94]Ibid., pp. 188-189.
[95]Ibid., p. 189.

including Awolowo, were found guilty. Awolowo was jailed for 10 years and the rest were sentenced to prison for periods that ranged from two to 10 years. Following the incarceration of Awolowo, Akintola quickly consolidated the UPP's alliance with the NPC, by terminating his coalition government with the NCNC in Ibadan. Instead, he announced the formation of yet another new party, this time called the Nigerian National Democratic Party (which soon had two of its members appointed ministers in the federal cabinet). The NNDP comprised of all members of the UPP, and most members of the NCNC who had 'crossed over' to the new party in response to an Akintola ultimatum.

Later, the NNDP and the NPC formed the Nigerian National Alliance to contest the December 1964 countywide elections. In turn, the NCNC, the AG, and their two electoral allies in the north (NEPU and UMBC respectively), launched the United Progressive Grand Alliance to challenge the NNA during these polls. And in the last six months of the life of the existing central parliament, the NPC-NCNC coalition, that political grouping through which the initial skirmishes of the immediate post-occupation phase of Nigeria's 'regionalist' politics were fought out, functioned barely in name.

IV. Strike and strife

By mid 1964, the intense and ever-widening crisis in Nigeria's political establishment was inevitably having its effects, and also being influenced by events elsewhere in the country. In July 1963, the United Labour Congress of Nigeria, the main workers' union, called on the central government to improve the deteriorating social conditions of workers. The workers demanded an urgent review of salaries and wages (including the introduction of a national minimum wage) to cope with growing inflation of prices of essential commodities, and the termination of the humiliating 'daily-wage' structure that had been in force since the British occupation. In a clear reference to the graft, the ostentatiousness, and the abuse of power that characterised the politics of the times, the labour organisation warned Nigerian leaders with a compelling foresight:

> In your luxurious surroundings, in your residential palaces far removed from the squalor of the worker's living condition, from his privation and generally depressed economic condition, you, dear compatriots, may be sitting on a power-keg. We do not begrudge you, but we give a timely warning. Please understand us properly. We want you to understand the present, and live in accordance with the

tenets of social and economic justice, so that we can all avoid the catastrophes of tomorrow.'[96]

The union also criticised the federal government's proposed legislation to detain citizens without trial in the name of the 'country's security' (later abandoned as a result of concerted opposition both in and outside parliament), which, it correctly observed, 'curtailed the necessary expressions of human dignity.'[97]

Three months later, the government replied, rejecting the workers' main demands, especially those on the upward revision of salaries and the provision of a minimum wage, and the abolition of the 'daily wage' system. It was willing to cancel regional variations in wage, even though employers still retained the right to fix wages in certain local circumstances. The workers turned down this offer, and declared a one-day strike on 27 September 1963. This action forced the government to appoint a special commission, headed by Justice Adeyinka Morgan to look into the workers' demands. The Morgan Commission completed its work in April 1964, but the government dithered over publishing its findings, which were later found to be generally favourable to workers. Indeed, two members of the Commission (O.I. Akinkugbe and C.O. Nwokedi) advocated, albeit in a 'minority report', a drastic cut in salaries paid to the higher echelons of the public services which they considered as still 'colonial in content and structure and not related to the capacity of the national economy, nor to the degree of responsibility shouldered by the beneficiaries.'[98] They also called for the termination of car allowances paid to various categories of state officials, another feature of the British conquest legacy. They had argued that this practice was extremely expensive (a point demonstrated acutely in the proportion of the 1962-63 federal and regional governments' recurrent expenditure allocated to car allowances alone: the west 2.4 per cent; the north 1.8 per cent; the east 1.5 per cent, and central 0.8 per cent[99]) and also that it was an impediment to the development of a coherently planned countrywide transport system. In yet another 'minority report', T.M. Yusufu called on the government to abolish allowances paid to children of top officials, another feature of the occupation's privilege, and implicitly attacked the non-existence of a countrywide housing policy by asking the

---

[96]Statement issued by Lawrence Borha, general-secretary, United Labour Congress of Nigeria (cited in Ananaba, *The Trade Union Movement in Nigeria*, p. 235.)
[97]Ibid., p. 234.
[98]Ibid., p. 245.
[99]Ibid., p. 246.

central government to also terminate the provision of statutory accommodation which was made to top state officials.[100]

The main thrust of the Morgan Commission's final report was to incorporate various strands of these 'minority' concerns within a number of recommendations, which amounted to some reforms of the pointedly anti-labour laws that were 'inherited' from the British occupation. In this regard, it was historically significant that the commission called for both a parliamentary legislation, which made it mandatory for all employers to publish their conditions of employment including workers' benefits (copies of which should be made available to workers), and the revision of the labour code act in order to 'guarantee certain basic minimum rights to all categories of workers with special reference to termination notices, leave entitlements, sick leave and medical care ... It should be illegal for an employer to refuse to recognise a duly registered trade union.'[101] In response to the workers' demands for an increase in their wages, the commission recommended the payments of a minimum wage, which took 'cognisance of regional variations', and which amounted to increases varying between 58-100 per cent of existing minimum wage scales.[102]

One 1 June 1964, Nigerian workers declared a general strike over the central government's reluctance to publish the report of the Morgan Commission. Two days later, the government published the report but rejected the commission's new wage recommendations. The strike spread. After its first full week, it had turned into a popular protest against the central government with calls for the prime minister to resign. As the strike moved into its second week, Nigeria was virtually paralysed with public transport, post and telecommunication, electricity power utilities, factories, banks, shops, schools, and the civil service ceasing to function. Not since the 1945 strike against the British occupation had the country witnessed such a manifestation of labour protest. The government was forced to negotiate, enabling the workers to call off the action on 13 June. Apart from minor adjustments, endorsed by workers during negotiations, the government and other employers accepted to pay both the 'Morgan' wages to workers and also implement the other longer-term proposals made by the commission.

But having barely survived the labour strike, the Balewa central government had more problems elsewhere. The strike itself had further weakened the coalition in Lagos where the NPC members accused the NCNC of supporting the protest, through the action of leading trade unionists sympathetic to the latter and the involvement of NCNC politicians in a number of solidarity labour rallies organised in several eastern towns

---

[100] Ibid., pp. 246-247.
[101] Ibid., pp. 244-245.
[102] Ibid., p. 241.

and cities during the period.¹⁰³ It was however in the west and the midbelt province of the north that the outcome of the strike had particularly bolstered the confidence of local populations who had embarked on a programme of defiance and resistance to the authorities of their respective regional governments. Balewa's ultimate capitulation to the labour strike demands had made his regime appear extremely vulnerable, and this was clearly detected by political forces actively opposed to the NPC and its NNDP ally in the west and the midbelt. More and more people in the west, who supported the Action Group and its jailed leader, were now openly calling for the resignation of the NNDP regime in Ibadan followed by a democratic election. NNDP officials, especially in the outlying districts of the west, were increasingly becoming targets of physical attacks, and fatalities mounted. Police and paramilitary reinforcements had been ordered to improve the general security situation, but without notable success. By the end of 1964, when elections to the central legislature were held, it had become obvious that the NNDP regime was immensely unpopular in most parts of the west.[104]

In the midbelt, the Tiv were in open revolt against the NPC government in Kaduna. Well-organised groups of the opposition UMBC attacked opponents and easily identifiable state officials and institutions, especially those associated with law and order. Scores of police, members of the judiciary and tax officials were killed, while several police posts, court houses, and local government establishments were destroyed during the campaign.[105] Hundreds of civilians died during the emergency,[106] many of whom were killed by the police during a scorched earth counter-insurgency operation. Whilst the deployment of the military ultimately suppressed the uprising, the political demands for Tiv self-government went unheeded.

V. Stalemate and coup

On the eve of the December 1964 elections to the central legislature, the overall political situation in Nigeria was extremely tense. The turmoil in the west continued unabated. An uneasy truce prevailed in the midbelt where hundreds had been killed and a total of 4,000 people had been detained for their involvement in the Tiv revolt.[107] The military were still responsible for the maintenance of security in the province.

---

[103] Ibid., p. 247.
[104] Anifowose, *Violence and Politics in Nigeria*, pp. 191-194.
[105] Ibid., p. 132.
[106] Ibid.
[107] Ibid., p. 133.

The campaigns for the elections emerged as another site of confrontation. The UPGA bloc of parties (NCNC, AG, NEPU and UMBC) was highly optimistic that they would defeat the NNA pact (NPC and NNDP) and break the entrenched hegemony that the Hausa-Fulani north exerted on Nigerian politics. The UPGA reckoned that it would be able to turn the tide of the mass anti-NNDP discontent in the west into its favour. There was a distinct possibility that the combined weight of 'traditional' AG and NCNC support in the region would ensure an UPGA victory there. Equally, the UPGA was optimistic that it would win in the troubled midbelt province in the north as a result of the strong local support of the UMBC. Finally, the UPGA was confident of victory in the east (where the NCNC had been the majority party since 1951), in the newly created midwest region (also led by an NCNC administration), and in the Lagos capital district where all the three incumbent legislators belonged to the NCNC. The UPGA appeared to be potentially in a position to exert considerable electoral control in all regions of Nigeria except the Hausa-Fulani north. Arithmetically, an overwhelmingly UPGA victory in these non-northern regions would ensure that the alliance either emerged as the majority party in the central parliament, or, at worse, end up with roughly the same number of seats as the NNA. Either way, the contentious 12-year old NPC electoral 'veto' in parliament would be destroyed. Going by past record during which the NPC had hardly won an electoral seat outside the 'guaranteed' constituencies of its Hausa-Fulani homeland, the prospects of an UPGA success at the forthcoming polls were real indeed.

The NNA reacted to this historic possibility of an NPC defeat by launching a frenzical strategy of intimidation directed at its UPGA opponents, especially in the north and west regions of the country, in the months to the run up of the elections. In the north, the local government police (linked to the emirate security apparatus but not integrated into the country's police service) detained scores of prospective UPGA candidates and their agents, particularly in the latter's political strongholds in the midbelt, plateau and Kano provinces. Several others were forced to go into hiding. As a result, many UPGA candidates were unable to file their election nomination papers. On the eve of the elections, 50 per cent of NPC (NNA) candidates in the north had been declared 'unopposed' by the regional electoral commission.[108] The intimidation of opposition candidates in the west was even more blatant. In spite of the availability of prospective UPGA candidates in all the electoral constituencies in the region, the government-controlled press and radio announced that the candidature of one-third of the NNDP (NNA) contestants had been reelected without opposition.[109] Coupled

---

[108]Dudley, *An Introduction to Nigerian Politic and Government*, p. 68.
[109]Ibid.

56 Biafra Revisited

with this, the security situation in the west was deteriorating ever sharply. A virtual state of war prevailed as rival political groups attacked each other, killing, maiming and burning. Thousands of people fled west to the neighbouring Benin Republic (then called Dahomey) into exile. Scores of officials in the electoral commission resigned from their posts, accusing some of their colleagues, in addition to pro-government functionaries, of bias against the opposition parties.

Alarmed by these election irregularities and the attendant violence, President Azikiwe called an emergency meeting of leaders of all political parties. The Lagos meeting, which was held a month before the December poll, agreed to a 'code of conduct' to ensure a free and fair election. But such a commitment was hopelessly late. In another initiative a fortnight later, the president broadcast to the nation, warning that Nigeria faced a particularly grim future if the violence and intimidation that had marked the preparation of the election in some parts of the country did not stop: 'The way and manner our electioneering campaign is being conducted leaves much to be desired. The politicians in power have no rights to employ the instruments of power in order to perpetuate their stay in office.'[110] The head of the police force, Louis Edet, was equally concerned. In a frank admission, Edet told the country in a special broadcast he made one week before the election: 'incidents involving violence [during campaigns] had reached alarming proportions.'[111] It was now clearly inconceivable that the political and security situation would improve radically to ensure that a free and fair election could be held in Nigeria by the end of December 1964.

In a dramatic move to halt the evidently fraudulent exercise, the UPGA called on the federal government to postpone the elections. Predictably, this was ignored.[112] The UPGA then announced its boycott of the polls. But the elections still went ahead. The UPGA boycott was most effective in the east (where no polling took place), the Lagos capital territory (polling took place in just one constituency, albeit with a recorded low turn out), and the west (with an 86 per cent boycott success[113]). A partial boycott occurred in the midwest and parts of the midbelt, but was unheeded almost overwhelmingly in the north. Regardless, the NNA announced that it had won the election. It claimed it won a total of 202 seats in the 312-member parliament (166 in the north, and 36 in the west), and called on the president to appoint the outgoing prime minister (Balewa) as head of a new government. The president, sensitive to the chicanery that went for an election, declined. A stalemate followed. The chief justices of the centre and the regions intervened. They

---

[110] Cited in Anifowose, *Violence and Politics in Nigeria*, p. 62.
[111] Ibid.
[112] Ibid.
[113] Ibid., p. 207.

advised the president to ask the NNA to form the new government because the country's constitution did not accord the president with explicit powers to deal with such crisis. The president accepted the advice and reappointed the NNA prime minister. Both agreed that the prime minister's new administration should be a multi-party 'broad-based' government, and that new elections should be held in regions and constituencies where boycotts had occurred.[114] They also agreed that a regional election should be held in west Nigeria.[115] The chicanery had now been *legitimised* and the real victor, the Northern Peoples' Congress, had once again cast its 'veto' to uphold the north's hegemonic control of the politics of Nigeria. Just as its census cousin, a free and fair election was now becoming virtually impossible to be held in Nigeria. On this score, the NPC was indeed demonstrating how thoroughly adept it already was in managing the riggings of these contests as its inveterate benefactor had taught during the course of the previous decade.

In October 1965, Nigeria's fraudulent election drama had its most farcical act played out in the poll to the west's regional legislature. Two days after the start of nominations for the election, the NNDP declared that 16 of its candidates had been 'returned unopposed' even though the UPGA opposition party were committed to contest all the 94 seats in the legislature. In an unprecedented move, a few days before the elections, the chair of the west's electoral commission, Eyo Esua, acknowledged that his organisation could not guarantee a free and fair poll,[116] and later accused the NNDP (the NPC ally) openly for rigging the elections.[117] On the election day itself, contradictory results were broadcast by rival political media organisations, even while focusing on the same constituency. In some cases, well-known opposition candidates who were initially declared losers by government-controlled media suddenly had their results altered (i.e. became winners!) after they had announced their support for the NNDP.[118] As was expected, the NNDP claimed that it had won the election (71 seats, and 17 for the opposition).[119] Its NPC ally was delighted, and the party leader's message of congratulations to the NNDP said, perhaps quite appositely, that the latter's victory was the 'work of Allah.'[120]

But this was an election outcome that did not help to stem the lynching and looting that had marked the political violence in the west for three years. On the contrary, the violence became exacerbated. There was now a popular

---

[114]Dudley, *An Introduction to Nigerian government and Politics*, pp. 69-70.
[115]Ibid., p. 70.
[116]Anifowose, *Violence and Politics in Nigeria*, p. 219.
[117]Ibid., p. 259.
[118]Ibid., p. 221.
[119]Ibid.
[120]Ibid.

and mass opposition to a regime, which the majority of the west's electorate felt had been imposed on them by the NPC and the north. There were also rumblings in the military over the violence in the west, and most importantly the Balewa government's inability to deal with the situation. For quite a while, but particularly since the December 1964 bogus elections, sections of the middle-ranking officer corps had been extremely incensed by the larceny and absolutism of the NPC rule, some of whose features had also affected the military itself in various fundamental ways. The fact that Nigeria appeared to be stuck indefinitely in an NPC, north-dominated political quagmire provided the impetus for the military coup d'état that occurred in the country in January 1966. The military intervention no doubt opened up a new front in the 20-year-old crisis. As we shall show in the next chapter the coup and subsequent events broadened the terms of contestation catastrophically: the north and its British allies organised the most gruesome genocide that Africa had witnessed in a century.

3

Three phases of genocide

On 15 January 1966, mutinous middle-ranking officers of the military toppled the central as well as all the regional governments across Nigeria in a coup d'état. A number of political (and military) leaders, including the prime minister and premier of the north region, were killed during the coup. Three officers were principally responsible for the planning and the execution of the coup: Majors Chukwuma Nzeogwu, Emmanual Ifeajuna and Adewale Ademoyega. According to Ademoyega, the planning of the coup began in July 1965 even though the lead officer of the trio (Nzeogwu) had contemplated such an action (as a way of tackling Nigeria's seemingly intractable socio-economic problems) as far back as 1961.[1] Ademoyega recalls:

> Nzeogwu was a good leader of men ... He drew the younger officers irresistibly to himself, endeavouring always to awaken in them both political and revolutionary consciousness, and above all, patriotism ... Throughout 1965 Nzeogwu spoke freely and openly to some younger officers about his intention to stage a revolution which would bring Nigeria to the path of greatness.[2]

Central to the these officers' opposition to the prevailing socioeconomics of post-conquest Nigeria was the hegemony which the north region wielded at the behest of extant British economic and strategic interests in the country, and whose political signification was openly displayed by the electoral 'veto' so perniciously exercised by the Northern Peoples' Congress. The military, just as other key institutions in Nigeria, was not immune to the impact and the long-term implications of the politics of the north's hegemony. In this regard, two areas of relevance must be cited. First, British conquest officers still occupied several senior positions in the military (including the post of chief of the general staff), despite the so-called restoration of independence in 1960. There was therefore resentment in the services by particularly south officers of the slow pace of the Nigerianisation

---

[1] Ademoyega, *Why We Struck*, p. 55.
[2] Ibid.

of the officer-corps, especially prior to 1963/64, in spite of the availability of a cadre of excellent local officers. Second, the introduction in 1961 of a recruitment quota system into the military which specified that the north had 50 per cent of each bi-annual intake, while the rest of the country shared the remaining 50 per cent, had created an intolerable level of tension between the north and south contingents with morale plummeting to an all time low.[3] This was yet another plank in the British architecture of intrigue and flagrancy to beef up the planted political supremacism of their NPC/north's clients.

This quota provision, as should be expected, had opened the military recruitment exercise to serious abuse – some of which had been very embarrassing to the services, as was evident in 1964 when a batch of Nigerian officer-cadets, mostly from the north, had had to be repatriated from Canada because the military academy there found them 'academically unfit' to pursue their career.[4] Regardless, these cadets were commissioned on arrival in Nigeria.[5] But apart from the incompetence and nepotism, which the quota system encouraged in the military, it also accentuated sectarianism within the officer-corps – north officers enjoyed a privileged induction, backed up by the political establishment, in contrast to their predictably resentful south counterparts who had to work evidently harder to win a commission.[6]

Britain, north hegemony, economy

Britain, however, remained the long-term beneficiaries of this discriminatory, unequal, and highly contentious political arrangement

---

[3] Ademoyega: 'Military aspirants from the South were frustrated. No wonder then that the army was not as insulated from politics ... The effects of these were made crystal clear by the events of 1966/167.' (*Why We Struck*, p. 24.)

[4] Ben Gbulie, *Nigeria's Five Majors: Coup d'état of 15th January 1966 – First Inside Account* (Onitsha: Africana Education Publishers, 1981), p. 13

[5] Ibid.

[6] Ademoyega recalls his own induction exercise in the Kaduna military academy in November 1961: 'When we were brought together with those cadets in the process of being tested, we observed that those of them who were Northerners were most carefree and more confident at sailing through. Those from the South were so afflicted by the fear of failing that they wore the look of anxiety and bewilderment ... Northerners were already billed to be 50% of the total number to be selected. Moreover, they already knew the eight Northerners to be selected and they knew that at least four of those Northerners would never have made it but for the quota system. This explains why [the southerner-would-be-cadets] were bewildered. *After all, we were all Nigerians, and there should be no cause for discrimination of any kind.*' (*Why We Struck*, p. 23; emphasis added.)

encapsulated in the post-conquest Nigerian military and across the country's other key socioeconomic institutions. For Britain, ascribed north privilege and political hegemony became the dual *internal* levers which it employed to reinforce its control of Nigeria's economy in the early years of the so-called restoration of independence. On the eve of the 1966 coup, the British success story was phenomenal. Apart from South Africa, Nigeria was the site of Britain's highest economic and industrial investment in Africa with the total worth of £1.5 billion. The British government controlled a near-50 per cent shares in Shell-BP (the predominant oil prospecting company in Nigeria) and 60 per cent shares in Amalgamated Tin Mining, a major prospecting tin, cobalt and iron ore mining company.[7] In the non-mining sector of the economy, John Holt, owned by a British family, was one of the two largest in the country with branches located in the principal towns and cities. The United Africa Company (UAC), another British enterprise, accounted for about 40 per cent of Nigeria's entire import and export trade.

The UAC was the major African subsidiary of the British transnational corporation, Unilever. It developed from the Royal Niger Company, which in association with Taubman Goldie, the entrepreneur, and Frederick Lugard, the first British occupation governor, harnessed the British conquest of the number of states in this southeast territorial stretch of West Africa between 1886 and 1941, and converted them into the amorphous political entity that Lugard's own mistress called 'nigger's area' or Nigeria.[8] The UAC, for its part, had wholesale and retailing enterprises run in most parts of Nigeria by its numerous subsidiaries, among which the following three were most prominent: Kingsway Chemist, G.B. Ollivant, and African Timber and Plywood.[9] In addition, the UAC had part interest in other well-

---

[7]For a discussion of the background to the British exploitation of Nigeria's tin mines, and the multilayered forms of labour resistance, see William Freund, 'Theft and Social protest among Tin Miners in Northern Nigeria,' in Donal Crummey, ed., *Banditry, Rebellion and Social Protest in Africa* (London and Portsmouth, New Hampshire: James Currey/Heinemann, 1986), pp. 49-63.

[8]An account of Unilever's strategic interests in the Nigerian economy can be found in Ikenna Nzimiro's excellent study, 'The Political Implications of Multinational Corporations in Nigeria,' in Carl Widstrand, ed., *Multi-National Firms in Africa* (Dakar and Uppsala: African Institute for Economic Development and Planning/Scandinavia Institute for African Studies, 1975), pp. 210-243. See also Margery Perham, *Mining, Commerce and Finance in Nigeria* (London: Faber and Faber, 1948), Claude Ake, ed., *Political Economy of Nigeria* (London and Lagos: Longman, 1985), especially chaps. 1-4., Robert Shenton, *The Development of Capitalism in Northern Nigeria* (London: James Currey, 1986) and Falola, ed., *Britain and Nigeria*.

[9]Nzimiro, 'The Political Implications of Multinational Corporations in Nigeria,' pp. 212-214.

established companies in the country such as Gulf Oil of Nigeria, Nigerian Prestressed Concrete, Nigerian Breweries, Taylor Woodrow, and Nigelec. Ikenna Nzimiro's often-quoted aphorism, 'UAC was Nigeria and Nigeria was UAC', does not therefore exaggerate UAC's effective control of Nigeria's economy at the time.[10] Finally, in the finance sector, Barclays Nigeria (subsidiary of the British Barclays Bank) and Standard Bank Nigeria (owned largely by the British Lloyds Bank and Westminster Bank) controlled 90 per cent of Nigeria's effective banking system. Once again, these institutions had branches across the country. The 25,000 Britons resident in Nigeria were employed in this extensive network of businesses and related services in the economy.

As we shall soon show, the economic restructuring of the Nigerian society envisaged by the January 1966 coup leaders' 'programme of action',[11] amounted to a direct challenge of the economic stranglehold Britain exerted on the country. The immediate source of pressure on the military to overthrow the Balewa regime was due, however, to the deteriorating internal security situation created by the virtual state of wars in the west and the north's midbelt province.

Military and ongoing strife

Coup leader Nzeogwu had long been particularly distressed by the crisis in the west. In a December 1965 coup planning session he had with Captain Ben Gbulie, who would play a key role in the coup, Nzeogwu had stressed: 'The killings in the West must be stopped ... These narrow-minded, blood-thirsty politicians have been spilling innocent blood, unchallenged, for far too long.'[12] Nzeogwu was alarmed by the Balewa government's extensive and indiscriminative deployment of military contingents (based in Ibadan and Abeokuta) to suppress the west revolt, a strategy reminiscent of the regime's counter-insurgency programme developed while dealing with the Tiv uprisings in the midbelt earlier on. Nzeogwu was especially incensed by the 'fanaticism' displayed during the military operations in the west by its leader, Colonel Largema, who was also the commanding officer of the army garrison in Ibadan. Largema had played a central role in mounting the 'security cover' for the rigging of the October 1965 elections to the west legislature, which the NPC's regional ally, the Nigerian National Democratic Party, claimed it won.

In its quest to overthrow the north political 'establishment' (the Northern People's Congress/Nigerian National Alliance), Nzeogwu and his group no

---

[10]Ibid., p. 217.
[11]Ademoyega, *Why We Struck*, pp. 33-48.
[12]Gbulie, *Nigeria's Five Majors*, p. 27.

doubt sought to confront, and hopefully expurgate what had become the internal source and acute manifestation of Nigeria's desperate post-conquest emergency. The evidence from all central and regional elections in the country, since October 1960, had demonstrated the tenacity of the NPC/NNA/north to defend and uphold its hegemonic control of the socioeconomics of Nigeria without due process of *countrywide* democratic support. The NPC/NNA/north's flagrant and persistent utilisation and manipulation of the institutions of the state (including especially the electoral, demographic, and the military/police) in the pursuance of this objective, ensured that the electoral space available to challenge or indeed dislodge it from power constitutionally had become extremely marginal. In this context, it is of immense importance to recall, once again, the apparent pain and anguish that Nzeogwu felt over the NPC/NNA/north campaign to destroy the Yoruba revolt: 'The killings in the west must be stopped ... These narrow-minded, blood thirsty politicians have been spilling innocent blood, unchallenged, for far too long.'

Promises and failure

But going beyond the immediate considerations of Nigeria's post-restoration of independence socioeconomics (i.e. 1960-1966), the coup leaders' challenge to the north political 'establishment' was aimed at dismantling an essentially exploitative and dehumanising British-created political edifice, which rested structurally on the hierarchisation of Nigeria's constituent nations and regions – with the north positioned on the apex of indefinite political control and attendant privileges. As we have already shown, the British embarked on this goal in the 1940s with the aim of dislodging the *all-Nigeria* political project of the National Council of Nigeria and the Cameroons. It should be recalled that top on the agenda of the political programme of the coup majors, in the event of taking power, was the abolition of the regions and the creation of an 'incorporative political culture' across the country which no longer assigned 'definitive' roles and privileges targeted to constituent nations and regions.[13] Not since the enterprising all-Nigeria focused political activities of the NCNC in the 1940s/early 1950s had any social grouping aspiring to Nigeria's political leadership expressed a deeper vision of countrywide 'one-ness' as shown by the concerns and aspirations of the January 1966 majors.

Yet, this laudable vision of creating the opportunity for a Nigeria countrywide 'one-ness' was seriously impaired by the majors' intention to appoint Obafemi Awolowo, the jailed Action Group leader, to the position

---

[13]Ibid., P. 58; Ademoyega, *Why We Struck*, pp. 33-48.

of head of a provisional government after the coup.[14] It was inconceivable that Awolowo, the architect of the fratricidal regionalisation of Nigerian politics in the 1940s, could have played an *enabling* role in the attainment of the Nigerian 'unity' envisaged by the majors. It was after all Awolowo who had effectively paved the way for the British construction of the hierarchical political entity, which effectively precluded a functioning and responsive state that served all the constituent African peoples. Awolowo remained a chauvinist Yoruba leader as he left for the Calabar prisons in 1963, and there was no indication whatsoever, in 1965/66, that his essentially racist conceptualisation and track record in Nigerian politics had undergone any shift.[15] On the contrary, it is to Awolowo's eternal credit that he remained emotionally and politically an intemperate, exclusivist Yoruba overlord throughout his long career which ended with his death in 1987.

It is however unlikely that the coup majors were unaware of Awolowo's history, and they would have come to the conclusion that they, *themselves*, would spearhead this crucial 'unity' perspective of their political programme, within the auspices of their projected diarchal administration ('team ... of honesty, patriotic and reliable civilians ... and a number of specially chosen military men'[16]). Their intention to appoint Awolowo to chair the provisional government was therefore aimed as a goodwill gesture to the long-suffering west. But it was also a symbolic demonstration to the rest of the country, north and south, that supreme political leadership could not be lodged in one geographical region in the country (as had been the case with regard to the north since 1954) without creating the political alienation and hopelessness that prevailed in the south. Thus the Awolowo choice appropriately served the dual components of this psychological symbolism: he was a southerner, and he had had a tempestuous career as opposition leader in the Lagos central legislature, which ended in a 10-year jail sentence for treason and felony. The fact the Awolowo had been incarcerated by a north-dominated central regime on charges that he had planned the overthrow of the latter, was not lost on the sensibilities of the coup majors. After all, the majors were anxious to *institutionalise* their revolt as an extension, perhaps a decisive phase for that matter, of the 4-year old countrywide opposition and resistance to NPC/NNA/north authoritarianism. The majors' preference to inaugurate a civilian-military diarchy after a successful overthrow of the Balewa regime, served further to amplify that their political project was not marginally putschist or militarist.

---

[14]Gbulie, *Nigeria's Five Majors*, p. 58.
[15]Cf. Billy Dudley, 'The Political Theory of Awolowo and Azikiwe,' in Onigu Otite, ed., *Themes in African Social and Political Thought* (Enugu: Fourth Dimension Publishers, 1978), pp. 210-212.
[16]Gbulie, *Nigeria's Five Majors*, p. 58.

In the end though, the majors were not in the position to embark on this political goal. While their 15 January coup succeeded in seizing political control in the north, it failed in the south, especially in the Lagos-Ibadan-Abeokuta military district, where loyalist troops led by army commander General Johnson Aguyi-Ironsi succeeded in crushing the revolt. Apart from Major Ifeajuna who fled the country after the collapse of their coup, the other majors and the rest of the officers involved in the revolt later surrendered to the loyalist high command. On the following day (16 January), a meeting of the members of the central government cabinet who survived the revolt resolved to transfer power to the loyalist armed forces, a decision that was conveyed to the nation in a broadcast by senate leader Nwafor Orizu, acting for President Azikiwe who was abroad at the time for medical treatment. Aguyi-Ironsi, the highest-ranking surviving loyalist officer, became the new head of state. It is significant historically, and perhaps ironically, that a south military officer, an Igbo, led the contingent of loyalist forces in Lagos to defend the central government, one of the pivotal sites of the north's hegemonic rule in Nigeria, when this came under assault by the forces of the coup majors.

Aguyi-Ironsi, January majors, politics

This loyalist background to the Aguyi-Ironsi 'take-over' ensured that the new administration had to effect some measure of continuity in the running of Nigeria. While Aguyi-Ironsi suspended the constitution, the central and regional legislatures, and ordered the detention or the partial restriction of the movement of leading politicians, his government however retained the services of the permanent secretaries and their not-nonpoliticised bureaucracies. Aguyi-Ironsi appointed military governors, ensuring that each came from the local majority nation. But perhaps, most importantly, Aguyi-Ironsi's choice of Colonel Hassan Katsina, the son of the influential emir of Katsina as the governor of the north, was the clearest signal to the north, and the rest of the country, that his government was not about to undermine the north's two decades of political hegemony in Nigeria. Aguyi-Ironsi had already said as much in a number of discreet contacts he made with the north leaders, including the sultan of Sokoto, soon after the failed majors' coup. He was anxious to reassure the north of the 'good intentions' of his regime, especially in the light of the deaths of the prime minister and the north's premier during the coup attempt. In fact to underscore Aguyi-Ironsi's 'goodwill' to the north, the new head of state ordered the release of most of the north's politicians from detention by February (1966) without a reciprocal gesture to their south counterparts. The released politicians took up positions in the various local government services in the north emirates and, strategically, had ample opportunity to team up with those other crucially involved genocidist operatives (academics and students) centred at the Ahmadu Bello University (Zaria) to plan and execute the first phase of the Igbo genocide, beginning May 1966. One hundred thousand Igbo were murdered during the course of this orgy of massacres between May and October 1966. Aguyi-Ironsi himself was murdered during the period, as well as scores of other Igbo military personnel. Ironically, Aguyi-Ironsi's murder by a north death squad in July came soon after he had completed yet another conference with north emirs, reassuring the latter of the region's continued dominant position in Nigeria.

The other sphere of continuity with the policies of the Balewa regime, which Aguyi-Ironsi was keen to maintain, was of course in the area of the economy. There were no distinct departures in the minds of the military top brass (now in power) as regards the character of the economy from that of the overthrown civilians. Moreover, the British, who virtually controlled the economy, had quickly established a close relationship with Aguyi-Ironsi. Britain had offered to send in troops to support Aguyi-Ironsi and his loyalist forces after Nzeogwu threatened (on 16 January) to march on Lagos and the south (from his Kaduna base) to enforce the control of the January majors countrywide.[17] While Aguyi-Ironsi discreetly turned down the British offer, he however informed London that its interests in Nigeria, the overriding British pre-occupation, would be preserved by his government. This meant that the radical reforms of the Nigerian economy envisaged by the revolting majors,[18] now known by Aguyi-Ironsi and in diplomatic circles in Lagos, would not be implemented. But for the British, the very presence of the Aguyi-Ironsi administration, the fastidious circumstances of its origins notwithstanding, had already breached a cardinal tenet of the socioeconomic architecture of post-conquest Nigeria which they had worked so assiduously between 1952-1960 to construct: that political leadership within the country to oversee these enormous British interests should come from their Hausa-Fulani/north clients. As the political situation in Nigeria deteriorated further in the second half of 1966 and into 1967, with the Igbo genocide now devastatingly on course, Britain would hem in its fortunes with these clients even more aggressively and determinately as ever.

Discontinuities

There were noticeable zones of discontinuities in the trajectory of the Aguyi-Ironsi administration, which no doubt represented some break with the discredited heritage from the NPC/NNA/north regime. Aguyi-Ironsi brought the four years of unrelenting perpetration of carnage and chaos in the west

---

[17]Ibid., p. 100; Obasanjo, *My Command*, p. 146.
[18]Ademoyega, *Why We Struck*, pp. 33-48.

and midbelt to a dramatic end, enabling people to resume the existence of normal life activity that had long been disrupted in the regions. Tens of thousands of refugees who fled their homes (including the Yoruba who emigrated to the then Dahomey Republic) returned to begin the task of reconstructing battered towns, villages and farms. The regime's prompt abolition of the local government police auxiliaries in the north and west (no such forces existed elsewhere in the country), and the integration of their personnel in the country's regular police force, helped considerably in the restoration of peace in the west. The auxiliaries, especially the *dan doka* in the north, had been pointedly notorious in the way the NPC/NNA/north political authorities utilised their services for the intimidation of opponents and for the rigging of elections.

Aguyi-Ironsi's success in enforcing peace in the west and midbelt as well as his regime's dismissal of the corrupt politicians, engendered popular support, expressed so ecstatically by the media, students, trade unions, women's organisations, and other popular-based bodies, which organised rallies across the country in support of the 'dawn of a new era'. In its response, the National Union of Nigerian Students, the main university/tertiary-level students' organisation, observed: 'We are happy that this salvation has come.'[19] The mass-circulating *Daily Times* agreed in an editorial:

> For some time now ... the country has been, as it were, at the sick bay. We have been groping along – rudderless, hesitant, unsure which foot to put forward first ... Opposition was virtually reduced to a position of nullity. For a long time, instead of settling down to minister unto the people's needs, the politicians were busy performing a series of seven days' wonders as if the art of government was some circus show. John Citizen was not amazed, but he was powerless; he was helpless ... It was too much, it was enough, but none there to bell the cat, until the last straw that broke the camel's back. Today, there is a new regime in Nigeria, a new military regime. About time too! Something just has to be done to save the [country]. Something has been done. It is like a surgical operation, which must be performed, or the patient dies. The operation has been performed. It has proved successful. And it is welcome.[20]

In the same vein, the *Morning Post* recalled in its own editorial:

---

[19]*Morning Post* (Lagos), 18 January 1966, quoted in Gbulie, *Nigeria's Five Majors*, p. 156.
[20]*Daily Times* (Lagos), 18 January 1966, quoted in Ademoyega, *Why We Struck*, pp. 113-114

Most of our politicians have behaved all along like spoilt, naughty children and have shown utter contempt for public opinion. They seemed to believe that they were a special breed, divinely ordained to lord it over the lesser beings that constitute 99 per cent of the people. Hence in the former regime corruption, greed, nepotism ... were rife. In fact, these evil ways have been taken for granted as if they did not matter. The politicians got so drunk with power that seeing themselves as tin gods, they saw lesser mortals as deserving only of tiny crumbs from their tables ... Nigerians today are glad and grateful that they see this day, the beginning of an era in which the agents of corruptions, greed, nepotism ... shall be swept away for all time.[21]

Two days later, another editorial from the *Morning Post* summed up the prevailing optimism in the country:

Gone are the days when, intoxicated with our dream-world euphoria, we saw little men and called them gods. Gone, too, are the days when every penny whistle in this country saw itself as a trumpet. No longer shall tin gods thrive on the simplicity of sycophants.[22]

Whirlwind of inheritance

No government, especially that which came to power in the wake of the most inauspicious of events, none of which was of its own making, could have wished for such a popular expression of support as that of Aguyi-Ironsi's. Yet, it was clear that in their support for the new government, the press and indeed other sectors of public opinion in Nigeria scarcely made a distinction between the position (political or otherwise) of the January majors, the leaders of what had in fact become a failed coup d'état, and that of General Aguyi-Ironsi's, whose regime now had to 'oversee' the majors' inheritance. On the contrary, public support for the 'new regime in Nigeria', often straddled both positions, their sharply contrasting objectives notwithstanding. It does appear that the background of this conflation, which was not done out of any mischief, not even on the grounds of some inability to make a distinction between these two contrasting ideopolitical tendencies in the Nigerian military, was due to the lasting impact of coup leader Nzeogwu's broadcast on popular consciousness across the country. In the

---

[21]*Morning Post* (Lagos), 19 January 1966, quoted in Gbulie, *Nigeria's Five Majors*, pp. 156-157.
[22]*Morning Post* (Lagos), 21 January 1966, quoted in Gbulie, *Nigeria's Five Majors*, p. 157.

broadcast on Kaduna Radio on 15 January (repeated intermittently throughout most of the day), after his forces were virtually in control of north Nigeria, Nzeogwu stressed:

> [Our aim] is to establish a strong, united and prosperous nation free from corruption and internal strife ... Our enemies are the political profiteers, the swindlers ... those that seek to keep the country divided permanently so that they can remain in office ... [T]hose that make the country look big for nothing before international circles; those that have corrupted our society and put the Nigerian political calendar back by their words and deeds ... [W]hat we do promise every law-abiding citizen is freedom from general inefficiency and freedom to live and strive in every field of human endeavour, both nationally and internationally. We promise that you will no more be ashamed to say you are Nigerians.[23]

There were no broadcasts made by Aguyi-Ironsi, during the period, which invoked comparable sentiments of focus, resolve or dedication as evident in the Nzeogwu statement quoted above. As a result, Nzeogwu's visionary address stuck in people's minds as the definitive point of departure for the country's progress – away from the ascriptive, reactionary, NPC/NNA/north neofeudalism of two decades and the uncertainties that encapsulated the imposition of military rule. And public perception did not waiver on this score, even after Aguyi-Ironsi crushed the majors' revolt the following day. Quite clearly, for the Nigerian public, the *raison d'être* for the 'new regime in Nigeria', i.e. the Aguyi-Ironsi administration, was the pursuit and concretisation of those *countrywide* sentiments articulated in the Nzeogwu address, which amounted to the negation of the scourge of inheritance that was the NPC/NNA/north epoch.

But while popular opinion discerned clearly the nature of the inheritance to be negated (namely, the NPC/NNA/north era) for the construction of an alternative Nigeria *à la* Nzeogwu, the choice for the Aguyi-Ironsi regime was not as straight forward as that. It indeed had a joint-inheritance to 'appropriate' – the NPC/NNA/north component which it had fought valiantly to save on 15 January, and the January majors' constituent which it had defeated militarily, but whose politics nonetheless had not only actuated *its own* existence, but now served as the inspirational source of the popular backing it received from the peoples across the country. These two components of the Aguyi-Ironsi inheritance were of course locked in fierce internal contradiction. The only way the regime could resolve this contradiction was to neutralise or in fact jettison altogether one of the dual

---

[23] Quoted in Ademoyega, *Why We Struck*, pp. 87-89.

constituents of its heritage. If it hoped to continue to enjoy the public support that had been so generous since its 16 January take-over, then the regime had to abandon the NPC/NNA/north component of its already chequered existence.

Phase I

The Aguyi-Ironsi administration did not however effectuate this break with the NPC/NNA/north past. Probably it was impossible for it to embark on such a move, even if it felt the urgency to do so. For instance, the regime was reluctant to yield to the persistent pressure from ex-north politicians and some sectors of the military to try the detained January majors and the rest of the officer-corps involved in the failed coup. It was aware that such a trial would cost it public goodwill because these officers were still held in high esteem in the country. Yet, the regime capitulated to these demands in May 1966 but was only compelled to postpone the trial at the last minute because it had to respond somehow to what turned out to be the beginning of the first phase of the Igbo genocide in the north.

Patrick Wilmot has argued that the sociopolitical leadership in north Nigeria has 'no tradition for managing social change. The only answer to dissent or rebellion is the massacre.'[24] Yet, to offer some rational explanation for a reason or reasons for a specific act of massacre of the Igbo carried out by this leadership is fraught with difficulties. For instance, when in November 2002 it ordered the murder of hundreds of Igbo immigrants in the north over the staging, in Nigeria, of the Miss World beauty competition (organised, not by any Igbo business interests, but by a London-based business conglomerate), it would have been most intriguing for any observer to discern the 'Igbo connection' that elicited this monstrous act. Similarly, an observer would be hard pressed to locate the 'Igbo connection' to astronomy as yet another gruesome example of an ordered Igbo pogrom in the north illustrates. In January 2001, hundreds of Igbo residents in the north city of Maiduguri were murdered by rampaging youths soon after a lunar eclipse was in progress. The émigrés' homes and business properties worth million of dollars were looted or destroyed during the carnage. For the north leadership, which has since 1945 regarded the Igbo émigrés in its region as a 'targeted population' or 'hostage population' to attack at will in furtherance of its myriad sociopolitical positions and objectives, 'dissent' or 'rebellion' or indeed any other factors need not be necessarily associated or referenced to the Igbo directly for it to execute its deadly mission on the latter. We should therefore surmise, following from this, that for 1966, two immediate

---

[24]Patrick Wilmot, 'Poverty amidst riches,' *West Africa* (London), 15 August 1988, p. 1489.

factors may have prompted the carefully planned genocide of Igbo immigrants in the north. The first concerned the outcome of the official inquiry ordered by Aguyi-Ironsi into the failed coup. As part of his continuing disposition to assure the north of his regime's 'goodwill' to the region, Aguyi-Ironsi insisted that the 3-person board of investigators to the coup be made up of exclusively north officers: M.D. Yusuf, head of the country's special branch, who came from a prominent Hausa-Fulani family; Colonel Yakubu Gowon, who Aguyi-Ironsi had just appointed chief of army staff, and who would play a key role in the Igbo genocide and the murder of Aguyi-Ironsi himself; Captain Baba Usman, military intelligence.[25] The inquiry's terms of reference were comprehensive – to uncover the motives, the intentions, and the long-term objectives of the January majors' failed coup.[26] It took three months to complete its work. About two hundred officers and other personnel in the military, including the principal leaders of the event, were interrogated. Important coup documents retrieved from Lagos, Ibadan, Abeokuta, Kaduna, Zaria and elsewhere, were exhaustively evaluated. The report on the outcome of the inquiry showed that the plans to overthrow the Balewa government were restricted strictly to the military; there was no involvement by members of the civilian population. While the majority of officers involved in the action were mainly from the south, and particularly Igbo, there was no evidence whatsoever to suggest or indicate that the coup was a south or indeed some Igbo conspiracy to seize and control the country.[27] Nzeogwu and his group acted alone.[28] In May (1966), the board submitted its report to the government. But while the government studied it, prior to publication, Colonel Gowon (board member and army chief of staff, who also worked for British intelligence in Nigeria) leaked its main conclusions to the British diplomatic mission in Lagos and a number of ex-politicians and local government leaders in the north. Gowon's motive was essentially to coalesce the activities of the anti-Aguyi-Ironsi forces, whose interests he shared, into some form of revolt. The north leaders were extremely disappointed with the findings of the investigation, despite the fact that it was carried out by well-known and respected north security officers. The leaders had felt, all along, that the south, especially the Igbo, would be found culpable in the failed coup. They expressed their disappointment in a series of memoranda and other representations made on the subject to both the central government and the north region military administration in Kaduna. They specifically called on Aguyi-Ironsi not to

---

[25] Gbulie, *Nigeria's Five Majors*, p. 147, p. 152.
[26] John de St Jorre, *The Brothers' War – Biafra and Nigeria* (Boston: Houghton Miflin, 1972), pp. 29-47.
[27] Ibid.
[28] Ibid.

publish the commission's report. Pointedly, even General Obasanjo's 1987 study on the failed coup (21 years after the event!) comes to the same conclusion as the Yusuf-Gowon-Usman investigating board: namely, that Nzeogwu and his group's action was not an Igbo plot to seize power.[29] This is despite the fact that Obasanjo, the current Nigerian head of state who participated in the second phase of the Igbo genocide, commanded a notorious brigade, during the period, which destroyed hundreds of Igbo villages and towns, murdering thousands of people in the process. There is thus no love lost between him and the Igbo.

It should now be obvious that given the matrix of the evaluative characterisation, interests, and ambitions of the constituent nations in Nigeria of 1966 (Igbo, Urhobo, Ijo, Hausa-Fulani, Tiv, Yoruba, etc., etc), the majors' failed coup was effectively a *pro*-Yoruba project, aimed at achieving the following goals: (a) end the state of insurgency in Yorubaland; (b) ensure the return and rehabilitation of the mass of displaced Yoruba on exile, especially the thousands in the neighbouring Dahomey Republic; (c) release Obafemi Awolowo, the incarcerated Yoruba leader; (d) appoint Awolowo the prime minister in a provisional military-civilian diarchal government. The Igbo and the east had already made a strategic withdrawal from the all-Nigeria mission they embarked upon in the 1940s/early 1950s as a result of the series of British counter-measures of the subsequent years (which we have already discussed here). The east was a booming economy, much more advanced than any other part of Nigeria, and was on course to developing into a leading economic and industrial power in another decade. Neither this enterprising economy, which was in no way linked to the Nigerian military establishment (apart from a small army garrison in Enugwu, the British had effectively cut off the east from the country's military bases and allied infrastructure located in the north and Lagos/west regions), nor the Igbo's famed (some would say ultra-) republican society as a whole therefore stood to benefit whatsoever from a coup d'état in Lagos or elsewhere in Nigeria. The Igbo officers involved in *both* the putsch attempt and also in suppressing it, had no political nor popular constituency anywhere in Igboland. The military presence in the east was minimal (just a small army garrison in Enugwu, usually staffed by predominantly north and Yoruba personnel), a feature that had been the case right from British times. This was part of the occupation's long established anti-Igbo programme to install military bases away from the region – preferring, instead, to site these in its favoured north, and in the west incorporating the Lagos-Ibadan-Abeokuta district. As a result, the Igbo officers in the military lived most of their lives *outside*

---

[29]Olusegun Obasanjo, *Nzeogwu* (Ibadan: Spectrum Books, 1987). For an insightful essay review of this book, see Herbert Ekwe-Ekwe, 'Nzeogwu: Notes on a Controversy,' *West Africa* (London), 2 March 1987, p. 418.

Igboland and those especially in the west region developed life-long friendships with the Yoruba, particularly members of the intelligentsia in civil society (including, notably, Wole Soyinka, the playwright) and the military (including Colonel Victor Banjo, Major Ademoyega and Captain Gani Adeleke). They were therefore more likely to be in tune and responsive to local politics and development (i.e. west/Yoruba) than occurrences in Igboland/east. These were professionals, technocrats, who acted on their own as the Yusuf-Gowon-Baba investigating panel and the Obasanjo study have correctly stated. The presence of these excellent Igbo officers, the cream of the indigenous Nigerian military officers on the eve of the restoration of independence, in the January 1966 events (pro- and anti-) was essentially attributable to the high-level humanpower development that the east had made across the board (academia, research, production, economy, etc.) as a result of its 20-year societal transformation programme.

In the end, the only outstanding subject in Nigerian politics that was really of concern to the Igbo, particularly in the 1964-1966 period, was the fate of their 1.5 million immigrants in the north, many of whom ran successful commercial, medical, educational and leisure enterprises. These émigrés were often seen by the north leadership as a symbol of Igbo 'extra-territorial' ambitions and versatility, a discomforting reminder of the Igbo lead-role in the liberation of Nigeria, and their audacious 1940s/early 1950s' all-Nigeria transformation project. As a result, measures against the émigrés usually featured very highly on the set of policy options 'available' to the north leadership, whilst reacting to an astronomical phenomenon such as an eclipse or responding to periods of acute sociopolitical development or controversy in the country (as seen, for instance, in the leadership's ordering and organisation of pogroms against this Igbo population during the 1945 labour strikes/the NCNC campaigns for the country's liberation and the 1953 debates on dates for the termination of the British occupation) or indeed in respect to international politics. On the latter, as these lines are written (February 2006 – forty years after 1966!), the fundamentals remain tragically the same: the north's leadership ordered the murder of scores of Igbo immigrants across north cities, towns and villages over cartoons published in Danish newspapers, 4000 miles away, purportedly critical of the muslim religion. No Igbo artists were the authors of these cartoons, as the world knows; no Igbo newspapers or newsmagazines reproduced these cartoons; the Igbo, who are Africans, are not in any way related to the Danes, who are a European people. Some of those Igbo murdered in their homes, schools, businesses or places of worship, were probably never aware of the existence of these cartoons, let alone the controversy surrounding the drawings before they met their untimely deaths. Yet, the north leadership's choice of the Igbo for 'retaliation' over the cartoons, instead of venting their anger on the Dane (who are visibly resident in capital Abuja where they have their embassy) or in fact on any of the nationals from the other European Union member states in Nigeria, underscores the point of the haunting historical vulnerability of this immigrant population. It was of course the 1966-1970 Igbo genocide, which pointedly began with attacks on these émigrés, that demonstrated the latter's vulnerability most profoundly, and the depravity of the north leadership organisers, most chillingly.

Besides the outcome of the investigating panel on the failed January coup, the second factor that may have contributed to the ordering of the Igbo genocide by the north was Aguyi-Ironsi's May (1966) decree no. 34, which set out a series of administrative reforms in the country. The divisive region-based political structure was abolished, in favour of a more 'unitary' state composed of groups of administrative provinces. The reforms drastically curtailed the extensive sphere of political, economic and judicial authority that had in the past been exercised by the regions vis-à-vis the central government in Lagos, and which had been central to the fractious politics in the country since 1946. By embarking on these reforms, Aguyi-Ironsi was no doubt responding to the growing demands in universities (especially in Lagos, Ibadan and Nsukka), trade unions, and the media, for some concrete political initiative from his government to maintain the general optimism and goodwill, which the overthrow of the Balewa regime had generated in January. Moreover, there had been some criticism in the media of the lack of uniformity across the regions in the implementation of some programmes, which the public considered popular, especially those that affected disgraced politicians. For instance, while the east, west, midwest and Lagos military administrations set up judicial commissions to probe the disbanded political parties, the north's counterpart did not have such a programme (on the contrary, ex-north politicians got new jobs in the local governments and the various emirates while their south counterparts were clamped in detention).

Aguyi-Ironsi's reforms were also partly dictated by the sheer 'centralising' features demanded by a military organisation. It had become clear to his regime, after four months in office, that the regionalist compartmentalisation of the country's key institutions (civil service, education, industry, commerce) was evidently obstructive to the centralising dictates of a military administration. Furthermore, Aguyi-Ironsi expected these reforms to sort out the confusion which was already apparent within the chain of the military command structure, especially in the way this tried to 'rationalise' rank authority between those officers who performed clear-cut military duties (for instance, brigade commanders) and those whose assignments were more political (particularly regional governors). Apart from the governor of Lagos, whose military rank was that of major, all the other regional governors were colonels. While these officers were all members of the supreme military council, the highest ruling body in the country, and each was personally responsible to Aguyi-Ironsi (as commander-in-chief of the armed forces and head of state), there were at least a score of other officers with superior rank whose duties were specifically military but who did not serve on the council. One of the disquieting consequences of this arrangement was that governor-officers, who also benefited immensely from the public profile inevitably associated with their posting, tended to blunt the edge of their responsiveness to this other category of officers, higher up in the military hierarchy. In order to overcome any tension that this procedure may have caused within the officer-corps, the new arrangement explicitly categorised *all* appointments involving military personnel in every sphere of the administration as 'military'. Finally, Aguyi-Ironsi's reforms were aimed at 'appropriating', even if belatedly, some part of the all-Nigeria 'one-ness' ideas of Nigeria's future visualised by Major Nzeogwu and his group. As we have already indicated, the Nzeogwu vision remained the definitive term of reference upon which countrywide popular support for the military regime depended.

But the response of the leaders of the north to these reforms cast grave doubts on their eventual implementation. A wave of effectively organised and co-ordinated attacks was unleashed on Igbo immigrants in cities, towns and villages throughout the north beginning on 29 May with the chilling cries in Hausa and Arabic of '*a kashe kafir*' (kill the infidels), '*a kashe nyamiri*' (kill the damned Igbo), '*Allahu akbar*' (God is great), heralding the staged orgies of gruesome murders, raping, looting and arson day in, day out. The following cities and towns bear the stamp of perpetual shame as dominant sites of the perpetration of these crimes against humanity: Sokoto, Katsina, Zaria, Kaduna, Kano, Kaura-Namoda, Nguru, Bauchi, Gombe, Saminaka, Yola, Kafanchan, Damaturu, Ningi, Darazo, Gusau, Birnin-Kebbi, Bukuru, Numan, Jos, Yola, Keffi, Wase, Langtang, Takum, Mangu, Shandam, Kantangora, Minna, Gudi, Mada, Mokwa, Ayaragu, Wukari, Makurdi, Ilorin, Zungeru, Otukpo, Gboko, Ilorin, Lafia, Tanglawaja. The genocide went on intermittently through June, and became intensified after the overthrow and murder of Aguyi-Ironsi on 29 July by north military officers, and the extension of the hitherto territorial limits of the carnage to include Lagos, the capital, especially the suburb of Ikeja, and the Yoruba towns of Ibadan, Abeokuta, Osogbo and Oyo. Marauding mobs of youth recruited from across society, joined later by north military and police personnel after 29 July, armed with clubs, rock, axes, spears, poisoned arrows, machetes and the like, attacked Igbo individuals, families, homes and property with a staggering, unparalleled, indiscriminate savagery. Two months on, as from 29 July, heavily armed north military and police joined their civilian brethren in expanding even further the territorial range and intensity of the genocide. Attacks were now increasingly focused on transport facilities (trains, coaches, aircraft) carrying survivors fleeing to Igboland in the east. By late October, five months after it began, 100,000

Igbo had been murdered, mostly teachers, students, pupils, civil servants, technicians, artists, military/security officers, medical doctors, nurses and other medical staff, and businesspeople. Tens of thousands of others were wounded, many of them with horrific injuries that created permanent disability. A mass exodus of Igbo survivors from the north, as well as from Lagos, midwest and west regions ensued. By the end of the following month (October), nearly 2 million Igbo had returned to Igboland from across the rest of Nigeria.

Tradition

The Igbo genocide was organised and coordinated by a coterie of former north politicians and local government officials as well as academics and students of the Ahmadu Bello University, Zaria. The north operatives received full cooperation and coordination from the British diplomatic mission in Lagos right from the outset, as we shall soon elaborate, and also liaised closely with Colonel Gowon, chief of army staff and the north's lead personnel on the ruling military council. Several British nationals including academics at the ABU and those who worked in the north civil service in Kaduna and elsewhere in the region played varying crucial roles in the genocide. These included intelligence work, incitement, propaganda and distribution of material, financing, and the provision, especially by some of the British academics who taught at the ABU, of personal transport to facilitate the movement of rampaging north students and others across towns and cities on their way to murder the Igbo and loot their property.[30] Besides being generally unhappy with what they felt was the gradual 'displacement' of the north from the apex of control of Nigeria, which the occupation had enthroned, the British, particularly those resident in the north region, were riled by Aguyi-Ironsi's so-called 'unification' decree no. 34. They felt that it would jeopardise their heavily entrenched interests in the north. These Britons had in the previous six years particularly (i.e. since the so-called restoration of independence) turned the north into the consummate haven to continue to work and live with all the imperious privileges of the era of the occupation, unperturbed by the energised *Africanisation* of personnel in all works of life in the east and west of the country. The north government had effectively guaranteed the indefinite provision of this haven for Britons (and other favoured foreigners) with its late-1950s' 'northernisation' legislation, which barred south Nigerians from working in the north's civil service and schools/allied institutions. These Britons therefore supported and participated in the Igbo genocide because they were not prepared to contend with the inevitable competition that their exalted positions and life styles

---

[30]Madiebo, *The Nigerian Revolution and the Biafran War*, p. 41

would face from especially the teeming numbers of highly qualified Igbo and others from the south graduating from the universities of Nsukka, Ibadan and Lagos, and from overseas (Britain, United States, Federal Republic of Germany, Soviet Union, German Democratic Republic, etc.), now that exclusivist regional labour services in Nigeria had been abolished.

The nerve-centre for the planning and execution of the genocide was at the Ahmadu Bello University, with the key operational sites being the faculty of arts and social sciences, the faculty of engineering, and the institute of administration. For its sordid role, the ABU acquired the unenviable record as the first public-funded university in post-conquest Africa from where the most devastating genocide on the continent since the 19th century was planned, coordinated and executed. The planners sought three clear objectives in the genocide: (a) destroy the 1.5 million Igbo immigrants in the north; (b) destroy the Aguyi-Ironsi regime and neutralise the Igbo position in the military by eliminating their entire officer-corps and other serving personnel; (c) declare an independent north republic. Four months on, after the murder of 100,000 Igbo, the north had failed to annihilate the entire Igbo population in its region but it probably would have felt that with the complete exodus of Igbo survivors from the north to Igboland, objective (a) was to all intents and purposes successful. Just as in the past anti-Igbo pogroms in the north (1945, 1953), the north leaders would now assign the tens of millions of dollars' worth of 'abandoned' Igbo homes, businesses, and other assets across the region to its people as 'booty', for participating in this grand scale orgy of murder, rape, arson and other gradations of appalling inhumanity. It is instructive to note, with respect to the objective (c), that the clarion call at every manifestation of the waves of attack on the Igbo throughout the five months of the genocide was 'Araba!' (Hausa for 'Let us Separate!', 'Let us Secede!'). Indeed, for 18 days after the 29 July murder of Aguyi-Ironsi, the flag of an independent north republic flew over the headquarters of the north military headquarters at Ikeja, Lagos. By September (1966), objective (b) had indeed largely been achieved. Apart from the murder of Aguyi-Ironsi, 190 Igbo military officers and other personnel were murdered, many of them in horrific circumstances.[31] Having achieved (b), the north was persuaded to abandon objective (c) by Francis Cummings-Bruce, the head of the British diplomatic mission in Lagos, who all long had been in regular contact with the leading north officers who had seized Lagos including, especially, Colonel Gowon (army chief of staff), the

---

[31]Scores of these personnel were hacked to death in military bases stretching from Abeokuta, Ibadan and Lagos in the south to Zaria and Kaduna in the north. Several others were rounded up from their offices and apartments and shot. In some gruesome cases, Igbo officers were bound up, thrown into graves that they had been compelled to dig, and entombed.

pointsperson of the British intelligence in the heart of the Aguyi-Ironsi government since January, and a key operative in the overthrow and murder of his commander-in-chief and the perpetration of the Igbo genocide. It must have become clear to the north leaders both in Lagos and back home in Kaduna, Zaria, Kano and Sokoto then that after accomplishing objective (b), there was little incentive to extend their programme to (c). In fact, in a special broadcast made to the north, Colonel Gowon, who had since declared himself head of state, stressed that 'God, in his power, ha[d] entrusted the responsibility of this great country of ours, Nigeria, into the hands of another Northerner.'[32]

There was a streak of tragic inevitability that the Aguyi-Ironsi government was subjected to right from taking office. It had been thrown onto the centre stage of Nigerian politics by dramatic events which were none of its making, but which nonetheless placed it in a position of major *historic* relevance: it was the first central government in Nigeria's history to be headed by a citizen from the south, a *non-north* Nigerian. But it appeared that Aguyi-Ironsi did not fully appreciate the historic significance of his regime's ascendancy to power, precisely because he *did not* initiate the process of its emergence in the first place. Tragically, Aguyi-Ironsi had lodged his regime in the dreadful, debilitating, and ultimately destructive logic of trying to appease what was certainly the most brutish bloc of political forces in Africa of the mid-1960s. Aguyi-Ironsi did not fully appreciate the *nature* of power, especially that as ruthless as the one emplaced in Nigeria since 1952 by Britain and overseen by its local north clients to safeguard London's vast interests in what Peter Opara has described, aptly, as 'this Lugardian cage'.[33]

In fact Britain had essentially sentenced the Aguyi-Ironsi regime to death soon after it took office on 16 January 1966. It was not going to accept the dismantling of what it felt was a secured architecture of power to exploit Nigeria as it deemed fit, through its NPC/NNA/north levers. As far as Britain was concerned, in spite of six years of apparent restoration of independence in Nigeria, the north must be positioned at the apex of this architecture and anything that challenged or wished to change this would be resisted and crushed. The previous day's failed coup attempt had had a humiliating impact on British intelligence in Nigeria, which was completely caught unawares, despite having constructed its most extensive African network of operation in Nigeria besides South Africa. The British diplomatic mission in Lagos literally went on 'red alert' in response to the failed coup

---

[32]Quoted in Ananaba, *The Trade Union Movement in Nigeria*, p. 254.
[33]Peter Opara, 'Two Nigerians apart, naturally,' *Kwenu*, at http://www.kwenu.com/publications/opara/2006/Nigerians_apart.htl (accessed 15 March 2006).

Three phases of genocide 79

and the emergence of the Aguyi-Ironsi government. The mission felt affronted when Aguyi-Ironsi turned down Britain's offer to send in troops to confront the January majors when the latter threatened to march on Lagos and the south. Consequently, the mission mobilised British civil servants and academics who worked in the north to liaise with the north's emirs, ex-politicians (who now worked strategically in the local government services of the emirate system) and academics and students at Ahmadu Bello University, to plan for the termination of the Aguyi-Ironsi administration and the restoration of a north-controlled leadership. Furthermore, the British mission crucially strengthened, and, in some cases, reactivated its links and contacts in the Nigerian military, for this operation. In this regard, it was a major success for British intelligence on the ground when Colonel Gowon, who had worked diligently for it since he was recruited into the service whilst attending the Sandhurst military academy in England in the 1950s, was appointed chief of army staff by Aguyi-Ironsi. With devastating effects, Gowon strategically became the eyes and ears of British intelligence in the governing supreme military council as well as to the north's leadership back home in Sokoto, Kaduna, Zaria, Kano, Maiduguri and elsewhere. He informed and updated the Lagos British mission and the north on crucial policy decisions of the military council soon after its scheduled meetings, including such key subjects as the results of the investigating panel on the failed coup and the 'unification' decree. Such access to the very heart of the Aguyi-Ironsi government gave Britain and the north the priceless opportunity they needed to plan for the destruction of this government and embark on the Igbo genocide. Given his core-coordinating role during these six months of informing, updating, liaising and strategising with the British on the one hand, and the north-based leaders on the other, Gowon emerged in July (1966) as the head of the junta that murdered Aguyi-Ironsi, the 'another Northerner' in supreme power position in Nigeria, and the person who would oversee the 4-year Nigerian campaign of genocide against the Igbo people, resulting in the death of 3.1 million.

Aburi discourses

The immediate goal in August (1966) for Gowon and the north military officers who had murdered Aguyi-Ironsi, seized power, and embarked on the Igbo genocide, was the consolidation of their control across the entire country. Their coup had failed in the east region where the Aguyi-Ironsi-appointed governor, Colonel Chukwuemeka Odumegwu-Ojukwu, refused to recognise Gowon as the new head of state and supreme commander of the military. Odumegwu-Ojukwu had insisted that Gowon's assumption of power was an 'act of rebellion' which should be tried by a military tribunal. Secondly, and perhaps more importantly to eastern sensibilities at the time,

Odumegwu-Ojukwu accused Gowon and the junta that he led for supervising the mass murder of Igbo people across most of Nigeria. The east, he emphasised, could not entrust its security to a regime with such record, a point that was demonstrated dramatically in September 1966 when the constitutional conference which Gowon had summoned in Lagos was abandoned as the gruesome attacks on the Igbo worsened. As a result, east leaders decided not to attend any more meetings in Nigeria with representatives of the Gowon junta.

The rehabilitation of the 2 million Igbo who had returned to the east from the rest of Nigeria, following the genocide, was a major task that confronted the Odumegwu-Ojukwu government in Enugwu. The resources of the east had been stretched extensively between October-December 1966 after it allocated £3 million in emergency funding for the expansion of housing units, office space, schools, and health facilities to cope with the sudden influx of such a large number of people. Thanks to the region's booming economy and the remarkable intervention of its extended-family system in 'absorbing' a high proportion of the welfare needs of the returnees, the east was able to avert what was potentially a major humanitarian catastrophe. There was no outside aid involved in this resettlement programme, not from the Organisation of African Unity, not from the United Nations, and not least from the Gowon junta in Lagos that had itself coordinated the genocide after the end of July 1966.

The general mood in the east was that of intense outrage to the genocide. The last train that brought fleeing survivors from Nigeria in October 1966 was grotesquely symbolic. It had on board the body of a decapitated Igbo man and a woman passenger whose only possession in a suitcase was the head of her child. The child's body had been severed in the mother's presence when genocidist forces attacked the train during the journey to the east. News of the arrival of this train at Enugwu with its infamous cargo was extensively covered in the east media. This incident gave further impetus to demands, already being made in rallies, symposiums, lectures, and other forms of public meetings across the region, for the declaration of the east's independence in response to the genocide. Those in the vanguard of the independence movement were workers and tradespeoples (both categories suffered the highest casualties during the genocide), intellectuals and students. Ninety per cent of the victims of the genocide came from these professional groupings, and their pressure on Odumegwu-Ojukwu to declare the east independent between October and December 1966 was intensive indeed. There was, however, a considerable feeling of reticence in government circles in Enugwu to these calls for the east independence. It was clear to the east government that, following the genocide and the mass return of survivors, the east's relationship with Nigeria would undergo a radical restructuring. But apart from coping with the resettlement of the returnees, east leaders were further inhibited from breaking with Nigeria at this stage because of unfavourable security considerations. Scores of brilliant Igbo military officers, the very best in what was the Nigerian armed forces prior to July 1966, were murdered during the genocide. The 500 east military personnel who escaped the tragedy were still traumatised by their experience. Now back in the east, they needed more time to recover before they could provide the leadership required for the defence of the region, if the need arose. Even then, the east was devoid of any significant military installation, as we have stated elsewhere. It had no ammunition factory. There was a small army base in Enugwu, staffed by mostly north and Yoruba forces who the east had given 'free passage' to evacuate soon after the genocide in the north was underway. These forces had departed for their homes with the limited arms and ammunition allocated to the garrison, ensuring that the east was left with hardly any weapons that were worthwhile. It was clear that any plans in the interim to defend the region from an attack from Lagos and Kaduna, which were now in control of all military facilities in the rest of the federation, were fraught with immense difficulties. The east's security situation at this stage was therefore highly precarious and this evidently restricted the scope available to the region's leadership to respond more favourably to popular calls for the declaration of independence. What however remained the symbol of the east's determination to seek a completely new political association with the rest of Nigeria, after the genocide, was Odumegwu-Ojukwu's adamant refusal to recognise the Gowon junta, the architect of the monstrosity, in spite of the region's feeble defence capabilities.

While this political stance tended to assuage the various constituencies of the east's independence movement, who were well aware of the region's security difficulties, it however fuelled the demands in Lagos and Kaduna for an expansion of the genocidal mission begun in May to Igboland itself. Indeed throughout November-December 1966, the threats from Lagos and the north to invade the east continued unabated. A number of the genocidist officers in the north, including Colonel Katsina, the governor and future chief of army staff, and those in control of Lagos, especially the personnel grouped around Colonel Murtala Muhammed (who commanded an execution squad that murdered hundreds of Igbo men and boys in Asaba and other Igbo towns and villages west of the River Niger in 1967 and who would be head of state in 1975-76) and Major Theophilus Danjuma (who commanded the death squad that murdered General Aguyi-Ironsi and who would be defence minister in the future), pressed particularly for such an invasion because of their disappointment with the failure of their genocide to destroy the entire Igbo population in Nigeria, and consequently the larger-than-expected-extent of Igbo survival. They were also stunned by the 'apparent ease' with which the east had proceeded, *on its own*, to rehabilitate the 2 million survivors of the genocide without any outside support. They reasoned that the longer an extension of the attack on the east was delayed, the more likely the Igbo would be in the position to mount a greater resistance. Colonel Katsina was already boasting that his forces could overrun the east in '48 hours,'[34] given the fact that all Nigeria's military equipment and facilities were located in the north and west. The mass publicity facilities based in the north especially the Nigerian Broadcasting Corporation radio and television services (Kaduna), the *New Nigerian* daily newspaper (Kaduna) and *Gaskiya Ta Fi Kwabo*, the Hausa language weekly (Zaria), which had played a notorious role during May-October in inciting and propagating the genocide, seized on this theme of 'completing the task' begun in May, arguing and urging the Gowon regime to attack the east before the latter recovered from the trauma of the mass murder of recent months. These media outlets would move viciously into the vanguard of the mobilisation of the north population to embark on the eventual Nigerian attack of the east in July 1967 and the inauguration of the second phase of the Igbo genocide.

It was against this background that the head of Ghana's military government, General Joseph Ankrah, invited Odumegwu-Ojukwu, Gowon and the rest of the members of the military council to Aburi, Ghana, in January 1967 to discuss the Nigerian débâcle. After two days of talks, the delegates achieved an extraordinary degree of agreement, in spite of the horrors of the previous seven months. A brief examination of the key points of the agreement underscores our conclusion. Two areas require comment. First, the resolution that focused on the renouncement of force and the importation of arms:[35] (i) 'renounce the use of force as a means of settling the present crisis in Nigeria'; (ii) 'agree that there should be no more importation of arms and ammunition until normalcy [is] restored'. Second, the provisions that dealt with the ruling military council of which Gowon had declared himself 'supreme commander' since he seized power during the genocide and the reorganisation of the army. Four articles are relevant here:[36] (i) 'military is to be governed by the Supreme Military Council'; (ii) 'creation of area command corresponding with the existing region and under the charge of an area commander'; (iii) 'during the period of the military government, military governors will have control over their area commands on matters of internal security'; (iv) 'agree that any decision affecting the whole country must be determined by the Supreme Military Council and where a meeting is not possible such a matter must be referred to military

---

[34]Obasanjo, *My Command*, p. 15.
[35]Bernard Odogwu, *No Place to Hide* (Enugu: Fourth Dimension Publishers, 1985), p. 255.
[36]Ibid., p. 256.

governors for comment and concurrence'.

In effect, the Aburi decision to transfer the constitutional responsibility of the Nigerian military from the position of the supreme commander to the supreme military council, extensively limited the executive (and legislature) powers of position of 'supreme commander and head of state' which Gowon had exercised since the genocide (these powers were originally contained in Aguyi-Ironsi's January 1966 decree no. 1 which had made the occupant of that office, and not the SMC, the principal person in charge of decision making in the country). In future, following the Aburi accord, 'any decision affecting the *whole* country must be decided by the Supreme Military Council' (added emphasis) – namely, the eight members that made up the body gathered in Ghana including pointedly the military governors of the regions of which Odumegwu-Ojukwu, the only member that had refused to recognise Gowon in that position, was one. It is of immense significance that this provision on the new powers of the SMC also states that 'where a meeting [of the SMC] is not possible such a matter must be referred to military governors for *comment and concurrence*' (added emphasis). This referral procedure was aimed evidently at meeting Odumegwu-Ojukwu's contention, repeatedly stated during the meeting, that he would not attend any meetings in Nigeria where the Nigerian military, which had played a central role in the Igbo genocide, was positioned and operating. Odumegwu-Ojukwu had in fact converted the Aburi gathering into a peer-review session, unprecedented in recent African history. Here at Aburi, an African leader bluntly told his colleagues, who only 18 months earlier would have all shared the conviviality of an officers' mess or one of the other's residence to wine and dine, that he had no confidence in them and the troops they commanded because they had been involved in the perpetration of a genocide that claimed the lives of 100,000 Africans. This was indeed an historic rendezvous, the like of which has not been seen in Africa since. It would take another 40 years for the world at large to increasingly begin to lecture African leaders to openly condemn atrocities committed by one of their own.[37] Back to Aburi (1967), Odumegwu-Ojukwu had laid bare, for the crucial reckoning of African history, the apposite moral and juridical dilemma surrounding the status of lead-genocidist leader Yakubu Gowon. Odumegwu-Ojukwu had insisted at the talks that Gowon must neither be seen nor aided by his peers to appropriate the position and the powers invested in Nigeria's top political and military leadership after his perpetration of the mass murder of tens of thousands of people. Odumegwu-Ojukwu's reply to a question about Gowon's status, posed by Major

---

[37]See Herbert Ekwe-Ekwe, 'Why African leaders are leading them nowhere,' *USAfricaonline*, at http://www.usafricaonline.com/ekweekwe.nepad.html (accessed 26 September 2005).

Mobalaji Johnson (governor of Lagos), was undoubtedly the turning point at the conference. It led to the challenge and dramatic reconfiguration of Gowon's acquired position and powers that he had exercised so ruthlessly since 29 July 1966. Astonishingly, this outcome was approved and signed by *all* the eight principal participants at the meeting – Colonel Adebayo, west governor; Colonel Ejoor, midwest governor; Colonel Gowon, head of the genocidist forces in control of Lagos/west-north regions; Major Johnson, Lagos governor; Colonel Katsina, north governor, Colonel Odumegwu-Ojukwu, east governor; Mr Salem, head of the police, and Commodore Wey, head of navy.

Following objections that Odumegwu-Ojukwu had earlier made during the proceedings to one of the participants who referred to Gowon as 'supreme commander', Johnson had asked: 'Is there a government in Nigeria today? Is there a central government in Nigeria today?'[38] Odumegwu-Ojukwu: 'That question is such a simple one that anybody who has been listening to what I have been saying would know that I do not see a central government in Nigeria today. [Following the genocide] Nigeria resolved itself into three areas – Lagos, West and North area; the Mid-West area; and the East area.'[39] Odumegwu-Ojukwu was in effect highlighting the territorial reach and distribution of the Gowon-controlled genocidist forces across the country – Lagos/west-north regions where they occupied, and the east and midwest regions, which were still free of their presence. In the light of Aburi, Gowon's overall control of the Lagos/west-north regions had in fact come under question. With the newly acquired powers of individual governors on the supreme military council at the expense of those hitherto wielded by Gowon, it followed, for instance, that the governors of Lagos, west and north (where the Gowonist forces were entrenched) would in future be expected to exercise greater powers of control in their respective regions than Gowon. If an audio-recorded transcript of the entire deliberations of the Aburi conference did not exist today as a treasured historic document, it would have been extremely difficult to appreciate Odumegwu-Ojukwu's phenomenal success in persuading the rest of the participants to accept an extensively decentralised structural solution to Nigeria's crisis, after the devastating genocide, looting, and the displacement of 2 million Igbo people. That Gowon, *himself,* appended his signature to this Odumegwu-Ojukwu prepared text at a gathering that had, as a result of these developments, clipped his powers so extensively, was not just because the east governor was the 'cleverest ... the only one who understood the real issues,' as Walter Schwarz has observed,[40] or that the rest of the conferees

---

[38]Quoted in Dudley, *Instability and Political Order*, p. 172.
[39]Ibid.
[40]Quoted in Obasanjo, *My Command*, p. 10.

were 'too unserious[ly] minded to meet with [Odumegwu-]Ojukwu's compulsive logic,' as Joe Garba, a leading genocidist officer in the Gowonist forces and Nigeria's foreign minister in the 1970s, has noted.[41] On the contrary, Gowon and each of the other Nigerian leaders at Aburi (Adebayo, Ejoor, Johnson, Katsina, Salem, Wey – all of whom, bar Odumegwu-Ojukwu, had recognised Gowon as 'supreme commander and head of state' since end of July 1966) signed this extraordinary document because they were each and collectively in awe of the frankness and rectitude of Odumegwu-Ojukwu's strictures of them for executing such a despicable act of genocide during the course of 1966.

Overnight, the outcome of the Aburi discourses radically altered the contours of the political landscape of Nigeria. The centralising features of Aguyi-Ironsi's decree no. 34 dispensation of the previous year, since adopted by the Gowon junta despite the irony, had been abandoned. More importantly, though, the powers of the regions vis-à-vis the centre had become more enhanced – much more than at any time in Nigeria's history, even including the epoch of the feverishly-pursued British occupation's regionalisation drive of the 1950s. Aburi had in effect inaugurated a confederal, extensively decentralised constitutional solution to the Nigerian impasse, to the consternation of the British (who had followed the talks with nervousness), the north, the military, and the central bureaucratic establishment in Lagos. These critics launched a chorus of fierce opposition on the accord, forcing the Gowon junta to renege on the agreement a few days after returning to Nigeria from Ghana. The groups felt that Gowon and the rest of the non-east delegation at Aburi had capitulated to Odumegwu-Ojukwu's uncompromising censure of his former colleagues' involvement in the Igbo genocide. As a consequence, notes these critics of the Aburi outcome, Odumegwu-Ojukwu had out-manoeuvred fellow conferees in accepting as *de jure* the increasingly autonomous political direction which the east had embarked upon in the wake of the genocide, in addition to according this same status to the other regions of Nigeria – a move that further eclipsed Gowon's powers as 'head of state'.[42] But for the east, the implementation of the Aburi agreement was the minimal condition for maintaining further political links with Nigeria: 'It was Aburi or a clean break with Nigeria.'[43] In a radio broadcast in Enugwu in February 1967, Odumegwu-Ojukwu gave notice that the east would begin to implement the Aburi agreement as from the end of March (1967), even if Gowon and the rest of the accord's signatories did not do so. Gowon responded by threatening to attack the east if it went ahead to implement the agreement.

---

[41]*This Week* (Lagos), 13 July 1987, p. 23.
[42]See, for instance, Dudley, *Instability and Political Order*, p. 176.
[43]Odogwu, *No Place to Hide*, p. 262.

Ironically, Gowon's threat was itself a clear violation of one of the key articles of the accord, which pronounced unambiguously: 'renounce[d] the use of force as a means of settling the Nigerian crisis.' Odumegwu-Ojukwu nonetheless went ahead to implement the Aburi accord after 31 March. This move further enhanced the virtually autonomous position that the east had had in relation to the rest of the country since October 1966 – i.e. at the apogee of the genocide. For his part, Gowon imposed a total economic blockade of the east. Effectively, this was the prelude to his forces' invasion of the region, the expansion of the territorial reach of their yearlong genocidal campaign on the Igbo to Igboland itself. This 'solution' had increasingly become the proffered one sought by the British and their north Nigerian allies since Aburi. To defend itself from the obvious consequences of this renewed scourge, the east, Biafra, declared its independence from Nigeria on 30 May 1967, one year to the day since the Igbo genocide began.

Phase II

The developed confluence of opinion between the British and the north on the Aburi accord, soon after the end of the conference, no doubt facilitated the July 1967 invasion of Biafra by Nigeria. Britain was still reeling from its disappointment over Odumegwu-Ojukwu's refusal to attend its own planned December 1966 'conference of mediation', involving all the members of the governing military council (same group that ultimately met in Ghana) on board a British naval frigate anchored off Nigeria's waters. The east governor could not accept the presumption of 'neutrality' or 'even-handedness' inherent in London's invitation to host such a summit, considering Britain's activist role in the Igbo genocide of May-October 1966. Furthermore, Odumegwu-Ojukwu could not have ignored the lessons of a similar event in the 19th century. Then, King Jaja of Opobo, an Igbo nationalist monarch opposed to British territorial expansionism along the Atlantic coast of Igboland, was kidnapped by the British navy and exiled to the Caribbean (where he eventually died) after accepting, in good faith, a British offer of 'peace talks' on board a British vessel berthed off shore. So, on the Aburi agreement, Britain rejected its outcome out of hand and began to pressurise Gowon, who for two days during the Ghana conference was out of reach from his British intelligence minders for the first time in almost a year, to renege on it. Britain was therefore pleased when the north and other interest groups in Nigeria joined in the opposition against the accord. Gowon's ultimate renegation of an accord that he signed willingly in Ghana, in the presence of all the other seven members of the Nigerian governing military council, their five secretaries, and General Ankrah, their host, was a reminder, if ever such an evidence was sought, of who eventually called the shots at the crucial junctures of the course of the Igbo genocide. Such was the British disappointment of Gowon's performance in Abuja that they ensured that Gowon would in future no longer be 'exposed' to Odumegwu-Ojukwu or any of these Igbo with 'compulsive logic'. Subsequently, the often more coherent spokespersons who tried to put across some 'form of explanation' of the Anglo/Nigerian position on the Igbo genocide, especially in Britain where there was a groundswell popular opposition to the slaughter, were from a hired pool of consultants of ex-British conquest administrators who had served in Nigeria.

Nigeria resumed its campaign of genocide on the Igbo, which had been on hold since October 1966, by attacking Biafra on 6 July 1967. Gowon received full backing from the British government, which pledged its unflinching military and diplomatic support throughout the campaign. The Gowonist forces envisaged a very short campaign – '48 hours,' according to Colonel Katsina, who Gowon appointed chief of army staff to direct the operation. The Nigerian objective was to simultaneously overrun three strategic Biafran towns, all positioned within a 50-mile arc from the southern fringes of Nigerian territory: Nsukka, the university town, Enugwu, the capital, and Abakaliki, the headquarters of the rich agricultural province of the Ebonyi and Asu valleys. As we have already indicated, Nigeria's confidence of a swift victory over Biafra was based on the fact that it had not only 'inherited' the entire Nigerian military assets including seven-eights of the combatant personnel prior to the beginning of the genocide in 1966, but it had been involved lately, particularly since the Aburi conference, in the massive importation of arms. It could also count on British support, an important consideration given London's role as the leading global power in Africa of the mid-1960s.

The core units Gowon assigned to spearhead the invasion were the very ones that led the genocidal attacks on Igbo population centres across the north and elsewhere in the country during the previous year. The Kaduna radio and television services of the Nigerian Broadcasting Corporation, assisted by the *New Nigerian* daily and *Gaskiya Ta Fi Kwabo* weekly, went into a sustained bout of racist, vitriolic broadcast and publicity to mobilise and recruit for the campaign in Igboland. Such was the utter virulence of the anti-Igbo propaganda material on these media services that they constituted the most effective 'recruiting sergeant' for the tens of thousands of young men across Nigeria and the neighbouring states of Chad (the notorious *gwodogwodo* operatives), Niger, and north Cameroon who Nigeria and Britain would train and deploy across Igboland to murder, rape, burn, loot, and waste during three long years of genocide, not seen in Africa since Belgian King Leopold II's ravages of the countries of the Congo basin during the 19th century.

Nigeria inaugurated another maleficent 'first' in Africa of the epoch, to be copied with devastating consequences 40 years later by genocidist broadcasters in Sierra Leone, Rwanda and Congo Democratic Republic, when the Kaduna public-funded radio and television campaigned openly in their broadcast outputs for the Nigerian military and other recruits to march to Igboland and embark on the mass murder of Igbo people, the rape of Igbo womanhood, the looting and vandalisation of Igbo property. These radio and television stations aired the following fiendish jingles in Hausa (with spot advertisements or editorial comments on the theme regularly reproduced in both *New Nigerian* and *Gaskiya Ta Fi Kwabo* during the period) before and after the broadcast of each news bulletin and other current affairs programmes throughout the course of the second phase of the genocide – July 1966-January 1970:

Mu je mu kashe nyamiri
Mu kashe maza su da yan maza su
Mu chi mata su da yan mata su
Mu kwashe kaya su

(Let's go kill the damned Igbo/Kill off their men and boys/Rape their wives and daughters/Cart off their property)

Fully armed and reinforced continuously by Britain, which also had a contingent of advisors and instructors on the ground, the Nigerian forces descended on Biafra with unimaginable ferocity, turning the country into an extensive crime scene as the Radio Kaduna jingles beckoned. The Nigerians began to murder, rape, burn and loot as they were unmistakably expected to perform. The hallowed justice of the world must urgently investigate this crime thoroughly. Thankfully, its lead organisers and perpetrators such as Generals Gowon, Obasanjo, Abubakar, Babangida, Buhari, Haruna, Akinrinade, Brigadier Adekunle, Captain King and Messrs Enaharo, Ayida and Aminu are still alive. They are more likely to be seen today strutting across the world's capitals as dubious democrats and statespersons instead of being sequestrated at The Hague International Criminal Court house to answer charges against genocide. Forty years before its routine operationalisation in Rwanda, the Nigerians established on the ground of Igboland, in 1967-1970, the use of rape and the public executions of men and boys as pivotal instruments in waging a war of genocide in Africa. Every Igbo town or village overrun by the Nigerians became a haunting milestone in an inexorable march of rape, death, and destruction: Obollo Afo … Obollo Eke … Enugwu-Ezike … Opi … Ukehe … Nkalagu … Owgwu … Abakaliki … Eha Amufu … Nsukka … Enugwu … Agbaani … Asaba … Ogwashi-Ukwu … Isele-Ukwu … Umunede … Onicha … Oka … Aba … Udi … Evugbo … Evugbo Road … Okigwe … Umuahia … Owere … Abagana … Ugwuocha/Port Harcourt… Ahaoda … Obiigbo … Azumini …

Umu Ubani/Bonny ... Opobo ... Ugwuta ... Amasiri ... Akaeze ... Uzuakoli ...

In a courageous and admirable public admission made in 1970, Colonel Robert Scott broke ranks with his employer, the British diplomatic mission in Lagos where he worked as a military advisor, to acknowledge, gravely, that as the Nigerians unleashed their attacks on Igbo towns and villages, they were the 'best defoliant agent known'[44] – such was the destructiveness. Brigadier Adekunle, one of the most notorious of the Nigerian commanders during the period, does not disagree with Scott as he indeed told journalists in his theatre of operations then for the record, as we have already referenced in this study: 'I want to prevent even one I[g]bo having even one piece to eat before their capitulation. We shoot at everything that moves, and when our forces march into the centre of I[g]bo territory, we shoot at everything, even at things that do not move.' Adekunle was implementing to the letter the Anglo-Gowonist high command's 'starvation as weapon/quick kill' doctrine, articulated by Obafemi Awolowo, the imprisoned Yoruba political leader who had since been released by Gowon and made the latter's deputy to ensure a more activist Yoruba support for the genocide. Awolowo had insisted that 'starvation was a legitimate weapon of war' and that starving the Igbo to death was part and parcel of the Nigerian strategy in its mission in Biafra.[45] British Prime Minister Wilson confirmed his government's involvement in the implementation of this strategy, as we have already shown. According to Olusegun Obasanjo, another genocidist commander at the time and current president of Nigeria, it was left to Wilson and his government to 'sort out' the international outrage that had erupted in 1969 when the Nigerians deliberately shot down a clearly marked International Committee of the Red Cross relief carrying aircraft about to land in Biafra, in defiance of the infamous 'starvation as weapon/quick kill' doctrine.[46] The ICRC plane was shot down by Captain Gbadomosi King of the Nigerian airforce, who Obasanjo had known since 1966.[47] At the time of the outrage, King served in Obasanjo's unit in southern Biafra. Obasanjo remembers King affectionately as a 'dare-devil pilot'.[48] He had personally 'challenged' the pilot in May 1969 to 'produce results' in stopping further international relief flights into Biafra in keeping with the doctrine to starve the Igbo to death, to which King 'promised to do his best.'[49] 'Within a week [King]

---

[44]*Sunday Telegraph* (London), 11 January 1970, quoted in Suzanne Cronje, *The World and Nigeria* (London: Sidgwick & Jackson, 1972), p. 61.
[45]De St. Jorre, *The Brothers' War*, p. 244.
[46]Obasanjo, *My Command*, p. 165.
[47]Ibid., pp. 78-79.
[48]Ibid., p. 78.
[49]Ibid., p. 78.

redeemed his promise,' Obasanjo reflects nostalgically.[50] Finally, Obasanjo recalls the destruction of the ICRC aircraft, with the death of all crew on board, with perverse satisfaction: 'The effect of [this] singular achievement of the Air Force especially on 3 Marine Commando Division [the unit Obasanjo commanded] was profound. It raised the morale of all service personnel, especially of the Air Force detachment concerned and the troops they supported in [my] 3 Marine Commando Division.'[51]

One of the tragic features of the Igbo genocide, as we have already established in this study, was the lack of concerted effort from the rest of the world, including governments and peoples in Africa, to stop the Nigerian state's meticulously organised murders, rapes, lootings and destruction of Igbo lives and property that went on from May 1966 to January 1970. The world could have stopped this genocide, *should* have stopped this genocide, if it had really endeavoured to do so. In Nigeria, itself, there was a palpable lack of concern shown to the victims by most Nigerians elsewhere, particularly in the west region, a situation which has led Okwudiba Nnoli to observe that, '[a]t that time, Nigeria seemed morally anesthesized.'[52] In what was clearly an obscene postscript to the first phase of the genocide in October 1966, a group of Yoruba *obas* (kings) toured north Nigeria, soon after these horrific events, to 'thank' local community leaders and authorities there for 'offering protection' to the Yoruba domiciled in the region during the genocide from being murdered. It of course needs no reminder that the north leaders and authorities being praised by the Yoruba *obas* were the same who had played an instrumental role, on the ground, in spearheading the Igbo genocide up and down their communities during May-October 1966. The logistics entailed in ensuring the very 'success' of this 'protection' enterprise for the Yoruba during a time frame of five months as 100,000 Igbo were being murdered across north Nigeria, a land space that is about one-half of the entire west Europe, once again underlines the premeditated and rigorous planning in the execution of this crime.

In appreciation of the north leaders' success in safeguarding the lives of thousands of Yoruba émigrés in the north during the Igbo slaughter, the *obas* supported the rest of the Yoruba leadership, principally Obafemi Awolowo (who Gowon had released from prison and appointed his deputy), to send the Yoruba military to participate in the expanded phase of the genocide in Biafra when it began in July 1967. Awolowo, a rabid Yoruba exclusivist, thought that he now had an opportunity that he had sought frantically for 15 years to 'offset' his punishing electoral 'humiliation' brought about by his election defeat in his Yoruba/west region homestead by Nnamdi Azikiwe

---

[50] Ibid., p. 79.
[51] Ibid., p. 79.
[52] Nnoli, *Ethnic Politics in Nigeria*, p. 245.

and the NCNC all-Nigeria liberation party. Awolowo always believed that the enterprising and seemingly irreverent Igbo were the victor in the 30-year-old (1935-1965) classic Igbo-Yoruba competition/rivalry that dominated the history of economic, political and cultural transformation in south Nigeria during this epoch. He felt that this outcome had placed the Igbo at the position where it had developed a variegated high-level humanpower and regional economic base from which to 'dominate' socioeconomics relations in post-conquest Nigeria.[53] For Awolowo, the May-October Igbo genocide was a 'shattering blow' to Igbo historic fortunes and it was in the *national* interest of the Yoruba to lend its support to the north in the latter's expanded attack on the Igbo. In gratitude, the north assigned the entire south Biafra to the Yoruba military, led initially by Brigadier Adekunle and later Colonel Obasanjo, to ravage. In the meantime, the Yoruba began to fill the plum positions in academia, the bureaucracy, business, industry, military, police, etc., etc., across Nigeria 'vacated' by the ubiquitous Igbo who had either been murdered during the earlier phase of the genocide, or were awaiting the new onslaught in their homeland launched in July 1967. They also seized, as had been the case in the north, 'abandoned' Igbo businesses and property in Lagos and the west some of which were established 50 years earlier. The apparent 'Yoruba Age' in Nigeria had, at last, dawned but on sheer greed and opportunism.

Phase III

Awolowo soon emerged as the lead-ideologue of the Nigerian state genocide against the Igbo. If Awolowo were alive today, he would have been one of the lead-defendants of the grouping of Nigerian genocidist military and civilian officials to be arraigned at The Hague International Criminal Court for crimes against humanity in Biafra. In his absence, his co-defendants, especially those who worked very closely with him such as Gowon, Obasanjo, Adekunle, Enaharo and Ayida would no doubt be expected to inform the world fully of all they knew about the infamous 'starvation as weapon/quick kill' doctrine. Awolowo was the formulator of the doctrine, a strategy that was implemented with devastating success by particularly the Yoruba air force and marine units operating in south Igboland. Following the truce in the carnage declared by Nigeria in January 1970, Awolowo formulated yet another strategy on the Igbo, this time aimed at impoverishing the 9 million of them that had survived the genocide – such was the virulence of Igbophobia that drove this man's policy programmes as Gowon's deputy and minister of finance during the period. In this new phase, Awolowo approved a banking edict which invalidated all bank

---

[53]Cf. ibid., p. 227.

accounts operated by the Igbo throughout the four years of the genocide. As a result, Nigeria earned £4 million from a people that had lost 3 million of their population, and had had most of their cities, towns, villages, homes, schools, hospitals, businesses, everything, destroyed. The meagre flat rate of £20.00 was given in exchange for the value of the Biafran currency (whatever the amount) held by the head of the Igbo family, if the person could be 'certified' to have survived. Finally, Awolowo initiated a raft of confidential memoranda and protocols which effectively barred Nigeria's rehabilitation of the economy of Igboland in perpetuity – 'an atrocity,' as Nnaemeka Ikpeze has unambiguously described the measure.[54] If anyone thought that the savagery of this holocaust would cease with the formal end of *direct* Nigerian military operations in Biafra on 12 January 1970, they were extremely mistaken. As decreed by Awolowo, all successive Nigerian regimes since then (headed by Generals Gowon, Muhammed, Obasanjo, Buhari, Babangida, Abacha, Abubakar and Messrs Shagari and Shonekan) have pursued a brazen policy of economic siege on the Igbo country: blanket freeze on worthwhile development projects, atrocious communication infrastructure, nonchalant disposition to grave environmental degradation caused by soil erosion/land slides particularly in the northwest provinces bordering the River Niger. And to undergird this virtual economic boycott/blockade of Igboland both politically and culturally during the period, the Nigerian genocidists have shut the Igbo off from accessing and occupying critical levers of power in the country. Furthermore, they have, through the relentless promotion of *Igbophobia*, popularised this policy of exclusion across Nigeria.

Olusegun Obasanjo, the most avid Awolowoist of these leaders and current head of state, is most fanatically desperate on the subject of the Igbo, Igbo exclusion, and Igbophobia. Obasanjo has often reminded the Igbo and others that the 1966-1970 genocide campaign had not achieved its 'final solution' when the 12 January 1970 truce came into effect. After all, he reckons, the Igbo, *as a people*, did not disappear ... They survived; they were, therefore, victorious. For Obasanjo, this outcome was 'incomplete'. It falls short of the defeat of the Igbo that he and his forces had envisaged: erasure, total erasure. It is in this context that Obasanjo's recent public acknowledgement in Igboland that Nigeria still has a policy to exterminate the Igbo must be taken seriously by all, most especially the Igbo. He should be expected to elaborate fully on this plan of annihilation when he faces the justices at The Hague International criminal Court. As a result, of the nine Nigerian heads of state since the genocide, Obasanjo suffers and exhibits the

---

[54]Nnaemeka Ikpeze, 'Post-Biafran Marginalization of the Igbo in Nigeria,' in Ifi Amadiume & Abdullahi An-Na'im, eds., *The Politics of Memory* (London and New York: Zed Books, 2000), p. 106.

most virulent contagion of Igbophobia. His is in fact only surpassed by that of Awolowo's. Obasanjo refuses to be content with the genocidist state's encoded economic boycott of Igboland and the political marginalisation of its people. This is enforced by the blanket military and police cordon slammed on the Igbo country by this state since January 1970. Obasanjo therefore does not believe that his state's continuing dual-track violation of the fundamental human rights of the Igbo in the past 36 years is having its desired effect – namely, to 'seal the fate' of the Igbo permanently, as the Nigerians had wished at the height of the genocide.

Evidently, Obasanjo's trenchant Igbophobia is a telling metaphor for the utter frustration felt by the inability of the Awolowoist wing of the Nigerian genocidist state, an indolent and capricious lot, to transform the Nigerian society after the Igbo genocide. It was always keen to boast at the time that it would accomplish this goal within a couple of decades. The Igbo had now 'gone', including their academics who, as Ali Mazrui reflects on the times, with amazingly undisguised indifference, 'had become too visible for their own safety at the Univeristy of Ibadan.'[55] As a consequence, Yoruba professors at the University of Ibadan and elsewhere in the west now saw themselves as the intelligentsia of this wing. They never tired during the course of the 1970s/1980s to inform whoever cared to listen that with the 'elimination' of the Igbo from the 'dominant position' in Nigeria, the Awolowoists were poised to build a Nigerian super state. To underscore such confidence, the wing's top military personnel, Obasanjo, who also doubled as the head of the state's military junta during the period, made the following public declaration to the world in 1979: 'Nigeria will become one of the ten leading nations in the world by the end of the century.'[56]

Almost 20 years to the day after his boast, Obasanjo returns to the political scene once again as head of state but instead of leading 'one of the ten leading [states] in the world,' he was in fact president of one of the 10 poorest and most depressed countries on earth. He spends the four years of this term as president junketing around the world, with bowl in hand, asking Nigeria's presumed overseas creditors to 'forgive' and cancel the country's US$34billion 'debt', which he himself had begun to accumulate in the 1970s. Meanwhile, Allison Ayida, one of Obasanjo's close genocidist colleagues who was a top bureaucrat during the genocide and had traversed African capitals reminding his audiences of the 'legitimacy' of his regime's 'starvation as weapon/quick kill' doctrine, had published a book on Nigeria with the following amazing stark title: *The Rise and Fall of Nigeria*. Even then, it is not yet certain if, 40 years since the beginning of the genocide, the

---

[55] Ali Mazrui, 'Conflict Resolution and Social Justice in the Africa of Tomorrow,' *Présence Africaine*, 3rd and 4th Quarterlies, Nos. 127/128, 1983, p. 311.
[56] See Achebe, *The Trouble with Nigeria*, p. 9.

Awolowoists, who currently are in the vanguard of its third phase, in addition of course to the Anglo/north region dominant wing, realise that genocide coupled with greed and opportunism are definitely no routes to the transformation of state and society. Nigeria 1966-2006 underscores just that.

Besides the generalised African silence or complicity in the Igbo genocide, there is, finally, an equally pernicious feature of the continent's response to this carnage, which is best illustrated by the position of Ali Mazrui, the Kenyan-born leading ideologue of islamic expansionism in Africa. Not only does Mazrui condemn the right of the Igbo to defend themselves from the genocide (natural law, rights to life and property guaranteed by the relevant articles in the Nigerian constitution at the time, United Nations declaration of human rights to which the Nigerian state was – and still remains – a signatory), he also derides their very act of defence through his novel, entitled *The Trial of Christopher Okigbo*. Mazrui has written expansively in the past 45 years, valorising every conceivable islamic cause or project in Hausa-Fulani north Nigeria as well as other parts of west Africa, the rest of Africa, the Middle East, and elsewhere in the world. As a result, Mazrui has never condemned the Igbo genocide unambiguously nor its Hausa-Fulani/north perpetrators, who, in addition, have carried out other series of pogroms against the Igbo since 1945 under the ideological rubric of islam, nor their British accomplices. Mazrui is fully aware that the Hausa-Fulani/north muslims categorise the Igbo as belonging to the *dar el harb* (abode of war) zone of the islamic conceptualisation of the world, unlike the *dar el islam* (abode of islam) of the muslim faithful, the other region of this dichotomised universe.[57] The Hausa-Fulani/north muslims have therefore always felt that it is 'legitimate', 'justifiable', 'fair game', to murder the Igbo and pillage their property in their *sabon gari* residential districts or enclosures dotted across the north (*dar el harb*) during the spates of anti-Igbo pogroms that have occurred here in the past 61 years (1945, 1953, 1980, 1982, 1985, 1991, 1992, 1993, 1994, 1999, 2001, 2002, 2004, 2005, 2006) or during the first phase of the Igbo genocide in the north (May-October 1966) or indeed during the second phase of the Igbo genocide that was carried out in Igboland itself (July 1966-January 1970). Each and every manifestation of this outrage, it must be emphasised, is preceded and accompanied by the familiar anti-Igbo chants and obscenities of 'kill the damned Igbo' or 'kill the infidels' which are invigorated by the tempo of the exhortative signatures of '*Allahu akbar*', all of which seemingly help focus the minds and brawn of the rampaging gang as it zooms unto that targeted zone of perpetual genocide, expropriation and wasting called *dar el harb*.

---

[57]For an insight into this islamic view of the world, see, for instance, Ali Mazrui, 'The Reincarnation of the African State,' *Présence Africaine*, 3rd and 4th Quarterlies, Nos. 127/128, 1983, p. 116.

In his *The Trial of Christopher Okigbo*, it is clear which of the two islamic classificatory zones in Nigeria, sketched above, has Mazrui's sympathies. The novel focuses on the active involvement of the poet, Christopher Okigbo, in the defence of his people during the second phase of the Igbo genocide in Biafra. Okigbo lost his life in the resistance. In its imaginary trial of Okigbo after his death by some 'after-life' tribunal, the novel attacks the poet for 'putting society before art in his scale of values.'[58] Furthermore, it alleges, '[n]o great artist has a right to carry patriotism to the extent of destroying his creative potential.'[59] This is indeed a bewildering criticism coming from Mazrui who is a trained historian and political scientist and who is surely aware that hundreds of Igbo artists and intellectuals and hundreds of thousands of potential ones were murdered during the genocide. Igbo artists and intellectuals were not immune from the bullet or cudgel of the genocidist horde. The great Chinua Achebe, for instance, barely escaped with his life from Lagos to Igboland after being trailed and hunted for days by the horde. His cousin, Lieutenant Achebe, was not so fortunate. He was murdered by the genocidists.

Artists and intellectuals over the ages have supported the defence of the human rights of their people. This defence has ranged from artists and intellectuals focusing actively on the subject in their areas of creative endeavour to physically defending their people, their homeland, from whatever is perceived as a danger to these rights. The African humanity has been no exception to this trend. Alioune Diop, the critic, philosopher and founding publisher of the respected *Présence Africaine* has noted that '[w]e live in an epoch where artists [and intellectuals] carry testaments, where they all more or less are committed. One has to take sides ...'[60] African World artists and intellectuals such as Eze Nri, Olaudah Equiano, Chukwuemeka Odumegwu-Ojukwu, Nelson Mandela, Malcolm X, Martin Luther King, Chinua Achebe, Mary Seacole, Pius Okigbo, Cheikh Anta Diop, Onwuka Dike, Christopher Okigbo, Sojourner Truth, Angulu Onwuejiogwu, Zora Neale Hurston, Philip Emeagwali, Ralph Uwazurike, Chimamanda Ngozi Adichie, James Africanus Beale Horton, Edward Wilmot Blyden, Adiele Afigbo, George Washington Carver, Eni Njoku, John Coltrane, Molefi Kete Asante, Morgan Freeman, Donatus Nwoga, J.E.K. Aggrey, Bill Cosby, George Russell, Nina Simone, Amiri Baraka, Ella Fitzgerald, Oscar Pettiford, Walter Rodney, Sun Ra, Nnamdi Azikiwe, Charles Mingus, Frederick Douglass, Clark Terry, Danny Richmond, Flora Nwapa,

---

[58] Ali Mazrui, *The Trial of Christopher Okigbo*, at http://www.complete-review.com/reviews/nigeria/okigbo2.htm (accessed 30 January 2004).
[59] Ibid.
[60] Quoted in Ihechukwu Madubuike, *The Senegalese Novel* (Washington D.C.: Three Continents, 1983), p. 63.

Thelonious Monk, James Brown, Harriet Tubman, Joe Henderson, Woody Shaw, Elvin Jones, Chike Obi, Frantz Fanon, Uche Okeke, Horace Silver, James Baldwin, King Jaja of Opobo, McCoy Tyner, J.B. Danquah, George Duvivier, Ray Charles, Toni Morrison, Andrew Hill, Léopold Sédar Senghor, Louis Armstrong, Ben Enwonwu, Charlie Parker, Okot p'Bitek, Duke Ellington, Mbonu Ojike, Jackie McLean, Theophilus Enwezor Nzegwu, George James, Jimmy Garrison, Ousmanne Sembene, Aretha Franklin, Patrice Lumumba, Wynton Marsalis, Maurice Bishop, Michael Echeruo, Eric Dolphy, Agostinho Neto, Emmanuel Obiechina, Billie Holiday, Bud Powell, Efua Sutherland, Ossie Davis, Ruby Dee, Aimé Césaire, Clifford Jordan, Martin Delaney, Pharoah Sanders, Nicolas Guillen, Sam Rivers, Amilcar Cabral, Mahaila Jackson, Ladipo Solanke, Booker Little, Jacob Carruthers, Steve Coleman, Steve Biko, Sunny Murray, Marcus Garvey, Albert Ayler, Casely Hayford, Alice Coltrane, Dizzy Gillespie, Funmilayo Ransome-Kuti, Richard Davis, Spike Lee, Ron Carter, Marcus Roberts, Countee Cullen, Cecil Taylor, David Diop, David Murray, Kofi Awoonor, Peter Tosh, Ivan Van Sertima, Danny Glover, Tony Williams, Claude MacKay, Herbie Nichols, Don Ohadike, Lee Morgan, Gani Fawehinmi, Art Tatum, Oprah Winfrey, Don Cherry, John Henrik Clarke, Fela Anikulapo-Kuti, Jay Wright, Edward Kamau Brathwaite, Art Farmer, Miles Davis, Théophile Obenga, George Lamming, Max Roach, Chancellor Williams, Jimmy Cobb, Billy Higgins, Julius Nyerere, Ornette Coleman, Maulana Karenga, Roy Haynes, Ama Ata Aidoo, Denzel Washington, Ngugi wa Thiong'o, Jaki Byard, Kofi Anyidoho, Léon-Gontran Damas, Wynton Kelly, Mariama Bâ, Bob Marley, Sydney Poitier, E. Franklin Frazier, Stevie Wonder, C.L.R. James, Johnny Coles, Langston Hughes, Sonny Rollins, Mariamba Ani, W.E.B. Du Bois, George Coleman, Wayne Shorter, Herbie Hancock, Billy Strayhorn and Alioune Diop himself have duly carried such 'testaments' of commitment for the defence/liberation of threatened or subjugated African interests in recent history.

It was not different in the history of the Igbo people, especially in defending themselves against the rampaging forces of genocide when it began in north Nigeria on 29 May 1966. Igbo resistance to the genocide began right from the outset in the north Nigerian city, town or village where they were being attacked. The objective of the resistance was to save one's life, the lives of family, relatives, friends, from the marauding hordes dispatched to kill, rape, maim, burn, waste ... Every Igbo caught up in this unfolding tragedy – whether they were a mother, a father, medical doctor, a school teacher, a hotelier, a pilot, a shopkeeper, a judge, a carpenter, a builder, a university professor, an artisan, a student, an engineer, a writer, a painter, a musician, etc., etc., was involved in the desperate effort to save a threatened life (or lives), beginning with theirs. No Igbo person was immune from instant death if caught by the mob ranged against them and theirs. No professions were spared. The horde's target was defined unproblematically: 'the damned Igbo'. The defence of life, the defence for life, was therefore organised and coordinated by the Igbo in the collective spirit of a shared threat and shared desire to survive. The local or base committee of the Igbo State Union/Igbo town/Igbo village family organisations at most sites of the genocide played a central role in this defence and escape strategy to Igboland. The resistance took innumerable, highly imaginative forms and feat of trying to keep people alive, if they managed to escape the immediate encircled encampment of terror – as they tried to make their way across an ever increasingly hostile territory on their way back to the safety of Igboland, 300-500 miles away. The phrase that captures the Igbo resistance here and indeed in the subsequent phases of this genocide is 'quest for survival'. The 1.5 million Igbo population facing death as the genocide got underway did not want to be slaughtered by their very determined assailants. They neither wished to submit themselves personally nor collectively to their assailants in some act of suicide. All they wanted was to *survive* the impending holocaust by trying to return to their east homeland. And they embarked on the measures to achieve this, to survive. Unfortunately, tragically, several did not make it back to Igboland safely. These were murdered. A total of 100,000 Igbo were murdered across north Nigeria during the period – 29 May-31 October 1966. But 1.4 million, thankfully, escaped the genocide and returned to the safety of Igboland. This was an extraordinary feat of survival. The survivors had been aided tremendously, after breaking out of the boxed tenement of the assailants, by the successes of a catalogue of defence measures that they adopted in days, weeks, and in some cases, months of tortuous efforts to travel back to Igboland: the guises, the decoys, the intelligence and counterintelligence work to determine the assailants' intentions and manoeuvres, intercepts of the assailants' intentions and manoeuvres by employing the Hausa language skills which most Igbo had, mapping out safe routes/exploration of new passages of departure, especially across the notorious Benue River bridge railway/road crossing points where genocidist troops and police mowed down thousands of would-be survivors who, having travelled precariously for hundreds and hundreds of miles deep in the north region, were just about 130 miles from the Igboland frontier. Finally, there was the rerouting of some survivors to Igboland via the neighbouring countries of Benin Republic, Chad, Niger and Cameroon.

An examination of the Igbo defence strategy during the second and third phases of the genocide shows that these are generally a variation on the themes of safety and survival that they learnt during the brutal and bloody sieges of their 'sabon gari' abodes in the north. This accounts for the extraordinary Igbo success in defending their homeland (Africa's most densely populated area outside the Nile valley, which was not contiguous to any friendly or sympathetic country for refuge or respite) for 30 months, during the second phase. This is despite the ferocious encirclement and bombardments by the Gowonist/British military, strengthened even further by support from the then Soviet Union, the then German Democratic Republic, Egypt, Sudan, Chad, Guinea, Algeria, Saudi Arabia and Iraq. In a word, 'survival' is indistinguishably linked to the Igbo response to this genocide. Igbo survival at the end was therefore a triumph over the forces that had tried determinably for four years to destroy them. Indeed, following the 12 January 1970 'truce' that Nigeria proclaimed on its campaign, the Igbo prefaced their exchange of greetings with each other for quite a while with the exaltation, 'Happy Survival!': 'Happy Survival! *Nne*', 'Happy Survival! *Nna*' 'Happy Survival! *Nwannem*', 'Happy Survival! *Nwanna*', 'Happy Survival! *Nwunyem*', 'Happy Survival! *Oriaku*', 'Happy Survival! *Dim*', 'Happy Survival! *Kedu*?', 'Happy Survival! *Ndeewo*', 'Happy Survival! *Ke Kwanu*?', 'Happy Survival! *Odogwu*', 'Happy Survival! *Okee Mmadu*', 'Happy Survival! *Dianyi*', 'Happy Survival! *Umu* Igbo', 'Happy Survival Ndiigbo'.

So, contrary to Ali Mazrui's assertion, no effort could have been nobler by any Igbo person, *including* artists and intellectuals, than to offer their support for such defence or resistance against genocide. It was at once a resistance for the personal as well as for the community/nation. There was therefore a concerted 'testament' of commitment by several artists and intellectuals in support of the defence of the Igbo at each phase of the genocide as the following examples show: Flora Nwapa, Michael Echeruo, Ifeagwu Eke, S.J. Cookey, Sam Mbakwe, Janet Mokelu, Uche Chukwumerije, Kalu Ezera, Philip Efiong, Ignatius Kogbara, Alvan Ikoku, Celestine Okwu, Benedict Obumselu, Donatus Nwoga, N.U. Akpan, Adiele Afigbo, Michael Okpara, Akanu Ibiam, C.C. Mojekwu, Okoko Ndem, Agwu Okpanku, Tim Onwuatuegwu, Chudi Sokei, Pol Ndu, Ben Gbulie, Dennis Osadebe, Osita Osadebe, Chuba Okadigbo, Chukwuemeka Odumegwu-Ojukwu, Okechukwu Ikejiani, Anthony Modebe, Alex Nwokedi, Chukwuedo Nwokolo, Pius Okigbo, Godian Ezekwe, Felix Oragwu, Ogbogu Kalu, Kevin Echeruo, Emmanuel Obiechina, Uche Okeke, Onuora Nzekwu, Chukuemeka Ike, Cyprian Ekwensi, Nkem Nwankwo, John Munonye, Gabriel Okara, Chinua Achebe, Onwuka Dike, Eni Njoku, and of course Christopher Okigbo.

As we demonstrate shortly, Mazrui's choice of focusing on Christopher Okigbo in his novel, as a means of attacking the Igbo people's right to defend themselves from the genocide, was more calculated than it might otherwise appear. This is not just the case of a non-literary scholar trying their hands on some form of literary criticism or work of fiction as some studies have suggested.⁶¹ Much more than that, *The Trial of Christopher Okigbo* was an ideopolitical statement by Mazrui, indicating, quite clearly, that in this worst act of genocide in Africa of the 20th century, his sympathies definitely did not lie with the besieged and bombarded Igbo humanity that supposedly habituate the *dar el harb* enclosures of islamic formulations. For Mazrui, the extraordinary Igbo defence of their lives and property in these enclosures under attack, whether in north Nigeria or in the Igbo homeland of Biafra, was an affront to the seemingly hallowed diktat of this example of extra-African continental ideoreligious dogma – the proselytisation of which has been the hallmark of Mazrui's writings throughout his career. Extra-continental ideoreligious dogmas and sensibilities, which have in the main been *anti*-African – both in their propagation and their ready-use for the rationalisation of the millennium-long, dual Arab/muslim and European World conquests and occupations of Africa – were precisely part of the compendium of ideas and themes which Okigbo's formidable African-centred poetry wrestled with during the early 1960s' so-called restoration of independent Africa. There was no comparable intellectual working on Africa between 1960 and 1967 who pursued with rigour and perspicacity a wide-ranging stretch of subjects from history to the arts, politics and spirituality/religion as Christopher Okigbo. As we now show, Okigbo posits the primacy of African spirituality and religiocultural system in the quest for the African renaissance, in the wake of the Arab/European World conquest and occupation of Africa and the contemporary realities of murderous African regimes. Okigbo's is undoubtedly a clash of ideas, a 'clash of civilisation' with Mazrui's self-serving 'African-triple heritage' construct under which the latter's islamic expansionism agenda has been proselyetised so relentlessly.⁶²

Okigboan humanism

Christopher Okigbo is Africa's most celebrated poet. He occupied the poetry chair of the continent's post-conquest literary academy in the 1960s – with Chinua Achebe in charge of the novel institute and Wole Soyinka as head of drama. Since then, Okigbo's poetry has influenced the work of several poets including those of his generation such as brothers Michael and Kevin Echeruo, Pol Ndu and Okogbule Wonodi, and the post-genocide generation poets especially Ezenwa-Ohaeto, Sesan Ajayi, Chukwuma Azuonye, Onuora Enekwe, Obiora Udechukwu, Chimalum Nwankwo, Akomaya Oko, Olu

---

⁶¹Cf. Benedict Obumselu, literary critic and historian and very close friend of Okigbo's, in an interview with James Eze, entitled 'Ali Mazrui's submission is rubbish,' *Daily Sun* (Lagos), 21 August 2005.
⁶²Mazrui, 'The Reincarnation of the African State'.

Oguibe, Esiaba Irobi, Niyi Osundare, Maik Nwosu, Uche Nduka, Nnorom Azuonye and Nnamdi Azuonye. Elsewhere, *Heavensgate*, Okigbo's 1962 published poetic work, enriches the concluding thoughts in Jay Wright's poem, "Beginning Again" (from his *The Homecoming Singer*[63]), an exquisite exploratory journey into self-discovery and African American affirmation across time and space. With immense satisfaction shown by the protagonist as he is about to complete his voyage, Wright quotes four lines from that Okigboan landmark signature inscribed in the opening cycle of poems in *Heavensgate* that has been the focus of intense scholarship and debates in the past 40 years:

> And now my ancient rhythm calls me,
> Out of ashes and fraternal death,
> 'Before you, mother Idoto,
> naked I stand ...
> a prodigal ...
> lost in your legend ...'
> An aching prodigal,
> Who would make miracles
> To understand the simple given.

Okwuonicha Femi Nzegwu has in *Love, Motherhood and the African Heritage*, her path breaking study on African literature, discussed the respective seminal contributions that Chinua Achebe and Flora Nwapa have made in the development of contemporary African literature, following decades of the European conquest and occupation of the continent. Beginning with *Things Fall Apart* (1958), Achebe focuses on what Nzegwu describes as the 'high drama of state politics, international politics and racism' discourses[64] that have raged variously on invasions, seizures, expropriation, alienation, liberation and restoration. Nwapa, on the hand, launches a 'new theatre of discourse focusing on women centrally' in her publication of *Efuru* (1966) – to interrogate the African 'home or domestic life environment' in the wake of the occupation, as Nzegwu observes.[65] Okigbo's own contribution at this historic site of mapping out the tenets of Africa's renaissance scholarship is his focus on redeeming the occupation's assault on the spiritual embodiment of African existence. He must have wrestled intensely with that crucial question posed by the Umuofia interlocutor in *Things Fall Apart* when the Africans engaged a representative

---

[63]Jay Wright, *The Homecoming Singer* (New York: Corinth, 1971).
[64]Nzegwu, *Love, Motherhood and the African Heritage: The Legacy of Flora Nwapa*, p. 96.
[65]Ibid.

of the British occupation regime in a brief exchange of ideas on the pressing existentialist subject of the day: '"If we leave our gods and follow your god," asked another man, "who will protect us from the anger of our neglected gods and ancestors?"'[66] Okigbo surely considered the answer to this question and other girding features related to it as a momentous task that required a rigorous and expansive scholarship of contemplation. He reflects upon these meditatively in *Limits*, which he published in 1964: 'AND THE gods lie in state/And the gods lie in state/Without the long-drum./And the gods lie unsung,/Veiled only with mould,/Behind the shrinehouse./Gods grow out,/Abandoned;/And so do they ...'[67]

For Okigbo, the spiritual is a crucial sphere of resistance and restoration because the ultimate objective of the occupation's assault is aimed at funnelling a catastrophic fault-line in the soul of the people – to complicate their determined process of recovery on the morrow of the restoration of independence. Such is the paramount status of this subject that towards the end of the haunting meditations in *Heavengate* (1962), Okigbo evokes his saintly mother's memory, the poet's organic link to his ministering duties at Idoto (his hometown and where his maternal grandfather was a priest of the local river goddess), to come to his aid: 'Time for worship:/*Anna of the panel oblongs,/protect me/from them fucking angels;/protect me/my sandhouse and bones.*'[68] Evidently, Okigbo responds to this emergency by weaving a multi-layered and panoramic canvass of often-complex fabric of overarching architecture of ideas that meditate on the variegated ensemble, which constitutes the spiritual landscape of the people. This is the creative background from which the 'poet of destiny', about whom the distinguished critic Emmanuel Obiechina has discussed so authoritatively, emerges.[69] In this context, Okigbo's extraordinary interrogative insights anticipate the lethal amalgam of crank religiosity, violence, despair and immiseration that would constitute Nigerian politics from the mid-1960s. The retrograde religiosity and brutishness that can be codified easily as the *working ideology* of heightened self-conceit and repression, if ever there was one, links the regimes of the seven notorious Nigerian dictators of the era: Generals Gowon, Mohammed, Buhari, Babangida, Abacha, Abubakar and Obasanjo. These are self-styled 'papa' or 'baba' or '*kabiesi*' or 'father' of the country, each of whom sees himself unquestionably as a baron and

---

[66]Chinua Achebe, *Things Fall Apart* (London: Heinemann Education Books, 1980), p. 103.
[67]Christopher Okigbo, *Labyrinths with Path of Thunder* (New York & Ibadan: Africana Publishing in association with Mbari Publications, 1971), p. 34.
[68]Okigbo, *Labyrinths with Path of Thunder*, p. 17.
[69]Emmanuel Obiechina, *Language and Theme* (Washington, D.C: Howard University, 1990), p. 207.

Nigeria as some medieval fiefdom where all human and non-human resources therein are theirs and theirs alone for control, appropriation or rather misappropriation. Each and everyone of the heptarchy feverishly invokes the muslim religion and its symbols (or the christian religion and its symbols, in the case of Generals Obasanjo and Gowon) willy-nilly, such that an observer would not be mistaken if they were to think that Nigeria is some theocratic state despite the clearly stated secularity of its constitution. Even when they murder their opponents (a frequent and common denominator linking regimes), the dictators are ready with some 'God's Will' or 'God's Wish'-of-an-'explanation' or a 'Nigeria Prays' phantasm of recourse to offer their traumatised populace. In the very few weekends that he is in the country and not junketing across the world's capitals, General Obasanjo, otherwise known as the 'travelling supremo who runs the state from the air or from overseas,'[70] always insists that proceedings of his Sunday morning church service from his private chapel (built with public funds and located in the presidential villa) is broadcast live on national radio and television. Franz Schurmann's observation that Africa's dictators are not 'traditional but rather a phenomenon of modernity ... fighting for power in a Western-type state with its armies, police, bureaucracies, control over economic institutions ...'[71] could not have been more informative. One should also add to this list the import of self-serving fragments of distorted or twisted extra-continental religious tracts and packs, employed by the tyrant as cover to cheat, lie, steal, kill and oppress the people. Each of these seven dictators in Nigeria (and their counterparts elsewhere in Africa) has a characteristic streak of *anti-Africanness* in their worldview, programmes and policies that does not cease to astonish even the most cursory of observers.

In 1962, Okigbo published *Heavensgate*, which received extensive critical acclaim. The work is organised in five sections that map out the protagonist's spiritual awakening and life's quest: 'The Passage', 'Initiations', 'Watermaid', 'Lustra' and 'Newcomer'.[72] Four years earlier, shortly after his 26th birthday, Okigbo had come to the definitive conclusion of what he felt his life's mission was, as he recalled later:

> I am believed to be a reincarnation of my maternal grandfather, who used to be the priest of the shrine called Ajani, where Idoto, the river goddess, is worshipped. This goddess is the earth mother, and also the mother of the whole family. My grandfather was the priest of this shrine, and when I was born I was believed to be his reincarnation,

---

[70]See Ekwe-Ekwe, 'Why Nigeria and Africa's leaders are leading them nowhere'.
[71]Franz Schurmann, 'Africa is Saving Itself,' *Choices: The Human Development Magazine*, Vol. 5, June 1996, pp. 4-5.
[72]Okigbo, *Labyrinths with Path of Thunder*, pp. 3-19.

that is, I should carry on his duties ... And in 1958, when I started taking poetry very seriously, it was as though I had felt a sudden call to begin performing my full functions as the priest of Idoto. That is how it happened.[73]

Yet, besides his poetic engagement, Okigbo found time for other tasks and these are incredibly eclectic by any standard. Between 1956 and 1967, Okigbo had been a civil servant, a high school teacher, a literary journal editor, west African representative of the Cambridge University Press, business associate in an industrial enterprise, university librarian, co-founder (with novelist Chinua Achebe) of a book publishing company, and a major in the Biafran resistance against the Gowonist/British genocidist forces during the latter's second phase of their campaign against the Igbo people. But it was Okigbo's poetic work that preoccupied him. As the opening lines of 'The Passage' demonstrate, Okigbo had indeed completed the necessary labour required, since his 'call', to embark on his exalted mission. The poet-protagonist would now await his initiation for service as he stands before the shrine of his people's river goddess – the goddess, Okigbo reminds his readers, who is at once 'the earth mother and ... the mother of the whole family':

BEFORE YOU, mother Idoto
    naked I stand;
before your watery presence,
    a prodigal

leaning on an oilbean,
lost in legend.

Under your power wait I
    on barefoot,
watchman for the watchword
    at *Heavensgate*;

out of the depths my cry:
give ear and hearken ...[74]

---

[73]Marjory Whitelaw, 'Interview with Christopher Okigbo, 1965,' *The Journal of Commonwealth Literature*, No. 9, July 1970, p. 36.
[74]Okigbo, *Labyrinths with Path of Thunder*, p. 3.

'Earth mother' or the *ani* goddess is arguably the most revered deity in the Igbo pantheon as she is the guardian of society's moral order. Okigbo's maternal grandfather, as was indicated earlier, was the priest at the shrine where *ani* or Idoto is worshipped. As Okigbo reminds us in the quote above, he was perceived by his family at birth as the reincarnation of his grandfather who had died earlier. The grandson was therefore expected to 'carry on' with the grandfather's 'duties' later on in his own life; hence, the very intensive and extensive scholarship of the spiritual and religious heritage of diverse experiences of humanity within which Okigbo's formidable poetic enterprise is typecast. As the poet himself does recall, '... in 1958, when I started taking poetry very seriously, it was as though I had felt a sudden call to begin performing my full functions as the priest of Idoto.'

The outcome of this scholarship would incorporate syncretic excursions across the world's faiths and traditions with its discourse presenting at times daunting challenges to the reader. These features of Okigbo's work have attracted criticism from some, a reaction that barely bothered the poet. Chinua Achebe has rightly observed that Okigbo 'relished challenges and the more unusual or difficult the better it made him feel.'[75] Okigbo would have equally felt unperturbed by those critics, particularly after his death in 1967, who indicate their 'preference' for his last poem cycle (contained in *Path of Thunder*) in contrast to his earlier works on the grounds that the former was 'less obscure.'[76] Okigbo had insisted all along that all his published poetic output 'are, in fact, organically related,'[77] a point he restated in his introduction to *Labyrinths*, his collected works. Whilst *Path of Thunder* was first published posthumously in 1968, there is no compelling evidence here to suggest that this is not also *related organically* to the ensemble of the Okigboan poetics that emerged in 1962. The robust poetic voice that had spoken so eloquently on his people's fate, since the overrun of their lands by those conquering forces from Britain, was equally resilient to pronounce rigorously on the gathering storms of a catastrophic genocide that this same people would confront as from 1966 – this time, led by an African genocidist force armed, trained and reinforced by the *same* Britain of the earlier encounter. The poet himself was killed, defending the people's homestead during the genocide.

---

[75]Chinua Achebe, *Hopes and Impediments* (Oxford: Heinemann International, 1988), p. 79.
[76]See, for instance, Chinweizu, Onwuchekwa Jemie and Ihechukwu Madubuike, *Toward the Decolonization of African Literature, Vol. 1* (Enugu: Fourth Dimension Publishers, 1980), p. 276.
[77]Okigbo, *Labyrinths with Path of Thunder*, p. xi.

In 'Initiation', the second segment of *Heavensgate*, the poet had in fact articulated the salient features of the ideological facade of the British occupation regime that was of utmost importance to his long-term project:

so comes John the Baptist
with bowl of salt water
preaching the gambit:
life without sin, without

life; which accepted,
way leads downward
down orthocenter
avoiding decisions.

Or forms fourth angle –
duty, obligation:

square yields the moron,
fanatics and priests and popes,
organising secretaries and
party managers; better still,

the rhombus – brothers and deacons
liberal politicians,
selfish selfseekers – all who are good
doing nothing at all;

the quadrangle, the rest, me and you ...[78]

Okigbo's poetry is constructed at various levels of an intensely pursued labour of exposition. It is studious, insightful, if not prophetic; it is vividly picturesque: intimate, interactive, meditary or intercessional, dialogical, monological, haunting, incantatory, improvisational, lyrical. Okigbo sings, sings and sings. He is town crier, *griot* and diarist. He chronicles the people's everyday life experiences – individual, at home with the family, during meditations, at school, on the farm, at the market place, their joys and celebrations, their aspirations, their fears, their disappointments, at the community, and the debates on society's course of direction. Everything, everything, seems to be a subject for intense scrutiny and record. Okigbo's scholarship and influences are expansive: Igbo history, Nri, mythology, art and philosophy, ancient world religious and spiritual heritage encompassing

---

[78] Okigbo, *Labyrinths with Path of Thunder*, pp. 6-7.

Kemet ('ancient Egypt'), Babylon, Judaism, Hinduism, Buddhism, Christianity, Greece and Roman, as well as the poetry of Ovid, Virgil, Dante, Milton, Yeats, Mallarmé, Eliot, Pound, Hopkins. Equally, Okigbo's aesthetic appreciation was varied and virtuosic. As he wrote *Heavensgate*, Okigbo, who was a multiinstrumentalist who played in jazz bands and whose favourite jazz composers included Ellington, Parker, Monk and Mingus, recalled that he was 'working under the spell of the impressionist composers Debussy, Caesar, Franck, Ravel ...'[79] In his emotionally charged 'Lament of the Lavender Mist' (from the Four Canzones – poems he wrote between 1957-61), the pain of disenchanted love in a couple's relationship in the final lines of the poem is palpable enough: 'The moon has ascended between us-/Between two pines/That bow to each other;/Love with the moon has ascended,/Has fed on our solitary stems;/And we are now shadows/That cling to each other/But kiss the air only.'[80] Was Okigbo listening to that interrogative, reflective and captivating 2-way dialogue on 'What Love' between Mingus (on bass) and Eric Dolphy (on bass clarinet) in the *Charles Mingus Presents Charles Mingus* seminal album[81] as he worked on 'Lament of the Lavender Mist'? If indeed he was, it is tempting to speculate that Mingus's very humorous composition (on the same album) entitled 'All The Things You Could Be By Now If Sigmund Freud's Wife Was Your Mother' provided the creative musical background mood as Okigbo wrote his lines on Kepkanly (the 1930s primary school teacher in occupied Igboland) in 'Initiations', in his *Heavensgate* poem cycle. This is an exhilarating parody of the seeming confidence and exacting arrogance of the British occupation regime, which the poet compares with Kepkanly's mathematical preoccupation:

Elemental, united in vision
of present and future,
the pure line, whose innocence
denies inhibitions.

At confluences, of planes, the angle:

---

[79]Angus Calder, review of Christopher Okigbo, *Labyrinth*, in *New Statesman* (London), 28 April 1972, at http://www.complete-review.com/reviews/nigeria/okigbo1.htm (accessed 10 May 2003).
[80]Christopher Okigbo, 'Lament of the Lavender List' (1961), Web Concordance to the Poetry of Christopher Okigbo, at http://echeruo.syr.edu/okigbo/19Okigbopoems.htm (accessed 30 January 2004).
[81]Charles Mingus, *Charles Mingus Presents Charles Mingus*, Candid CCD 79021 (personnel: Charles Mingus, bass; Ted Curson, trumpet; Eric Dolphy, alto saxophone, bass clarinet; Dannie Richmond, drums), New York, October 1960.

man loses man, loses vision;[82]

Yet, just as Kepkanly's experience later shows (the teacher dies of 'excess of joy'[83] after receiving salary arrears awarded by a salary-review commission appointed by the regime), the occupation's apparent confidence – and therefore long term stability is at best tenuous; it does not have the organic stranglehold in society that it often portrays.[84]

In 1964, Okigbo published *Limits* and *Distances*. Both continue to focus on the poet's concerns in *Heavensgate*, namely the state of Igbo religion and culture, in the aftermath of the British invasion. The poet's syncretic strides across the globe's ancient cultures continue apace. *Distances* is an intrusive sequence of reminiscences as the protagonist embarks on his journey to accept the calling of his destiny. We are reminded time and time again that 'I was the sole witness to my homecoming …'[85] The journey is long and enduring with the vividly mixed fortunes that such an enterprise would entail. These include coming across sites of promising and profound beauty ('Serene lights on the other balcony:/redolent fountains bristling with signs – '[86]) to encountering some danger and challenges ('DEATH LAY in ambush that evening in that island;/voice sought its echo that evening in that island.'[87]), to yet more danger and challenges in the form of some ku-klux klan-like procession (with 'an immense crucifix/of phosphorescent mantles:'[88])[89] but arriving safely at last to an ecstatic welcome: '*Come into my cavern,/Shake the mildew from hair;/Let your ear listen:/My mouth calls from a cavern* …'[90] The journey of initiation now over, the protagonist only knows that this signals the beginning of yet another phase of his mission, but the outcome of the one just completed is a resounding success as he, now a town-crier, proclaims:

I have fed out of the drum

---

[82]Okigbo, *Labyrinths with Path of Thunder*, p. 6.
[83]Ibid., p. 7.
[84]Unlike Elaine Savory Fido's, this is a more historical reading of the significance of this subject. See Fido, 'Okigbo's Labyrinths and the Context of Igbo Attidues to the Female Principle,' in Carole Boyce Davies and Anne Adams Graves, *Ngambika: Studies of Women in African Literature* (Trenton: African World, 1986), pp. 232-233.
[85]Okigbo, *Labyrinths with Path of Thunder*, pp. 53 and 60.
[86]Ibid., p. 53.
[87]Ibid., p. 54.
[88]Ibid., p. 57.
[89] Cf. Fido, 'Okigbo's Labyrinths and the Context of Igbo Attitudes to the Female Principle', p. 233.
[90]Okigbo, *Labyrinths with Path of Thunder*, p. 59.

I have drunk out of the cymbal

I have entered your bridal
chamber; and lo,

I am the sole witness to my homecoming.[91]

Limits brings together two poems, 'Siren Limits' and 'Fragments out of Deluge' which Okigbo had published earlier in the *Transition* journal. *Limits* is a lush environment with rich and lively flora of palm grove, bamboo towers, poplars, oil bean and the like. Rivers abound and it also boasts of an impressive birds' sanctuary (sunbird, weaverbird, eagle) and a variety of other fauna including elephants, lions, and tortoise and python – 'the twin-gods of the forest'. Significantly, the tortoise and the python, as well as the oil bean constitute the totems for the worship of the river goddess, Idoto. This evergreen lush of life is indeed the reverential and regenerative shrine for the priest of the goddess, engaged in his spiritual task of rebirth and service for the people. The poem is suffused with a range of symbolisms that underscores the solemnity of worship in progress: the 'moonlit' sweep of night (very much associated with time for worship, as well as the crucial *egwu onwa* story-telling sessions that children love – highlighted, in this context, with the presence of *mbekwu nwa anuga*, the wily tortoise), eggs ('I hang my egg-shells'[92]), *manya nkwu* or palm wine ('Hang, dripping with yesterupwine'[93]), a tiger mask and a spear. As it is the case with Okigbo's symbolic interplays, they vary from the very subtle to the distinctly diverse and expansive. Here, he continues to pursue his interest in the image of the lioness ('Oblong-headed lioness – /No shield is proof against her – '[94]) which he had begun in *Heavensgate* ('BRIGHT/with the armpit-dazzle of a lioness,/she answers,/wearing white light about her;/and the waves escort her,/my lioness,/crowned with moonlight.'[95]). Okigbo wishes to stress the element of *continuity* in some features of Igbo religion with those of Kemet, as he reflects on the 'Kemet Thesis' of Igbo migratory origins. He introduces the popular Igbo story of the monkey and the lioness in this multi-layered imagery in which the former is so dazzled by the armpit of the latter that it destroys itself. The revered, powerful and dependable Idoto obviously protects her own. Idoto is linked to Isis, the Kemet goddess, who had the grand title of the 'lioness of the sacred assembly' among others. Moonlight,

---

[91] Ibid., p. 60.
[92] Okigbo, *Labyrinths with Path of Thunder*, p. 23.
[93] Ibid.
[94] Ibid., p. 27.
[95] Ibid., p. 11.

eggs, pythons, wine, rivers, lush vegetation, are also associated with the worship of Isis as is Idoto. Just as the worship of Isis and the feminine order in the ancient world was violently suppressed by an ascending patriarchy, so is the assault on Igboland by a rampaging British occupation regime via its ideology of clearly anti-feminine/people religion:

> Past the village orchard where
> Flannagan
> Preached the Pope's message,
> To where drowning nuns suspired,
> Asking the key-word from stone;
> & he said:
>
> *To sow the fireseed among the grasses,*
> *& lo, to keep it till it burns out ...*[96]

It is to uproot this 'fireseed' of conquest that Okigbo focuses on increasingly in his subsequent poetic enterprise. This begins in 1965 with the poet's 'Lament of the Masks', which is his contribution to a book commemorating the life of W.B. Yeats, edited by D.E. Maxwell and S.B. Bushrui. Okigbo has until now referred to 'the elephant' or 'the big white elephant' in a number of his poem sequences without much elaboration.[97] This is now the opportunity to work through the theme, which, in this poem, refers to Britain but could also be used in describing brutal African regimes as he certainly does in *Path of Thunder*. As usual, Okigbo picks up a 'common thread' in his cyclical reading of history and juxtaposes seemingly disparate events along the course within a controlled time frame to enable us focus our minds more intensely on pressing issues of human concern. The 'common thread' here is twin-track: aggression and universal human quest for justice, which the Igbo people would soon have to confront as the Nigerian state, backed by Britain, unleashes a devastating genocide against them. 'Lament of the Masks' focuses simultaneously on Yeats on Britain in Ireland, that first experimental outpost of the march of British conquest and occupation, and on the challenges that those far-flung events have had, and would have on artists, like him, responding to the subsequent British outrage in Igboland/Africa. In that case, 'Lament of the Masks' can also be read as a commentary by Okigbo on Britain in Igboland/Africa or Okigbo on the genocidal Nigerian state on the Igbo. For the latter, it is important to note that Okigbo's contribution to the Yeats study would have been written sometime between 1964-65; only 2-3 years after, Britain would emerge as

---

[96]Ibid., p. 30.
[97]In ibid., for instance, p. 26 and in 'Lament of the Drums', p. 46.

the principal state in the world that supported, to the core, the Nigerian state genocide campaign against the Igbo which cost 3.1 million lives. The resplendent musicality of the lines on the resistance to the 'white elephant', which evokes Parker, Monk, Ellington, Mingus, Powell, Coltrane, Dolphy and Davis, is vintage Okigbo:

> THEY THOUGHT you would stop pursing the white elephant
> They thought you would stop pursing the white elephant
> But you pursued the white elephant without turning back –
> You who chained the white elephant with your magic flute
> You who trapped the white elephant like a common rabbit
> You who sent the white elephant trembling into your net –
> And stripped him of his horns, and made them your own
> You who fashioned his horns into ivory trumpets –
> They put you into the eaves thatch
> You split the thatch
> They poured you into an iron mould
> You burst the mould;
>
> For like the dog's mouth you were never at rest,
> Who, fighting a battle in front,
> Mapped out, with dust-of-combat ahead of you,
> The next battle field at the rear
>
> That generations unborn
> Might never taste steel –
>
> Who converted a jungle into marble palaces
> Who watered a dry valley and weeded its banks
>
> For we had also forgotten
> Your praise-names –
>
> Who transformed a desert into green pasture
> Who commanded highways to pass thro the forest –
> And will remain a mountain
> Even in your sleep ...
>
> BUT WILL a flutist never stop to wipe his nose?
> Two arms can never encircle a giant iroko.
>
> Night breezes drum on the plantain leaf:

Let the plantain leaf take over the dance ...[98]

Before 1965 was over, Okigbo published *Silences*. He also planned to reissue all his poems to date under the title *Labyrinths*. In his 4-page introduction to this new edition, Okigbo notes: 'although these poems were written and published separately, they are, in fact, organically related.'[99] *Labyrinths*, for him, is a 'fable of [a person's] perennial quest for fulfilment ... [A] poet-protagonist is assumed throughout ... a personage for whom the progression through "Heavensgate" through "Limits" through "Distances" is like telling the beads of a rosary; except that the beads are neither stone nor agate but globules of anguish strung together on memory.'[100] *Labyrinths* was not published until 1971, four years after the poet's death. By the time it came out, *Path of Thunder* (his last poetic output published posthumously in 1968) and *Silences* were added to the volume. *Silences* was Okigbo's last publication before his death in 1967. It contains two poems – 'Lament of the Silent Sisters' (first published in *Transition* in 1963), which is a variation on a number of themes on culture, love and spirituality that he had earlier dealt with in his works, and 'Lament of the Drums'. The latter is a poem of support for two influential African politicians – Patrice Lumumba, and Obafemi Awolowo, who has already been a subject of quite an extensive discussion in this study. Lumumba was the leader of the Congolese liberation movement against the Belgian occupation of the country and prime minister of the new republic of the Congo (Democratic Republic of Congo) in the early 1960s. Lumumba was overthrown in a coup d'état shortly after the country's restoration of independence by the then Colonel Mobutu, the army commander, with the complicity of the Belgian military garrison in the country. Mobutu would later transform himself to a dictator and embark on a 30-year old terrorisation of his population and the exploitation of the country that would only rival that of Belgian King Leopold II the previous century. Awolowo was of course the Action Group party leader who had been jailed for 10 years in 1962 for apparently plotting a coup against the Northern Peoples' Congress-led central government in Lagos. Okigbo is sceptical of the fairness of Awolowo's trial and incarceration. He agrees with the popular opinion in the country that the government that had imprisoned Awolowo and rigged the general elections of 1964, still planned to impose its illegal rule on the people: 'The robbers

---

[98]Christopher Okigbo, 'Lament of the Masks' (1965), Web Concordance to the Poetry of Christopher Okigbo, at http://echeruo.syr.edu/okigbo/19Okigbopoems.htm (accessed 30 January 2004)
[99]Okigbo, *Labyrinths with Path of Thunder*, p. xi.
[100]Ibid., p. xiv.

will strip us of our tendons!'[101]; 'The robbers will strip us of our thunder ...'[102]

Awolowo was later released from prison by the Gowon junta that had seized power in July 1966 and began to coordinate and expand the territorial reach of the Igbo genocide. In a quirk in the course of history that would have been a fascinating challenge for Okigbo himself at his typewriter, if he had survived the genocide during its second phase the following year, Awolowo failed to reciprocate Okigbo's immense gesture of solidarity against state injustice and arbitrariness. Awolowo instead supported and championed the Nigerian state genocide against the Igbo. In return, he was appointed deputy to Gowon (head of the junta) and minister of finance. As we have noted here, Awolowo formulated the infamous 'starvation as weapon/quick kill' strategy during the genocide which, three years on, accounted for 80 per cent of all Igbo 3 million dead.

It is with the advantage of hindsight that the world is now able to evaluate the incredible foresightedness evident in Okigbo's last poem cycle, *Path of Thunder*, which he worked on before the outbreak of the Igbo genocide. Okigbo had intensely studied the unfolding political development in Nigeria between 1962-66 particularly, and came out with a 'testament', his last 'testament', in which he 'prophesised' mass murder as an outcome of the crisis and which, astonishingly, ended with a foreboding of his own likely death:

AND THE HORN may now paw the air howling goodbye ...

For the Eagles are now in sight:
Shadows in the horizon –

THE ROBBERS are here in black sudden steps of showers,
of caterpillar –
THE EAGLES have come again,
The eagles rain down on us –

POLITICIANS are back in giant hidden steps of howitzers,
of detonators –
THE EAGLES descend on us,
Bayonets and cannons –

THE ROBBERS descend on us to strip us of our laughter, of our thunder –

---

[101]Ibid., p. 46.
[102]Ibid., p. 49.

THE EAGLES have chosen their game ...

POLITICIANS are here in this iron dance of mortars, of
generators –
THE EAGLES are suddenly there,
New stars of iron dawn;

So let the horn paw the air howling goodbye ...

O mother mother Earth, unbind me; let this be
    my last testament; let this be
The ram's hidden wish to the sword the sword's
    secret prayer to the scabbard –
...

BEYOND the iron path careering along the same beaten track –

THE GLIMPSE of a dream lies smouldering in a cave,
together with the mortally wounded birds.
Earth, unbind me; let me be the prodigal; let this be
the ram's ultimate prayer to the tether ...

AN OLD STAR departs, leaves us here on the shore
Gazing heavenward for a new star approaching;
The new star appears, foreshadows its going
Before a going and coming that goes on forever ...[103]

    Christopher Okigbo's contribution to the development of 20th century African literature is extraordinary, given the slim volume of his 'collected works' of poetry. Kevin Echeruo, the 22-year old poet and painter whose work was very much influenced by Okigbo and who, himself, was killed in 1969 defending the Igbo against genocide, had dedicated the following poem, 'Lament of an Artist', to the memory of Okigbo soon after the older poet fell at Ekwegbe, near the university town of Nsukka in 1967:

SHE will weep for me,
now the priest has left
the palm grove,
left the palm groves
the masks dance
in blood ...

---

[103]Ibid., pp. 71-72.

Am I Christ for sacrifice?

Lord hear our prayers,
give the faithful departed
his pen and deep ink-pot
and Idoto shall rejoice
when ögbanje and his bangles
shall return,
never to leave
The Palm Grove for the Theatre.[104]

The *ögbanje* has indeed since returned and on this occasion, gratefully, he does not seem to be in a hurry to depart soon. Thanks to the *ögbanje*'s selfless dedicated service to the Igbo resistance and that of Echeruo's and those of tens of thousands of others, the Igbo humanity survived the genocide of 1966-1970.

---

[104]Kevin Echeruo, 'Lament of an Artist', written 1967, first published in *Nsukka Harvest: Poetry from Nsukka*, 1972, available at
http://echeruo,syr.edu/okigbo/kevin%20on%20okigbo.htm (accessed 7 February 2004)

4

In these times ...

Nigeria has, in the end, handed over Liberian fugitive leader Charles Taylor to the Freetown-based United Nations court investigating war crimes in conflicts in and around Sierra Leone. Taylor had lived in Nigeria for three years in exile since his forced departure from Liberia at the height of the war there in 2003. Despite the persistent calls on Nigeria to extradite Taylor to the Freetown court by an array of international human rights organisations including the Campaign Against Impunity (an association of 300 African and international human rights and civil organisations),[1] the Obasanjo regime in Abuja had always argued that it was against its 'national honour' (whatever this means) to respond positively to the court's request.[2]

Taylor has been indicted on 11 counts of 'greatest responsibility for war crimes, crimes against humanity and serious violations of international humanitarian law' during the decade's long war of the 1980s-1990s in the neighbouring state of Sierra Leone. These crimes include 'widespread and systematic killings of civilians, deliberate amputation of limbs, rape and other forms of sexual violence, the use of child soldiers, abduction and forced labour.'[3] A total of 1.3 million people were slaughtered in Sierra

---

[1] Kenneth Roth, 'Surrender Taylor to War Crimes Court,' *The Guardian* (Lagos), 15 August 2005.
[2] Obasanjo's reluctance to hand over Taylor all along was based on his assertion that Nigeria had played a 'leading role' in negotiating the 'terms' that led to Taylor's agreement to relinquish power in August 2003 as Monrovia, his capital, was being besieged by Liberian insurgents. According to Obasanjo, an 'asylum package' for Taylor and his family and close aides was an 'important feature' of the agreement and that Nigeria would be violating the latter were it to hand Taylor over to the Freetown court.
[3] See Amnesty International South Africa, 'Obasanjo must surrender Charles G. Taylor,' http://www.amnesty.org.za/campaigns/charles_taylor.htm and Human Rights Watch, 'Letter to President Obasanjo on Bringing Charles Taylor to Justice,' http://www.hrw.org/press/2003/11/nigeria-ltr111703.htm (both accessed 27 April 2006).

Leone as well as in the *associated* wars in Liberia itself and southern Guinea during the period. Thanks to the insistence of the US government, the Obasanjo regime finally succumbed to the international pressure and dispatched Taylor to Freetown.

The irony is of course not lost on any keen observer of this development. Whatever may be the US's strategic interests on this subject (possible Taylor links with al-Qaeda,[4] possible Taylor involvement in millions of dollars' worth of money laundering, possible Taylor complicity in the January 2005 attempted coup in Conakry to remove the president of neighbouring Guinea who has good relations with the US), it has taken the intervention of a non-African power to force a disreputable African regime to hand over the head of a fellow murderous African regime to face trial for the murder of 1.3 million Africans – *not* 1.3 million non-Africans. African democrats are surely unencumbered by this irony. African regimes have murdered 15 million Africans across the continent in the past 40 years in appalling spates of genocide. Even if the devil itself were to lecture African leaderships to stop murdering their peoples and, in the process, help prevent just one more African being annihilated by their depraved overlords, that would be readily welcome. African populations are under siege by brutal regimes replete across Africa. The peoples require unremitting support from wherever in the world for the right to safeguard their lives and progress. Not less.

If indeed the US administration had threatened to block Nigeria's current 'bid'[5] for a permanent seat on a possibly enlarged UN security council if it continued to keep Taylor away from facing justice, as some press reports indicate,[6] then Washington did well. But the Americans should not lift their threat yet, even now that Nigeria has, reluctantly, dispatched Taylor to Freetown.[7] It is breathtakingly obscene for Nigeria to wish to be considered

---

[4]Louise Dunne and Kim Renfrew, 'Charles Taylor has al-Qaeda links, says Sierra Leone Special Court,' *Radio Netherlands*, http://www.radionnetherlands.nl/currentaffairs/region/africa/lib050525 (accessed 29 April 2006).
[5]See, for instance, *The Guardian* (Lagos), 11 April 2006.
[6]See, for instance, Amby Uneze, 'US pressure: Taylor May Leave Nigeria,' *ThisDay* (Lagos), 14 May 2005. See also Samuel Obukwelu, 'For Nigeria, Charles Taylor or the UN Security Council?' http://www.utexas.edu/conferences/africa/ads/725.html (accessed 27 April 2007).
[7]The purported Taylor 'escape' from his exile home in south Nigeria on the eve of his 27 March 2006 planned extradition to Freetown, and his 'recapture' two days later by the Nigerian military and police, underscored how utterly reluctant the Obasanjo regime was in returning Taylor to face justice. Many informed observers (see, for instance, 'Nigerian Government planned Taylor's escape, says Ex-UN Prosecutor,' *The Punch* [Lagos], 11 April 2006) believe that the Abuja regime may

for a permanent seat at the security council, given its genocide against the Igbo people during the course of 1966-1970 and other dreadful human rights record of successive Nigerian regimes since – *including* the current one where statecraft is at best run as some medieval baronial fiefdom. The US and the rest of the world should reject this 'bid' out of hand.

Relay baton

Pointedly, Nigeria's 'bid' to join the security council could not have provided the world with a better opportunity to deal with the crux of contemporary Africa's malaise: the non-accountability of African leaders who employ genocide and the pillage of the economy as a twin-track instrument of power. No country in Africa is more compellingly placed for the enforcement of this accountability than where the disease first emerged on the continent – Nigeria, the quintessentially genocide-state. Few observers would have missed the gripping irony on display during the Charles Taylor extradition saga in March 2006: namely, that it was a leading representative of the notorious circle of Nigerian generals who planned and executed the Igbo genocide, 40 years ago, who was forced by the US government to hand over the ex-Liberian president to an international court to face trial for 'crimes against humanity'.

Taylor, who was born in 1948, was still in school during 1966-1970 when commanders Adekunle, Obasanjo, Gowon, Abubakar, Mohammed, Danjuma, Haruna, Buhari, Babangida, Rotimi, Akinrinade, Yar'Adua, Abacha and several others led their squads and regiments to hunt down and murder and rape and starve the Igbo and devastate and plunder their property and homeland. The final outcome of this holocaust was the extermination of 3.1 million people. Because Africa and the world did not bring Adekunle *et al* to trial immediately for crimes against humanity, the mid-1960s/early 1970s schoolboy Charles Taylor in Liberia would, within 40 years, re-enact these dreadful crimes in his native Liberia and other states contiguous to it. These tragic replays would similarly be mounted across the other regions of Africa including eastcentral (Rwanda, Burundi, Uganda, Democratic Republic of the Congo, Congo Republic) and northcentral (Sudan) during the same timeframe. Young African men who, like Taylor, were schoolboys in the mid-1960s/early 1970s or were toddlers or just babies would, in these

---

have indeed facilitated Taylor's 'escape' plan but changed its mind at the last minute (just as Taylor was about to leave the country through one of its northeast crossing points into neighbouring Cameroon or Chad) because of the US government's blunt threats of 'dire consequences' on Nigeria (interestingly, Obasanjo had just arrived in Washington as this 'escape' drama got underway) should the ex-Liberian dictator succeed in absconding from Nigeria and (consequently) the Freetown court house.

territorial theatre extensions from genocidist Nigeria, lead in the execution of these crimes. Dreadfully, the 'child-soldiers'[8] that have commanded rape/murder/arson/pillage squads and regiments in Sierra Leone, Liberia, Rwanda, Democratic Republic of the Congo, Congo Republic, Uganda, etc., etc, *à la* Nigerian military forces against the Igbo in Nigeria and Biafra in 1966-1970, were born a decade later – in the mid-1970s/early 1980s. So, in carrying out its 1966-1970 Igbo genocide, Nigeria has no doubt created a catastrophic precedence that has poisoned the African human landscape almost inexorably.

Even then, the Nigerian perpetrators of this precedence, most of whom are still alive, have remained unapologetic, unremorseful, even totally defiant. This is precisely because they have yet to be apprehended by the global court of justice to account for their crimes against humanity. Yakubu Gowon, the general commander of the genocidist forces, told the press in Enugwu (political and cultural capital of Igboland) in April 2005, almost 39 years to the day since the outbreak of the mass slaughter, that he had 'nothing to apologise' to the Igbo for the genocide.[9] Before he shot himself in a Berlin bunker in 1945, few would have expected Adolf Hitler to apologise or show remorse for his organised genocide of six million Jews and others across Europe during the Second World War. Hardly anyone, though, would wish to contemplate a Hitler travelling to Jerusalem today to address a press conference in which he would insist, categorically: 'I have nothing to apologise for the six million Jews my forces annihilated between 1939 and 1945. What I did was right.' That would be an unimaginable monstrosity. But this was precisely what Gowon did at Enugwu in April 2005. Benjamin Adekunle, a leading Awolowoist commander who relished particularly in the bestiality of his campaign during the genocide, was given the opportunity in 1987 by the editors of *ThisWeek* (a leading Nigerian newsmagazine) to apologise to the Igbo for the atrocities of his troops 20 years earlier. He scoffed at the idea in the same characteristic vein as he did whilst addressing the international media at the limits of encircled towns and villages of Igboland in 1968. Adekunle insisted in his *ThisWeek* interview: 'Starvation is a legitimate weapon ... what's the ... fuss about starvation?'[10] General Ibrahim Haruna, who with General Murtala Mohammed (a one-time head of state, also known as the 'butcher of Asaba' by the survivors of the

---

[8]Of the 300,000 'child-soldiers' fighting in the world's wars, 80,000 or approximately one-quarter of the total are Africans – actively involved in the continent's major conflicts in the east, central and west regions – see 'Children Under Arms,' *The Economist* (London), 10 July 1999, p. 22.

[9]*The Vanguard* (Lagos), 26 April 2005.

[10]*ThisWeek* (London), 13 July 1987, p. 28.

genocide in west Niger Igbo) were involved in appalling crimes of executions of Igbo men and boys west of the Niger during the period, has been equally blunt in his own lack of remorse for participating in the genocide. Speaking publicly in October 2001 at the Justice Oputa Commission on the Nigerian state's violation of the human rights of the citizens since the 1960s, Haruna was adamant: 'As the commanding officer and leader of the troops that massacred 500 men in Asaba, I have no apology for those massacred in Asaba, Owerri and Ameke-Item.'[11] Finally, Olusegun Obasanjo, another Awolowoist who commanded a notorious death regiment in south Igboland, which committed indescribable atrocities as it overran cities, towns and villages, has never apologised nor shown remorse for his crimes against humanity. On the contrary. Since 1999 when Obasanjo's current 2-term presidency began, there has been widespread anecdotal information in Nigeria, quoting presidential aides, to the effect that the president often raves around in his villa in disturbing bouts of rage and angst, screaming of 'teaching the Igbo a lesson', or 'crushing these Igbo who don't seem to have learnt the lessons of 1966-1970' or 'ensuring that these Igbo never rule this country in my life time ... Never!' Consequently, Obasanjo has expanded the 36-year-old established Nigerian political and economic 'encirclement' of the Igbo (genocide phase III) to incorporate an added military/quasi-military sphere of confrontation. In November 2004, this latter sector of hostility was exemplified by Obasanjo's dispatch of vandals to destroy every conceivable asset of state institutions including executive, legislative, judiciary, and information/communication infrastructure in the northwest Anambra region of Igboland. The total cost of the rampage ran into millions of dollars. Thirty people were murdered during the brigandage. It was clear at the time that this act of terrorism was Obasanjo's response to his visceral disappointment over the decision by Chinua Achebe, the world-renowned novelist who comes from this part of Igboland, to turn down a Nigerian 'state honour' because of the writer's opposition to the generalised anti-Igbo trajectory and institutionalised dictatorship of the Obasanjo regime.[12] As if the Igbo needed a reminder of the import of the Anambra brigandage, Obasanjo, through to type, was not going to forego the opportunity when in January 2006 he personally went to Amichi, in Anambra, to inform the Igbo that Nigeria still had a policy to

---

[11] See Sufuyan Ojeifo and Lemmy Ughegbe, 'No regrets for the Asaba massacre of Igbo – Haruna,' *The Vanguard* (Lagos), 10 October 2001.
[12] Wale Akinola & John Nwokocha, 'Chinua Achebe to Obasanjo: Keep your CFR award – "Nigeria's condition under your watch is too dangerous for silence",' *The Vanguard* (Lagos), 17 October 2004. See also Herbert Ekwe-Ekwe, 'Igboland: Why Obasanjo must be stopped now,' *Kwenu*, http://www.kwenu.com/publications/ekwe-ekwe/igboland_stop_obasanjo.htm (accessed 18 November 2004).

exterminate them – well beyond the 12 January 1970 so-called truce on the genocide campaign announced by General Gowon.[13]

Now is surely the time for the world to insist that each and every member of the Nigerian regime who participated in the murder of three million Africans 40 years ago, and who in effect triggered off the chain of mass killings of 12 million others elsewhere in the continent must be made to account for their action. This move will at once uphold the rule of law and elevate the sense of justice in Africa exponentially. Besides, if Nigeria has been ultimately forced by the US to hand over Taylor to face trial for the murder of 1.3 million Africans in the 1980s-1990s, then his former hosts (Obasanjo, Abubakar, Babangida, Buhari, Gowon, Danjuma, Haruna, Rotimi, Akinrinade, Adekunle, King, Enaharo, Ayida, Aminu, and several others) must also be apprehended and sent to the International Criminal Court in The Hague to stand trial for the murder of 3.1 million Africans in Nigeria and Biafra in 1960s-1970s.

Failed-State?

It is perhaps difficult not to conclude from the portrait of Nigeria presented in this study that this state is symptomatic or even indicative of that term that several scholars and political commentators increasingly employ in characterising most countries of Africa – the 'failed-state'.[14] The concept 'failed-state' of course has a melodramatic import! It designates the outcome, penned in professorial manner, of a project that evaluates the state's performances or otherwise on a set of empirical indices (security, governance, health, education, housing, etc., etc.) supposedly observed and assessed over time and space. There is a presumption in this exercise that the recipient or audience to which this outcome is conveyed is well in tune with the progress or otherwise of the subject matter. The problem though is that the evaluative parameter of this enterprise, including the constitutive timeframe of assessing and therefore concluding that this or that 'African state has failed', is often not as clear or certain as practitioners portend. Or is it? Was Nigeria, for instance, a 'failed-state' during the course of May to October 1966 (i.e., six years after its so-called restoration of independence following 60 years of British occupation) when it murdered 100,000 of its Igbo citizens in the first phase of the genocide that it would expand subsequently between 1967-1970 to murder three million additional Igbo?

---

[13]*ThisDay* (Lagos), 12 January 2006.
[14]For instance, see Foreign Policy & the Fund for Peace, *Failed States Index – July/August 2005*, 2006,
http://www.foreignpolicy.com/story/cms.php?story_id=3098 (accessed 2 May 2006).

As we have shown, Britain spent 15 and one-half long years (March 1945-September 1960) working assiduously to ensure that Igbo people, who spearheaded the liberation movement to terminate the British occupation of Nigeria, did not assume a leadership position in a post-conquest/occupation Nigeria. Did this elaborate programme of *institutionalised* exclusion of one of the leading constituent nations of occupied Nigeria by the occupying foreign power render Nigeria a 'failed-state' on the eve of the presumed restoration of independence in October 1960? Parallel to the above-mentioned project, Britain also spent 15 and one-half long years (March 1945-September 1960) fashioning the institutions and processes that, in effect, choked off the possibilities of the emergence of a coherently organic state that would serve the interests of most of the African constituent nations in a future *independently-restored* Nigerian state. Was the outcome, the Nigeria that emerged at 12 midnight 1st October 1960, already a 'failed-state'? Somalia has been without a functioning central government since 1991. Does this make it a 'failed-state'? Was it already a 'failed-state' prior to this event (i.e., between 1960, following its restoration of independence from Italian and British occupations and 1991 when the central government collapsed) when rival regional-based insurgent organisations battled for influence and control across the country? Successive central governments in Kinshasa, Democratic Republic of the Congo, have for nearly 20 years hardly exercised effective authority over a quarter of the country's territory, which is twice the size of west Europe; is the DRC a 'failed-state'? According to the current survey of the world's 'failed-states' by the *Foreign Policy* journal and the Fund for Peace published in May 2006, Sudan tops the list.[15] Since when? This can't just have occurred more recently as the conclusions of this study suggest! Wasn't Sudan *already* a 'failed-state' in 1956 when, on the eve of the Sudanese restoration of independence, the British occupation governor, James Robertson, handed over supreme political power to the Arab minority population? This action effectively excluded the African majority in the south, Darfur and elsewhere in the country, *à la* South Africa, triggering off the sustained African resistance movement that has gone on till this day – 50 years on. The same Robertson would head south to Nigeria to rig the 1959 pre-restoration of independence election in favour of the Hausa-Fulani muslim north region, Britain's historical client in the country, to reinforce this region's burgeoning hegemonic power base. This power base would within six years embark on executing the worst genocide in Africa of the 20th century. Did the outcome of this election rigging and the earlier British rigging of census results to favour the same north region (1952) ensure that Nigeria had *already* become a 'failed-state' prior to the 1st October 1960 restoration of independence?

---

[15]Ibid.

All of Africa, since 1981, has become a net exporter of capital to the West with a large proportion of this being interest payments on 'debts' that the West claims Africa owes it.[16] In 1981, Africa recorded a net capital export of US$5.3 billion to the West. In 1985, this figure increased to $21.5 billion. Three years later, this net capital transfer was $36 billion or $100 million *per day*. In 1995, this figure jumped to $100 billion and on the eve of the new millennium in 2000, Africa's net capital transfer to the West hit the $150 billion mark. Africa has exported a total of $400 billion in the past 25 years in this way – these are funds that could and should easily have provided a comprehensive health programme across the continent, the establishment of schools, colleges and skills' training, the construction of an integrative communication network, and finally, the transformation of agriculture to abolish the scourge of malnutrition, hunger and starvation. Would this outlandish export of critical resources merit designating all of Africa as 'failed-states'?[17]

Christopher Clapham has argued that the concept 'failed-state' is 'one of those categories that is named after what it isn't, rather than what it is.'[18] This makes a crucial point in the discourse to the effect that a *state*, such as Nigeria or Sudan for instance, that embarks on the genocide of its population or does not provide basic services for its people or immanently churns out successive regimes that fleece the collective wealth of the country can hardly merit such a definition in social science. All we need do to highlight the obvious flaw in applying this concept in Africa is to reflect on the fact that crucial state functions such as the provision of security, rule of law, a rationalising but flexible structure of management, accountability and open and unfettered competition, especially with respect to regime change, have not been in operation in any African state since the conquest and occupation of most of the continent by a constellation of European countries in the 19th century. Tragically, in the 50 years since the concerted African drive towards the restoration of its independence resulted in the supposedly 1956 breakthrough in the Sudan, followed soon in 1957 by Ghana, the situation

---

[16]For details and analysis of the African World-West politics of 'debt' and Africa's net capital transfers to the West during the era, see Ekwe-Ekwe, *African Literature in Defence of History*, pp. 3-7 and pp. 156-162.

[17]It should be stressed that none of the figures referred to above includes the national accounting of the Arab states in north Africa – namely, Morocco, Algeria, Tunisia, Libya and Egypt – but the rest of the 47 countries on the continent which also contain the majority of Africa's 650 million-population.

[18]Christopher Clapham, 'Failed States and Non-states in the Modern International Order,' paper presented at conference on failed states, Florence, Italy, April 2000, http://www.ippu.purdue.edu/failed_states/2000/papers/clapham.html (accessed 15 September 2003).

has not changed significantly in Africa for the realisation of these attributes of the state.

Ultimately, the major limitation of the use of the 'failed-state' concept to assess the catastrophic situation in contemporary Africa is that it confers an unjustifiable presumption of rationality to an enterprise in which a spectrum of outcomes ranging from perhaps 'failure' to 'outright failure' to 'disaster' is predetermined; it is assumed that those who run the state in Africa (Obasanjo, Idi Amin, Taylor, Moi, Habre, Doe, Gowon, Mobutu, Ahidjo, Rawlings, Obote, Babangida, Mengistu, Abacha, Mugabe, Mohammed, Banda, Abubakar, Bokassa, Eyadema, Buhari, Toure, Museveni, Biya, Al-Bashier ...) are aware of this test and its evaluative scruples and, like any rational participant, would want to succeed ... If they do not do so well, at some instance, so goes the logic, they will try to improve on their previous score and, hopefully, do better ... Success is always a possibility! It is on the basis of this possibility that Roland Oliver concludes his own controversial contribution to this debate. If one, for a moment, ignores the gratuitous racism and paternalism embedded in the premise of Oliver's contribution as well as the highly contestable analytical category on which it is hinged, Oliver notes: 'With its overriding population problem, Africa can hardly expect to achieve First World standards of economic development within the next century [i.e. 21st century] but with just a little more day-to-day accountability, it could at least recover the confidence to continue the uphill struggle with more success.'[19] On the contrary, there is limited indication on the ground that African state operatives currently or indeed in the past 50 years have approached statecraft as a challenge to succeed in transforming the lives of their peoples. 'Success' is never a goal set along the trajectory of their mission. To that extent Oliver's conclusion is, ironically, quite optimistic. Furthermore, it should be noted that given the evidently limited concerns on just 'measuring' the scoreboard of performance, 'failed-states''s discourses tend to overlook the much more expansive turbulence of underlying history – the kind of project that has been mounted here in this study.

So, rather than relations that bring benefits to many of its people, the state in Africa has 'evidently been a source of suffering,'[20] to quote Clapham, an imagery consistent with Basil Davidson's description of the impact of this state on the African humanity as a 'curse'.[21] Richard Dowden also uses a health metaphor in capturing the legacy of the African state when

---

[19] Roland Oliver, 'The condition of Africa,' *Times Literary Supplement* (London), 20 September 1991, p. 9
[20] Clapham, 'Failed States and non-States in the Modern International Order'.
[21] Basil Davidson, *Black Man's Burden: Africa and the Curse of the Nation-State* (London: James Currey, 1992).

he notes, alluding to its genesis: '[this European]-scissors and paste job [has indeed caused Africa] much blood and tears.'[22] For her own observation, Lynn Innes is in no doubt that the African state has created what she describes as a 'deeply diseased [outcome]' on the continent.[23] The health metaphor stretches even to the psychiatric as Thomas Pakenham observes: 'One has only to think of the bloody ... wars that followed decolonisation to see the craziness of these lines drawn on maps in Europe by men ignorant of African geography and history.'[24]

Chester Crocker points to the fundamental problem of the state in Africa. It is 'not the absence of nations; it is the absence of states with the legitimacy and authority to manage their affairs ... As such, they have always derived a major, if not dominant, share of their legitimacy from the international system rather than from domestic society.'[25] It is this question of *alienability* that is at the crux of this grave crisis. Crocker may have had the Igbo experience especially in mind as he wrote those lines. In Nigeria, on 29 May 1966, this form of state, supported fully by Britain, which created it in 1900, turned on its Igbo population in north Nigeria murdering, raping, burning, pillaging. By 1970, this genocide had claimed 3.1 million Igbo lives, the worst in Africa for a century.

While it is true that Biafran independence was declared formally a year later on 30 May 1967 in Enugwu, it was in fact on that fateful May day in 1966, 29 May, that the Igbo ceased to be Nigerians forever. That resolve, that renunciation of Nigerian citizenship, was the permanent Igbo indictment of a state that had violated its most sacred tenet of responsibility to its citizens – provision of security. Instead of providing security to these citizens, the Nigerian state murdered 3.1 million of them. Nigeria's 12 January 1970 so-called truce on this campaign of genocide did not therefore, in any way, alter the fundamentals of this Igbo resolve. The resolve is irreversible. The Igbo *did not* return to Nigeria on 12 January 1970. To suggest otherwise would be a contradiction in terms. There could be no question of the Igbo returning to Nigeria just as the African nations in this southeast part of west Africa that made up Nigeria, before 29 May 1966, could not return to the British conquest and occupation enforcement of the 1900-1960 epoch. What has happened since 12 January 1970 has been a Nigerian state military, police and bureaucratic occupation of Igboland. As all occupations in history, this too shall end. The current events on the

---

[22]Richard Dowden, 'Redrawing the outmoded colonial map of Africa,' *Independent* (London), 10 September 1987.
[23]C.L. Innes, *Chinua Achebe* (Cambridge: Cambridge University, 1990), p. 151.
[24]Thomas Pakenham, 'The European share-out of the spoils of Africa,' *Financial Times* (London), 15 February 1988.
[25]Chester Crocker, *Foreign Affairs*, September/October 2003, p. 37.

ground in Igboland, particularly the politics of the de-Nigerianisation of Igbo social existence spearheaded by the Movement for the Actualisation of the Sovereign State of Biafra, point to a much earlier termination of the occupation that only few would have predicted with great certainty just a few years ago.

Pointedly, the Igbo created the state of Biafra on 29 May 1966 – right there on the ground of those death camps in the *sabon gari* residential districts and offices and railway stations and coach stations and airports and churches and schools and markets and hospitals across north Nigeria to protect the Igbo people from the genocide unleashed by the Nigerian state and its myriad of allies. In other words, the Igbo created Biafra, the first African peoples'-centred state on African soil since the 1885 formal loss of African sovereignty, to safeguard an African population subjected to genocide by the Nigerian state, actively propped up by its European originator and overlord as this appalling crime got underway. 29 May 1966 therefore emerges as a more *historic* date in the annals of African reckoning than the 1 October 1960 so-called restoration of independence in Nigeria or indeed the 1 January 1956 restoration date in the Sudan – often tagged the 'post-occupation breakthrough' in Africa.

Biafra was tasked to provide security to the Igbo and prevent the Nigerian state, a genocide state, from accomplishing its dreaded mission. And contrary to the British-inflected, Nigerian declaration of 'no victor, no vanquished' on 12 January 1970, the Igbo were indeed the victor in this encounter. They survived. This was an extraordinary triumph of human will and tenacity. The Igbo overcame an amalgam of desperately brutish forces, some of whom were otherwise antagonists or nominal rivals in regional or the broader contours of international politics in the post-World War II epoch: Hausa-Fulani, Britain, Yoruba/Oduduwa, Soviet Union, Tiv, Egypt, Berom, Yergam, Nupe, Ishan, the Sudan, Angas, Urhobo, Itsekiri, Igala, Bachama, Poland, Bini, Sura, Algeria, Jarawa (central Nigeria), Jukun, Saudi Arabia, Gwari, Guinea, Kanuri, Syria, Idoma, German Democratic Republic, Iraq, Chad/gwodogwodo.

The Nigerian state and its allies failed to accomplish their goal. This is why Obasanjo has since not minced his words about the Nigerian state's stated desire to complete its 1966 envisaged task on the Igbo people. But Obasanjo must now know that the Igbo will never go under. For all intents and purposes, Nigeria collapsed as a state with any serious prospects in the wake of the Igbo genocide. Despite earning the stunning sum of US$650 billion in oil sales in the subsequent 40 years, a significant proportion of this from occupied Igboland in the Delta, Rivers, Imo and Abia administrative regions, Nigeria has cascaded into a degenerative slump politically, economically, intellectually, socially, morally and spiritually.

Expression

To live in the typical African state presently, as we have argued in this study, is to live in the most oppressively centralised, alienated and alienating state in the world – a state that denies most peoples in *constituent* nations their fundamental human rights. This has been a debilitating legacy for most Africans since Europeans created this state during their occupation of the continent. It was, and still remains a conqueror's and a conquest state, just as the old Soviet Union or Yugoslavia, having cobbled together peoples of varying political, cultural, religious and ideational heritage with no identifiably-embracing organic transnational sensibility, save an ensemble or organisation to rationalise the exploitation of critical resources for transfers to the Western World and elsewhere. It is precisely in this context that what P. Chabal and J-P. Daloz have ironically called 'disorder as political instrument,'[26] actually works in Africa: it offers immense opportunities to those Africans who control the instrument of the state but who clearly lack or do not subscribe to the domestic or internal legitimacy, as in William Reno's 'shadow state' scenario,[27] to work the system for their purpose and their external allies. Just as in Nigeria, some of these African state controllers would have initially worked against the liberation of the state from European occupation. It must never be forgotten though that this sociopolitcal infrastructure of 'disorder' was and still remains a boon to the European occupation project which created it. The British example in Nigeria, for instance, illustrates that fact as we have shown in this study. Hussein Solomon and Nikki Funke surprisingly ignore the saliency of the genesis of this 'disorder' and the continuing paramountcy of its European creators when they assert: 'It is ironical that western states, traditional representatives of human rights and democracy, should support an unaccountable and self-enriching leader [in Africa].'[28] On the contrary. It was the West that, in the first instance, created these 'shadow states' of 'disorder' on the African scene. Britain has profited enormously from Nigeria especially in its active involvement in the 1966-1970 genocide of the Igbo people. In more recent times, British arms exporters were the leading

---

[26]P. Chabal and J-P Daloz, *Africa Works: Disorder as Political Instrument* (Oxford: James Currey, 1999).
[27]See, for instance, William Reno, 'African Conflicts and Contemporary Intervention,' Key Note Address, African Studies Association of Australasia and the Pacific 2003 Conference Proceedings – Africa on a Global Stage, http://www.snn.flinders.edu.ac/global/afsaap/conferences/2003proceedings/reno.PDF #search='william%20reno%20on%20shadow%20state' (accessed 6 May 2006).
[28]Hussein Solomon and Nikki Funke, 'Revisiting Shadow States in Africa,' http://www.ac.za/academic/cips/Publications/Revisiting%20Shadow%20States%20in %20Africa.doc (accessed 5 May 2006).

beneficiaries of the billions of dollars that Nigeria spent on arms and other 'state security-related' imports during the 16 years (1983-1999) of the appalling military dictatorships of Generals Buhari, Babangida, Abacha and Abubakar. At the time, budgetary allocations to the Nigerian military and other paraphernalia of the juntas' repressive apparatus averaged US$2 billion per annum with Britain enjoying 60-70 per cent of all imports. The dictatorships were therefore fully equipped to pursue their notorious state of siege on the populations with such devastating consequences: a run-down economy, the murder of scores of political opponents, the detention of several others, the catastrophic military interventions in Liberia and Sierra Leone, which cost the country at least US$12 billion[29] and thousands of casualties (never acknowledged officially by any of the latter three military regimes that were involved in the intervention nor indeed the so-called 'civilian' Obasanjo successor government), and the flight of tens of thousands of intellectuals and professionals into exile.

Contrary to popular expectations across Nigeria in 1999, the formal end of military rule did not necessarily reverse the underlying anti-democratic policy and manifestation of militarisation. The situation has not least been helped by the leadership of the new government, headed by none other than an ex-military dictator himself – General Obasanjo, who led a junta for three years in the 1970s. This era of the juntas in Nigeria also provided Britain with another crucial asset in the country. It consolidated even further its dominant position in both the ownership of capital and trade. It enjoyed a fantastically more advantageous balance of trade with Nigeria at a time a number of countries, including the United States, had extensively restricted their relations with the country as a result of the generals' appalling record on human rights. In the first six months of 1995, at the height of Nigeria's ostracism by most of the world, Britain's exports to Nigeria stood at £250 million while imports from Nigeria amounted to £77 million.[30] As for the figures for the first six months of 2000, one year after the start of General Obasanjo's so-called 'civilinised' regime, Britain exported £230.8 million worth of goods and services to Nigeria while the total worth of its Nigerian imports was just £31.8 million.[31] Given this entrenched British role in the Nigerian economy, British banks and other financial services have emerged as favoured conduits used by corrupt Nigerian leaders and officials to siphon and transfer millions of capital assets from the country. In just one example, assets worth £600 million looted from the Nigerian treasury during the course of the 1990s by General Sani Abacha were initially deposited in

---

[29]'This General doesn't know when to stop talking,' *The Punch* (Lagos), 7 February 2006.
[30]*The Guardian* (London), 11 November 1995
[31]*The Vanguard* (Lagos), 20 October 2000.

British banks[32] before subsequent transfers of part of the haul to Swiss banks and elsewhere. The British Financial Services Authority has been very critical of the role of British banks to this effect, openly accusing 15 banks of 'significant weaknesses' in their anti-money laundering controls.[33] The BFSA found out that at least 40 personal and corporate accounts linked to Abacha's family and associates existed in Britain.[34] For the Hausa-Fulani leaderships and their latterly Awolowoist-Yoruba ally, Nigeria's relationship with Britain is dictated pivotally on the premise that they ruthlessly oversee the neo-Royal Nigeria Company estate, that is Nigeria, for the pervasive British interests of well over a century's old, as well as theirs – most of which are routinely exported to the same Britain as staggering capital assets. According to Joseph Stiglitz, the respected Nobel laureate in economics, these estate overseers have stashed away the huge sum of US$100 billion abroad over the years.[35] In the Transparency International's annual corruption perception index for 2005, Nigeria is ranked the sixth most corrupt country in the world.[36] Britain's entrenchment in the very lucrative business of African militarisation and wars is equally evident in central and southern Africa.

Despite its rhetoric of an 'ethical foreign policy', the British Labour party government that took office in 1997 was heavily involved in the Congo/ Great Lakes wars. Britain sold arms to *both sides* of the principal protagonists – Democratic Republic of the Congo itself, Rwanda, Namibia, Zimbabwe, Burundi and Uganda. In an interview with the BBC at the height of the conflict in 2000, Charles Onyango-Obbo, the editor of the respected Ugandan independent newspaper, *The Monitor*, did not fail to stress the duplicity of the British role in the region:

> Britain is supporting both sides – it just robs them of any moral authority and a lot of people rightly do despise the British government in this affair.[37]

The West fully supports the continuing existence and benefits immensely from Africa's 'shadow states' of 'disorder'. Former French President François Mitterand was once quite categorical about the extent of these benefits: 'Without Africa, France will have no history in the 21st century.'[38] The African

---

[32]*The Financial Times* (London), 9 February 2001.
[33]*The Guardian* (Lagos), 10 March 2001.
[34]Ibid.
[35]See *The Guardian* (Lagos), 31 May 2004.
[36]The Guardian (Lagos), 8 November 2005.
[37]'UK arming African countries,' *BBC*, http://news.bbc.co.uk/1/hi/uk_politics/699255.stm (accessed 3 April 2000).
[38]Tom Masland, 'African Duel,' *Newsweek* (New York), 30 March 1998, p. 19.

'shadow state' of 'disorder' was the instrument that its Western creator employed to harness and enforce the African occupation in its entirety and maximise the expropriation of the spoils of conquest. The African take-over of this state as from the 1950s, without any efforts to dismantle it and create new state forms imbued with African peoples'-centred ethos and enterprise, witnessed a new era of even greater disregard for domestic legitimacy with cataclysmic consequences. This has created that 'deeply diseased [outcome]' Innes has referred to: the slaughter of 15 million, colossal decapitalisation of the economy, degenerative poverty during the timeframe of 40 years. The flip side of the coin that tells the tale of the annual stupendous levels of profits and other returns that accrue to the West as a result of its favourable trade and military relations with Africa, coupled with Africa's staggering capital transfers to the Western World, day in, day out (as we highlighted above), is the emaciated, starving and dying child, woman or man that has for long been the harrowing image of the African humanity on television screens across the world. In effect, Franz Schurmann is right to note in his illuminating study on the subject (already referred to) that African regimes which oversee the *non-deconstructed state* of the European conquest 'are not traditional but rather a phenomenon of modernity. They are fighting for power in a Western-type state with its armies, police, bureaucracies [and] control over economic institutions.' Chancellor Williams captures the consequences of this sordid history in his haunting portrait, which could, for instance, summarise the Igbo experience in Nigeria:

> Now the shadows lengthened. The Europeans had also been busily building up and training strong African armies. Africans trained to hate, kill and conquer Africans. Blood of Africans was to sprinkle and further darken the pages of their history ... Indeed, Africa was conquered for the Europeans by the Africans [themselves], and thereafter kept under colonial control by African police and African soldiers. Very little European blood was ever spilled.[39]

Pertinently, these African regimes have failed to incorporate into the state structures 'inherited' in the aftermath of the European occupation pre-conquest institutions of politics and governance, aimed at maintaining a democratic, fully participatory process and government to respond to the needs and aspirations of individuals and constituent nations.[40] The resulting imbalance in power relations so widely witnessed in Africa today between

---

[39]Chancellor Williams, *The Destruction of Black Civilization* (Chicago: Third World, 1987), p. 218.
[40]A.E. Afigbo, 'Nigeria and the myths of modern democracy,' *The Champion* (Umuahia), 12 December 2000.

the state and its constituent nations or peoples, among constituent nations or peoples, and between men and women, have their roots in this systematic marginalisation of Africa's traditional democratic legacy. Thus, structural alienation from the political process typifies the overall disposition of peoples in the African state. The overwhelming majority of the people are not involved in the process of their own governance and of course one obvious and serious consequence of this is the ease with which political differences and disagreements often deteriorate into massacres, genocides or generalised wars. This is dictated largely by the unresolved nature and character of the state vis-à-vis the individual and constituent nations or peoples.

Evidently, the underlying structural basis of independence, or, more historically correct, the restoration of independence in Africa, has rarely been defined comprehensively. There is no rigorously worked-out agreement on the fundamental character and role of the state by the constituent nations that make up the polity. The broad sectors of African peoples are yet to be placed and involved centrally in the entire process of societal reconstruction and transformation. Not surprisingly, the nature of the state that emerged after the European conquest and occupation had, and still has limited organically shared values linking its peoples. Most African conflicts have therefore centred on the continuously thunderous demands made by desperately deprived and exploited nations and peoples in these states for the construction of decentralised and decentring alternative political structures and institutions which empower people at their locale. It is as a result of this unresolved historical factor of conquest that Africa remains a tinderbox, exploding uncontrollably from time to time, with the devastating consequences that the world has come to know in the past 40 years. Until there is a far-reaching restructuring of sociopolitical relations within the state to ensure *inclusive* participation by all nations and peoples, conflict in Africa will remain endemic. Decentralisation and democratisation are essential in creating a sense of inclusiveness amongst African peoples, a crucial ingredient in overcoming the present causes of disempowerment, instability and underdevelopment. Only within these parameters of justice, equality, freedom, and the cessation of violence *and* alienation, will true peace occur.

It is instructive to note, to return finally to Nigerian President Obasanjo's grave threats on Igbo existence made in Amichi in January 2006, that similar threats in the past 61 years of incessant pogroms and genocide of the Igbo in Nigeria have usually been made, and executed, during periods of acute political or social uncertainties or crises in the country. Obasanjo made his threats whilst campaigning in the country to subvert the current Nigerian constitutional provision of a maximum 2-term presidency of eight years for an incumbent, to enable him extend his time in office to a third term. This campaign has inevitably heightened political tension across the country since mid-2005, as most indications point to an overwhelming majority of the population opposed to the presidential extension.[41] Opposition has also been voiced against the project from abroad, including, importantly from the United States, whose officials have variously issued a series of warnings on the dire consequences that such an arbitrary presidential decision could have on the future of the country.[42] The Nigerian media have been replete with reports of Obasanjo literally fleecing the country's treasury to bribe legislators in parliament, whose support is crucial to ensure the success of the extension programme. The sum of US$14 billion is reported to have been withdrawn from the central bank in Abuja for this purpose,[43] with the tagged bribe for a senator being US$500,000 dollars and US$400,000 for a member of the lower house.[44]

Whether or not Obasanjo succeeds in his extension ambitions, the response of the Igbo and the rest of the world to his Amichi threats on Igbo existence must be treated with utmost priority. Given the history, these are serious threats indeed. It is utterly inconceivable that US President Bush would, for instance, visit Atlanta and inform his African American audience that 'there remain plans by United States government to murder its African American population' and not be forced to resign for such an outrage by the resultant political fallout across the country and the world. Similarly, it is inconceivable that British Prime Minister Blair would visit Birmingham in central England and make a similar threat to the Asian population in the city and not be forced to resign from office as a result. It is also inconceivable that South African President Mbeki would go to Pretoria and inform an audience of European South Africans that 'there were still plans by the South African government to murder European South Africans' without been forced by public opinion in the country and from abroad to resign from office for such an outrage.

Undoubtedly, Igbo prosecutors and others will be adding the Amichi threats to the other counts of 'crimes against humanity during the 1966-1970 Igbo genocide' charge to be brought on Obasanjo and those others mentioned elsewhere in this study at the International Criminal Court in The Hague. In the meantime, it is incumbent on the international community to respond to the outrage of the Amichi threats without equivocations immediately:

---

[41]R. Abati, 'Obasanjo in America,' *The Guardian* (Lagos), 2 April 2006 and Abati, 'Obasanjo: An exit strategy,' *The Guardian* (Lagos), 12 May 2006.
[42]C. Isiwu & C. Offor, 'US Intelligence Report Warns Obasanjo,' *Daily Independent* (Lagos), 7/2/2006. But both *The Economist* (*The World in 2006*, London, December 2005, p. 112) and *The Financial Times* (London, 5/1/2006) endorsed the project.
[43]*The Punch* (Lagos), 9 May 2006.
[44]*ThisDay* (Lagos), 9 May 2006.

1. The UN Security Council should declare a comprehensive ban on all arms sales and transfers to Nigeria. Nigeria does not have any legitimate external threats. All weapons currently sent to the country are used directly by the country's military (army, air force, navy) and police or indirectly sublet to state-procured hoodlums to terrorise peoples particularly in Igboland/Niger Delta.

2. International travel restrictions should be placed forthwith on President Obasanjo and his wives, children, and his extended family, and on Nigeria's military and police chiefs and other senior members of his regime.[45] The immense savings that these travel bans will generate for the Nigerian treasury should be used to pay thousands of teachers, doctors and pensioners owed many years of unpaid salaries. It is outrageous for Obasanjo to be received henceforth by world leaders and international statespersons after threatening the Igbo people, who lost 3.1 million children, women and men during the 1966-1970 genocide by Nigeria. The world cannot wait for the materialisation of these threats before responding. Now is the time to act.

3. All assets abroad (particularly in South Africa, Western Europe, the Americas and elsewhere) belonging to President Obasanjo and his wives, children and extended family, and those of all the members of his security cabinet (and their families) should be sequestrated immediately.

The Igbo must now expand, most comprehensively, the range of its non-violent campaign against the Nigerian occupation, already begun by the Movement for the Actualisation of the Sovereign State of Biafra with astonishing success since 1999. MASSOB starts from the premise that the Igbo have the ingenuity and inventiveness to free themselves from the quagmire of 36 years of the Nigerian occupation of Igboland. MASSOB has no doubt made the most advanced study known of the Nigerian neurosis presently, and has come up with the solution to confront and free the Igbo from this pathology through a non-violent campaign strategy modelled on the theories and philosophies of Martin Luther King and Mahatma Ghandi. It acknowledges that Nigeria failed in its sustained attempts to destroy the Igbo in 1966-1970. Nigeria will not stop now, but it is a much weaker and ravaged force than it was 40 years ago. Moreover, the enhanced politics of human rights worldwide and the ever-expanding strides made in the

---

[45]Obasanjo spent US$16 million dollars of public funds travelling around the world during his first presidential term 1999-2003 on fruitless missions to 'attract foreign investment' to the country (see Ekwe-Ekwe, 'Why African leaders are leading them nowhere') and, as we recently referred to reports in the Nigerian media, Obasanjo illegally withdrew US$14 billion from the country's central bank to use in bribing legislators opposed to his intention to extend his presidential tenure beyond the May 2007 constitutional requirement.

advancement of information technology ensure instant transmission and access to information. Nigeria and its overseas guardian forces of old (Britain, the Arab World, Russia/former states of the since collapsed Soviet Union) can no longer muster the same 'unity-in-atrocity' portfolio today that motivated their support for the genocide last time round. Presently, the opportunities for the Igbo quest for the restoration of its independence have never been more evident.

MASSOB has re-read the March 1967 Aburi proceedings of Nigeria's leaders and particularly Odumegwu-Ojukwu's sterling performance (and also listened intently to the several hours of audiotape recordings), and concludes that the moral staff of the Igbo quest for justice continues to tower over the morass of inanity that is Nigeria. MASSOB rejects the violence of the Oodua People's Congress, which has murdered 10,000 people since 1999 in its campaign for Yoruba autonomy in west Nigeria,[46] and insists that the Igbo will be freed from Nigeria by utilising the armoury of ideas instead of weapons and weapon systems.[47]

Under the slogan 'Don't be a participant in your subjugation', MASSOB has, within seven years of existence, exposed and dislodged the *nku-ukwa* opportunistic and collaborative pro-consul politics of the string of dysfunctional regimes imposed on Igboland by the Obasanjo regime (particularly those led by Orji Uzor Kalu, Peter Odili, Achike Udenwa, Chimaroke Nnamani, and Sam Egwu), as well as that of *ohanaeze*, the so-called cultural organisation, and its US-based affiliates, especially the World Igbo Congress, and that notorious circle of Igbo *obusonjoists* based in Abuja led by the triumvirate Ojo Maduekwe, Arthur Nzeribe and Chris Uba. MASSOB argues, correctly, that these bodies and personages currently aid the Nigerian state's clearly stated post-genocide plan to degrade and retard Igbo national reconstruction and transformation. Members of these bodies are quite content to latch unto the mangled wheel of the 36-year old Nigerian programme of total exclusion of Igboland from meaningful development (euphemistically tagged 'Igbo marginalisation' in the Nigerian political lexicon) without challenging it or proffering alternative, redeeming strategies, in exchange for mundane personal and family patronage. MASSOB insists that Igbo leaders should stop bemoaning their 'loss' and imploring the Nigerian state, the author of the degradation of the economy of Igboland, to reconstruct Igboland. For Nigeria to embark on such a task is

---

[46]*Daily Sun* (Lagos), 8 March 2006.
[47]Rafiu Ajakaye, 'Uwazurike and the theory of non-violence,' *Daily Independent* (Lagos), 12 November 2005. See also interview of MASSOB leader Raph Uwazurike by Fred Iwenjora entitled 'Why Igbo obeyed MASSOB's call to stay home,' in *The Vanguard* (Lagos), 4 September 2004.

for it to accept responsibility (at least at this level) of the genocide, which it is not yet prepared to do. MASSOB believes that this so-called Igbo political elite has tended to overplay the rhetoric of 'marginalisation' to the extent that it disempowers the Igbo collective sense of direction and, quite often, obfuscates the central issues at stake in the Igbo-Nigeria situation in the aftermath of the genocide. In brief, this elite has, since 1970, handed over to the *same source* of the genocide – the Nigerian state – the 'onus' of responsibility to terminate the very 'marginalisation' which is a crucial plank in the latter stages of the third phase of the Igbo genocide, as we observed in our discussion in the last chapter. Most other Igbo – the farmer, the entrepreneur, the student, the artisan, the intellectual, etc., etc. – came to a different, and correct conclusion soon after the war: that they couldn't entrust their destiny in the hands of such a despicable state of mass murderers. They would have to work for the Igbo reconstruction *themselves* and the thrust and breadth of this recovery so far has been extraordinary. To buttress the point, the 2-million strong Igbo émigrés in North America, Europe and Asia now dispatch an annual remittance of US$10 billion to Igboland which is directed in supporting relatives (feeding, clothing, healthcare, school fees), building new homes/maintaining existing homes, and development of community infrastructure.

MASSOB's unambiguously stated goal of restoration of Biafra independence, which is intercalated in the movement's actuating or *actualisation* elixir, underscores its impressive dynamism and the flexibility of its tactics that have not ceased to impress observers and confound the Nigerian state since 1999.[48] It has shown an increasingly sophisticated ability in organisation and conscientisation work, utilising, and in several occasions, exploiting the use of information technology (internet, mobile phone, texting, etc., etc) to its advantage. For a development, without precedence in the history of the African liberation movement, MASSOB already takes the entire Igboland (from Opobo, Umu Ubani/Bonny, Ahoada and Ugwuocha/Port Harcourt in the Niger Delta to Enugwu, Nsukka, Eha Amufu and Obollo Afo in the north to Onicha, Asaba, Ogwashi-Ukwu and Agbor in the west/northwest) as *liberated territory* that is presently just encumbered by some barriers, mostly internal, which are inhibiting the post-

---

[48]See, for instance, Okey Ndibe, 'MASSOB, Ohaneze, and representation,' *Nigeriaworld.com*, http://nigeriaworld.com/feature/publications/okey-ndibe/120805.html (accessed 8 December 2005); Christian Ochiama, et al, 'UNBELIEVABLE: MASSOB order cripples business in Lagos, South-East,' *Daily Sun* (Lagos), 27 August 2004; Joseph Ushigiale, et al, 'Nigeria: Biafra separatists cripple economic activities,' *ThisDay* (Lagos), 27 August 2004; Sonnie Ekwowusi, 'Is Massob Winning Battle?' *ThisDay* (Lagos), 13 December 2005 and Oluokun Ayorinde, 'MASSOB Has 2 Million Members – SSS DG,' *PM News* (Lagos), 12 April 2006.

genocide Igbo transformation. MASSOB is now dismantling these barriers; it is *actualising* this historic goal. History and the future appear to be configured in an engaging present of breathtaking tactical and strategic moves and outcomes. Such is MASSOB's ascendancy in Igbo politics in the past three years that the movement's goal for the restoration of Biafran independence and its very vocalised, ideational, non-violent strategy of liberation have attracted the overwhelming support of the 50 million Igbo people – both at home and the diaspora.

Kayode Are, the director-general of Nigeria's notorious state security service, recently stated in a press conference on MASSOB: 'From the registers I have seen, the organisation now has over two million members.'[49] This is undoubtedly an insidious declaration for several reasons, two of which should be stressed here. First, MASSOB is not the kind of liberation movement which keeps the sort of 'membership record' that Are has referred to. MASSOB has no such record. Besides, how many 'registers' contain these 'over two million members'? In what format are these 'registers' kept – hard copy or on computers? MASSOB is a liberation movement that focuses its work on ideas - ever raising and deepening Biafran consciousness at personal and collective levels; demonstrating discipline and tenacity in its organisational work; displaying credibility of purpose. This is why its sustained boycott programmes and other projected activities since 1999 that focus on crucial or pivotal Igbo affairs vis-à-vis the occupying Nigerian state (29 May remembrance day for the 3.1 million Igbo who were murdered during the genocide, annual commemoration of liberation day or day for the Biafran declaration of independence, reintroduction of Biafran currency, organisation involved in the mass Igbo boycott of March 2006 Nigeria census) have received such resounding approval and successful participation by most of the Igbo population. It is the extraordinary level of the Biafra-focused consciousness that MASSOB has generated in Igboland in the past three years, especially, that any serious observer should be studying. This has grown and continues to grow in leaps and bounds. It is therefore absurd to narrow MASSOB's colossal effort to some seemingly quantifiable sum of its 'membership', however impressively large (or otherwise) this may be. The strength of MASSOB and its concomitant dominant position in Igbo politics are not dependent on its 'membership' tally but on the resolve and clarity of its mission and the overarching sagacity of its organisation. Second, Nigeria is one of the world's most inefficiently-run states – it does not know how much 'debt' it owes the West and other foreign 'creditors', does not know how much oil it pumps out of its oil fields daily, despite being dependent on this commodity for most of its income, does not know the population of the peoples that

---

[49] See Ayorinde, 'MASSOB Has 2 Million Members – SSS DG'.

make up the country, does not know the number of civil servants in its employ, does not know the number of teachers in the country, does not know the number of doctors in the country, does not know the levels of its infant mortality, does not know the levels of its maternal mortality, does not know the levels of male/female life expectancy, does not know the number of people in its population affected by the HIV/AIDS virus, does not know the number of its citizens currently living abroad ... If this state has no ready, verifiable answers to these easily, quantifiable constructs, it is highly unlikely that it can exercise the competence to inform on the real membership profile of a movement such as MASSOB's. Indeed, Are's two million-MASSOB-'membership' public claim is not aimed at providing objective information on MASSOB. It is, instead, a publicity stunt geared towards preempting the expected local and international outrage that is expected in response to the Nigerian state's new plans, formulated soon after the March 2006 countrywide census (largely boycotted by the Igbo, thanks to MASSOB), to 'destroy MASSOB'. This plan was formulated in Obasanjo's so-called 'kitchen cabinet', chaired by Obasanjo himself, in which Are and his SSS outfit were specifically tasked to embark on 'mass arrests, executions and the disappearing of Igbo youth (especially male)' across Igboland, beginning from April (2006). It was the same Are unit, in collaboration with the local death squad it raised on the ground (led by the *obusonjoist* Chris Uba) that murdered 30 people as well as wreaking havok in the Anambra region in November 2004 as we highlighted above. The principal towns in Igboland targeted for this new campaign, which has an indefinite brief for its duration, are Onicha, Aba, Enugwu, Owere, Okigwe, Orlu and Abakaliki. Obasanjo has apparently planned this campaign 'in response' to MASSOB's successfully-led Igbo boycott of the March 2006 Nigeria census. Instructively, the new directive's emphasis is on 'Igbo youth' rather than MASSOB, contrary to Are's press conference 'concerns'. The point though is that Obasanjo now regards these two concepts as *interchangeable*, ensuring that the extent of his regime's newly planned military/paramilitary campaigns of arbitrary mass arrests/executions of Igbo *youngmen (and women)* on Igbo streets, at the ubiquitous military/police check points, highways, playgrounds, parks, market places, public transport, etc., etc, would be so extensive and widespread to give 'credence' to Are's already formulated high 'membership' mark for MASSOB.

Pointedly, MASSOB has, particularly, a groundswell support among the Igbo youth, especially the 16-40, who make up part of Africa's most educated and talented grouping but whose employment opportunities and career choices and prospects have been constricted or even blighted by the Nigerian occupation's siege on Igboland. MASSOB has embarked on building up institutions that cover education, healthcare provisions, social security and general welfare in community after community in Igboland. It has organised successful Igbocentric 'days of affirmation' including the very moving 'day of remembrance' stay-at-home in August 2004 and December 2005 for the memory of the millions who died during the genocide.[50] This event shut down schools, business and the like all over Igboland as well as Igbo business activities in Lagos, Ibadan, Abeokuta, Abuja, Benin, Warri, Yola, Kaduna, Kano and Maiduguri, and in the neighbouring states of Benin, Togo, Ghana and Côte d'Ivoire.

Crucially, in this strategy of the actualisation of Biafra, MASSOB has now institutionalised the use of Biafran currency, a potent symbol of national sovereignty, in several businesses in Igboland especially in the markets of Onicha (west Africa's largest market), Oka, Aba, Ugwuocha/Port Harcourt, Enugwu, Abakaliki, Nsukka, Umuahia and Owere.[51] The Biafran currency is not only legal tender here, but also increasingly traded/exchanged with the Nigerian naira, the US dollar, the euro, the British pound sterling, and the cfa used by the officially French-speaking west and central African countries.[52] The Biafran currency is also used in business activity in several parts of Nigeria including Lagos, Warri and Sapele. It is steadily competing with the cfa as a trans-west African currency, given its increasing use in business transactions in Benin, Togo, Côte d'Ivoire and elsewhere in the region.[53] What however remains MASSOB's most staggering high-profile success to date, in its pursuit of the reestablishment of Biafran independence, is its March 2006 organisation of the Igbo mass boycott of the Nigerian census. The line of MASSOB's campaign this time is straight to the political and strategic point at stake: 'We are Biafrans. We do not wish to participate in a census to find out the population of Nigeria.'[54] The outcome of the MASSOB intervention was that the overwhelming majority of the 50 million Igbo people boycotted this census. Interestingly, as an addition to the record, some observers are already predicting that the outcome of the exercise will most likely end up as fraudulent as the one the

---

[50]*Daily Sun* (Lagos), 27 August 2004.
[51]Dino Mahtani, 'Biafran voices of dissent grow ever louder,' *The Financial Times* (London), 5 January 2006 and Lawrence Njoku, 'Traders accept Biafran pounds in Enugu,' *The Guardian* (Lagos), 12 January 2006.
[52]Gbenga Osinaike, 'Biafran pound still being spent ... at Togo, Benin Republic,' *Sunday Punch* (Lagos), 5 June 2005. See also Osinaike, '... It's curious – Lagos State University don recounts experience,' *Sunday Punch* (Lagos), 5 June 2005.
[53]Ibid.
[54]News Analysis of the Voice of Biafra International, 7 January 2006, http://www.biafraland.com/NewsAnalysis2006/newsanalysis010706.htm (accessed 12 January 2006). See also 'Nigeria census stokes tensions,' News24.com, http://www.news24.com/News24/Africa/News/0,,2-11-1447_1897530,00.htm (accessed 18 April 2006).

British conquest regime rigged in favour of its client north region in 1952, along with the subsequent censuses in the country.[55]

The Igbo should now expand the parameters of their actualisation project even further. They should begin a phased evacuation of all the Igbo population in north Nigeria. The returnees would be absorbed in a radically transformed workhouse of the Igboland economy such as sketched below. The risks involved for the Igbo to continue to live in the north are tremendous. There is no central regime in place in Nigeria or in any of the regions in north Nigeria that can or will guarantee the safety of Igbo people from newly planned pogroms and genocides. As has been the case in the past 61 years, none of these regimes is prepared to punish those who premeditatedly murder the Igbo. It will now be an unpardonable oversight for the Igbo to wait in the north to be visited by yet another season of slaughter. There must be a closure to the perpetuation of this cyclical tragedy. It is equally incumbent on the Igbo to curtail its current levels of investment in Nigeria, especially in Lagos (and greater Lagos) and Abuja, which continues to increase exponentially, in contrast to the paltry state of direct investment in Igboland itself. The question must be asked: Given the history of the Igbo in Nigeria, is it really prudent that the Igbo should be owning 85 per cent of all hotel businesses in Abuja, the capital of Nigeria?[56] What happens to this multimillion-dollar worth of investment deep in Gwari/Hausa-Fulani north Nigeria, or indeed elsewhere in the country during the genocide next time?

The Igbo should withdraw support from the existing regimes enforced on them by Obasanjo, in the wake of his 2003 rigged elections across Igboland, in the following administrative regions: Edo, Delta, Rivers, Abia, Ebonyi, Imo, Enugwu, Benue and Kogi. They should stop paying taxes and rates to regimes that do not serve their interests but have instead rendered their cities such as Onicha, Ugwuocha/Port Harcourt (the well-known 'garden city' prior to the occupation), Aba, Umuahia, Abakaliki and Owere into pyramids of garbage. The Igbo should also stop cooperating with the occupation military and police especially at those notorious checkpoints and tollgates that dot across the Igbo country. Since 1970, the typical Nigerian police officer graduating from police college bribes his/her superiors to be sent to Igboland where he/she makes a fortune in just a few years of their posting at the checkpoints, extorting money or consumer products from the road users including even school children going to and from school. This is indirect taxation by the occupation and therefore amounts to huge sums of money to

---

[55]See, for instance, Reuben Abati, 'Census as robbery,' *The Guardian* (Lagos), 24 March 2006.
[56]See Chuks Iloegbunam, 'Governor Kure's apotheosis,' *The Vanguard* (Lagos), 5 August 2003.

the Nigerian treasury totalling hundreds of thousands of dollars annually. The Igbo should insist on not paying this peonage forthwith and demand an unconditional dismantling of these barriers of extortion and expropriation. They should also demand the evacuation of the military/police bases in their midst.

In the aftermath of the genocide, as MASSOB has shown on the ground, the emplaced *obusonjoist* regimes in Igboland and the occupation's military/police activity clearly obstruct durable Igbo sociopolitical reconstruction programme. The Igbo should, as a matter of urgency, retrieve from the archives that plan for the reconstruction and transformation of Igboland (referred to in chapter 2 of this study) drawn up in the 1950s by Mbonu Ojike, the cerebral African peoples'-centred economist, who was the minister of the east region's economic development and planning at the time. The Ojike Plan had envisaged a 20-year timeframe, beginning in 1954, during which the Igbo country would be transformed into a leading industrial and commercial power. Such was the impressive pace of this programme that by 1964, ten years later, the overall economic performance of Igboland had not only outstripped the rest of Nigeria, but was in fact Africa's fastest growing economy. But for the 1966-1970 genocide unleashed by the Nigerian state, the Igbo were on course to construct the Taiwan or the China or the South Korea or the India of Africa. The main thrust of the Ojike Plan of building an advanced multifaceted industrial and agricultural economy is still valid and should be reworked and adapted for 21st century priorities and the advantage of new technologies.

The Igbo should now resume this journey in earnest. Right from the outset, Igbo women, who in the past (i.e. prior to the British conquest and occupation) controlled and exercised extensive rights and authority over their own affairs as well as those of the rest of society,[57] must be repositioned at the epicentre of the shared dual-sex complementary spaces of responsibility, power and authority in this historic transformation of Biafra. The Igbo have one of Africa's best-developed, multidisciplinary humanpower contingents to work this transformation. Given their well-known hardworking ethic and entrepreneurial drive, the Igbo should be able to achieve an annual 10 per cent growth rate in their economy to effectuate this transformation without difficulty. They should immediately set up a trust fund foundation to finance the enterprise in the next 10 years. The foundation should have a core membership of distinguished Igbo men and women of which the Igbo have unlimited number. An appeal should be sent out at once, calling on every adult Igbo man and woman at home and in the diaspora in Nigeria and elsewhere in the world, to make an annual voluntary contribution of US$100 dollars to the fund, with allowances made of course

---

[57]Nzegwu, *Love, Motherhood and the African Heritage*, passim.

for those who wish to contribute more than this stipulated figure or indeed less. The foundation should set up *actualising* working/implementation committees made up of experts in their fields to focus on various sectors of the Biafran economy: power generation, town-city/urban revival/development, industrial manufacturing, agriculture, information technology, communication/infrastructure, healthcare, education, culture/national heritage/leisure, rural embodiment, environment/regeneration – particularly focusing on the heightened erosion and landslide occurrence in the northwest region.

Hubs of industrial and agricultural activities are already in place in their designated sites of operation in Igboland and these would form the foci of this transformation: the Onicha-Nnewi-Oka-Ihiala industrial conurbation for machine tools and heavy industry; the Enugwu-Emene-Nsukka information technology valley; the Aba-Umuahia-Abiriba-Ugwuocha/Port Harcourt precision equipment/light industry; the Uburu-Okposi-Egbema sodium carbonate deposits/other minerals for potential pharmaceutical manufacturing; reactivation of Enugwu-Udi coal fields for unlimited power generation to work this manufacturing enterprise and provide cheap lighting for all, with surpluses that would also be sold to countries across west Africa for the indefinite future; work on renewable energy sourcing such as solar, wind, refuse; enhanced agricultural activities in the central and east Asu/Ebonyi valleys/Abakaliki corridor and the Onicha/upper Anambra farming belt ... The involvement of Igbo expertise, especially that currently based abroad in north America, Europe, Asia and elsewhere in the world will be crucial in this transformation project. The utilisation of this asset will understandably be managed with utmost flexibility in the drive and implementation of the enterprise. This will involve opportunities for visiting/adjunct professorships with appropriate colleges/schools/hospitals/laboratories/industrial facilities in Igboland to work in, summertime slots, and sabbatical emplacements.

Restructuring the communication/infrastructure base of Biafra would appear to be the trigger that would impact tremendously on other sectors of the economy. Igbo road, rail, waterway and air networks should now be rehabilitated and expanded radically. The entire length and breadth of Igboland from Opobo, Azumini, Umuebelengwu, Umu Ubani/Bonny, Ahoada, Ugwuocha/Port Harcourt in the Niger Delta to Nsukka, Asaba, Onicha Aboh, Ogwashi-Ukwu and Agbor in the hinterland should be comprehensively networked by these services. There should, for instance, be daily express railway services linking Opobo and Ugwuocha/Port Harcourt in the south to Nsukka and Eha Amufu in the north, via Aba and Enugwu, and from Umu Ubani/Bonny and Ahoada in the Niger Delta to Orlu, Okigwe, Ugwuta, Onicha, Asaba and Agbor in the west/northwest. Other trains should be crisscrossing on the east-west routes originating from

Abakaliki to Enugwu, Oka, Onicha, Asaba and Agbor and vice versa. This transformation should envisage dredging the River Niger south of Onicha to the Atlantic coast and the construction of an international ocean-bound port facility at Onicha and a dry dock at Aba.

Another road and rail bridge should link the twin cities of Asaba and Onicha and a tunnel service under the Niger to carry these dual modes of transport should also be constructed. The two towns should also have a modern hovercraft service in operation. Commuter bus, coach, tram and rail services in Igbo cities and towns should quickly replace the ill-suited and unsafe *okada* or motorcycle provisions of the present. The Igbo, a much travelled people worldwide, must now establish direct flight access entry to Igboland from the outside world that is not dependent on Nigeria via Lagos, Abuja and Kano or any of the country's other 'entry points'. The Enugwu and Owere airports should be transformed immediately to the status of international airports to ensure the uninterrupted movement of people, goods and services overseas flying directly into Biafra and vice versa. Direct flight routes from Igboland to Equatorial Guinea, Gabon, São Tomé and Principe, South Africa, the United States, Canada, Britain, France and Germany should be in operation here as of utmost priority in the first phase of this implementation, given the high number of Igbo people who live and work in the cited countries. Igbo émigrés in these countries should negotiate with their hosts for the latter to establish or augment existing consular/diplomatic presence in Igboland to ease travel plans and processing especially for those starting their journeys from Igboland. Asaba, Onicha, Enugwu, Oka, Owere, Umuahia, Opobo, Aba, Abakaliki, Ugwuta and Ugwuocha/Port Harcourt should enjoy these upgraded facilities. International airports should also be built at Onicha, Asaba and Ugwuta to cater for the movement of people, goods and services in the west, and at Nsukka and Abakaliki to respond to demands in the north and east of the country respectively.

The restructuring of city and local governments in Biafra is crucial in this transformation project. Igbo cities and towns should enjoy extensive autonomous status in order to transform themselves into advanced modern spaces for living, working, recreating, and the growth and development of culture. Each Biafran city and town should have a municipal authority to raise its own taxes, power its own development including the establishment of educational institutions at all levels, transport systems, including buses, trams and rail services (underground and overground) and city airport facility, cultural institutions and recreational facilities such as parks, theatres, museums, galleries, concert halls, stadiums and the like. Every Igbo child must have access to a computer and every school in Igboland linked to the internet. Equally crucial, technical colleges should be set up in Igbo cities and towns to develop and expand on that sphere of humanpower resource upon which the advancement of society is largely predicated – growth of plumbers, electricians, draftspeople, carpenters, builders, etc., etc. Cities and towns such as Aba, Nnewi, Nsukka, Eha Amufu, Abakaliki, Umuahia, Owere, Ogwashi-Ukwu, Aboh, Agbaani, Akeze, Okigwe, Enugwu, Asaba, Ugwuocha/Port Harcourt, Isele-Ukwu, Opobo, Onicha, Ahoada, Evugbo, Evugbo Road, Uburu, Aguleri, Nnobi, Umu Ubani/Bonny should be sites for these colleges.

These urban centres should also have their own city universities to cope with the continuously high demands from Igbo youths who have since 1970 consistently maintained top position for the highest number of students seeking university places in Nigeria. The existing universities in Igboland need to expand even further to respond to these needs. The trust fund will no doubt be looking into ways to increase funding to these institutions after three decades of calculated neglect from the occupation regime. A radically revamped university at Nsukka, the first autonomous university in this southeast region of west Africa, must now jettison that anachronistic name, University of Nigeria, which is a dreadful burden to bear. Such a prestigious centre of learning should not be carrying the name of a genocidist state, but, instead, entitled appropriately: Christopher Okigbo Univerisity. Okigbo, Africa's leading poet, was a librarian at Nsukka before the outbreak of the genocide and was killed defending the university and its environs from the vandals who made a bonfire of one of Africa's best library collections.

The 50 million Igbo should now set to work as determinedly as ever. The prospects are indeed exciting. This resultant transformation of Biafra in the next decade will at once be a time-honoured memorial to the 3.1 million and the triumph of the inalienable right to freedom.

Select Bibliography

Abati, Reuben, 'Census as robbery,' *The Guardian*, Lagos, 24 March 2006.
Abati, Reuben, 'Obasanjo in America,' *The Guardian*, Lagos, 2 April 2006.
Abati, Reuben, 'Obasanjo: An exit strategy,' *The Guardian*, Lagos, 12 May 2006.
Achebe, Chinua, *Morning Yet on Creation Day*, London: Heinemann Educational Books, 1975.
Achebe, Chinua, *Things Fall Apart*, London: Heinemann Education Books, 1980.
Achebe, Chinua, *The Trouble with Nigeria*, Enugu: Fourth Dimension Publishers, 1983.
Achebe, Chinua, *Hopes and Impediments*, Oxford: Heinemann International, 1988.
Ademoyega, Adewale, *Why We Struck: The Story of the First Nigerian Coup*, Ibadan: Evans Brothers (Nigeria) Publishers, 1981.
Afigbo, A. E., 'Nigeria and the myths of modern democracy,' *The Champion*, Umuahia, 12 December 2000.
Ajakaye, Rafiu, 'Uwazurike and the theory of non-violence,' *Daily Independent*, Lagos, 12 November 2005.
Ajanaku, Idowu, 'Ex-colonial officer faults amalgamation of Nigeria,' *The Guardian*, Lagos, 28 April 2005.
Ake, Claude, *A Political Economy of Nigeria*, Harlow: Longman Group, 1981.
Ake, Claude, ed., *Political Economy of Nigeria*, London and Lagos: Longman, 1985.
Akinola, Wale, and John Nwokocha, 'Chinua Achebe to Obasanjo: Keep your CFR award – "Nigeria's condition under your watch is too dangerous for silence",' *The Vanguard*, Lagos, 17 October 2004.
Amnesty International South Africa, 'Obasanjo must surrender Charles G. Taylor,' http://www.amnesty.org.za/campaigns/charles_taylor.htm
Amoda, Moyiba, 'Background to the Conflict: A Summary of Nigeria's Political History from 1914 to 1964,' in Joseph Okpaku, ed., *Nigeria: Dilemma of Nationhood*, New York: Third Press, 1972.
Ananaba, Wogu, *The Trade Union Movement in Nigeria*, Benin City: Ethiope Publishing Corporation, 1969.
Anifowose, Remi, *Violence and Politics in Nigeria*, New York and

Enugu: Nok Publishers International, 1982.
Awolowo, Obafemi, *Path to Nigerian Freedom*, London: Faber and Faber, 1947.
Ayorinde, Oluokun, 'MASSOB Has 2 Million Members – SSS DG,' *PM News*, Lagos, 12 April 2006.
Barnett, Antony, 'UK arms sales reach £1 billion mark,' *The Observer*, London, 12 June 2005.
BBC, http://news.bbc.co.uk/1/hi/world/africa/4268733.stm
BBC, http://news.bbc.co.uk/1/hi/business/4238045.stm
BBC, http://news.bbc.co.uk/1/hi/world/africa/4586832.stm
BBC, http://news.bbc.co.uk/1/hi/in_depth/uk_politics/2001/conferences_2001/labour/1575135.stm
BBC, http://www.pbs.org/newshour/bb/remember/mitterrand_1-8b.html
Busch, Gary K., 'Bí a bá tò sílé, onípò a m? ipò' ('If someone wets the bed, each person should know where he or she slept'), http://www.ocnus.net/artman/publish/article_21647.shtml
Calder, Angus, 'Review of Christopher Okigbo, *Labyrinth*,' *New Statesman*, London, 28 April 1972, http://www.complete-review.com/reviews/nigeria/okigbo1.htm
Chabal, P. and J-P Daloz, *Africa Works: Disorder as Political Instrument*, Oxford: James Currey, 1999.
'Children Under Arms,' *The Economist*, London, 10 July 1999.
Chinweizu, Onwuchekwa Jemie and Ihechukwu Madubuike, *Toward the Decolonization of African Literature, Vol. 1*, Enugu: Fourth Dimension Publishers, 1980.
Clapham, Christopher, 'Failed States and Non-states in the Modern International Order,' paper presented at conference on failed states, Florence, Italy, April 2000, http://www.ippu.purdue.edu/failed_states/2000/papers/clapham.html
CNN, http://edition.cnn.com/2006/WORLD/africa/02/02/africa.guns.reut/index.html
Coleman, James, *Nigeria*, Berkeley: University of California, 1958.
Crocker, Chester, *Foreign Affairs*, September/October 2003.
Cronje, Suzanne, *The World and Nigeria*, London: Sidgwick and Jackson, 1972.
Crummey, Donal, ed., *Banditry, Rebellion and Social Protest in Africa*, London and Portsmouth, New Hampshire: James Currey/Heinemann, 1986.
Davidson, Basil, *Black Man's Burden: Africa and the Curse of the Nation-State*, London: James Currey, 1992.
De St Jorre, John, The *Brothers' War – Biafra and Nigeria*, Boston: Houghton Miflin, 1972.

Deschambs, Hubert, 'France in Black Africa and Madagascar between 1920 and 1945,' in L. H. Gann, and Peter Duiganan, *Colonialism in Africa, 1870-1960. Vol. Two: The History and Politics of Colonialism 1914-1960* Cambridge: Cambridge University, 1970.
Dowden, Richard, 'Redrawing the outmoded colonial map of Africa,' *Independent*, London, 10 September 1987.
Drechsler, Horst, *'Let Us Die Fighting': The Struggle of the Herero and Nama against German Imperialism, 1884-1915*, London: Zed, 1980.
Dudley, Billy, *Instability and Political Order*, Ibadan: Ibadan University, 1973.
Dudley, Billy, 'The Political Theory of Awolowo and Azikiwe,' in Onigu Otite, ed., *Themes in African Social and Political Thought*, Enugu: Fourth Dimension Publishers, 1978.
Dudley, Billy, *An Introduction to Nigerian Government and Politics*, London and Basingstoke: Macmillan, 1982.
Dunne, Louise and Kim Renfrew, 'Charles Taylor has al-Qaeda links, says Sierra Leone Special Court,' *Radio Netherlands*, http://www.radionnetherlands.nl/currentaffairs/region/africa/lib050525
Echeruo, Kevin, 'Lament of an Artist,' 1967, http://echeruo,syr.edu/okigbo/kevin%20on%20okigbo.htm
Ekundare, R. Olufemi, *An Economic History of Nigeria: 1800-1960*, London: Methuen, 1973.
Ekwe-Ekwe, Herbert 'Nzeogwu: Notes on a Controversy,' *West Africa*, London, 2 March 1987.
Ekwe-Ekwe, Herbert, 'Religion: Manipulation or Mobilisation?' *West Africa*, London, 7 December 1987.
Ekwe-Ekwe, Herbert, *Conflict and Intervention in Africa: Nigeria, Angola, Zaire*, Basingstoke and London: Macmillan, 1990.
Ekwe-Ekwe, Herbert, 'Africans and the European Wars of the 20th Century,' *African Peoples Review*, July-December 1995.
Ekwe-Ekwe, Herbert, *African Literature in Defence of History: An Essay on Chinua Achebe*, Dakar: African Renaissance, 2001.
Ekwe-Ekwe, Herbert, 'Senghor (1906-2001),' *The Literary Encyclopedia*, http://www.litencyc.com/php/speople.php?rec=true&UID=5154&PHPSESSID=21352bc3455ccec00131d9f2a1dac48a
Ekwe-Ekwe, Herbert, 'What the world should celebrate,' *openDemocracy*, http://www.opendemocracy.net/globalization-G8/africa_2662.jsp
Ekwe-Ekwe, Herbert, 'Ban all Arms Export to Africa,' *USAfricaonline.com*, http://www.usafricaonline.com/ekweekwe.africaarms.html
Ekwe-Ekwe, Herbert, 'Just ban all arms sales to Africa – nothing else

required for now,' *Nigeriaworld*, http://nigeriaworld.com/articles/2005/mar/142.html

Ekwe-Ekwe, Herbert, 'Ban arms sales to Africa – nothing else required,' *openDemocracy*, http://www.opendemocracy.net/democracy-africa_democracy/arms_2602.jsp

Ekwe-Ekwe, Herbert, 'Why African leaders are leading them nowhere,' *USAfricaonline*, http://www.usafricaonline.com/ekweekwe.nepad.html

Ekwe-Ekwe, Herbert, 'The bogey of African-French solidarity,' *USAfricanonline.com*, http://www.usafricaonline.com/ekweekwe.africafrench.html

Ekwe-Ekwe, Herbert 'Igboland: Why Obasanjo must be stopped now,' *Kwenu*, http://www.kwenu.com/publications/ekwe-ekwe/igboland_stop_obasanjo.htm

Ekwe-Ekwe, Herbert, 'Reflections on the quest of African renewal: Inclusion and People-Building,' lecture to faculty and students, African and African American Studies Program, University of Tennessee, Knoxville, United States, 10 October 2003.

Ekwowusi, Sonnie, 'Is Massob Winning Battle?' *ThisDay*, Lagos, 13 December 2005.

Fido, Elaine Savory, 'Okigbo's Labyrinths and the Context of Igbo Attidues to the Female Principle,' in Carole Boyce Davies and Anne Adams Graves, *Ngambika: Studies of Women in African Literature*, Trenton: African World, 1986.

Foreign Policy & the Fund for Peace, *Failed States Index – July/August 2005*, 2006, http://www.foreignpolicy.com/story/cms.php?story_id=3098

Gbulie, Ben, *Nigeria's Five Majors: Coup d'état of 15th January 1966 – First Inside Account*, Onitsha: Africana Education Publishers, 1981.

Human Rights Watch, 'Letter to President Obasanjo on Bringing Charles Taylor to Justice,' http://www.hrw.org/press/2003/11/nigeria-ltr111703.htm

Ikpeze, Nnaemeka, 'Post-Biafran Marginalization of the Igbo in Nigeria,' in Ifi Amadiume & Abdullahi An-Na'im, eds., *The Politics of Memory*, London and New York: Zed Books, 2000.

Iloegbunam, Chuks, 'Governor Kure's apotheosis,' *The Vanguard*, Lagos, 5 August 2003.

Innes, C. L., *Chinua Achebe*, Cambridge: Cambridge University, 1990.

Isichie, Elizabeth, *Junior History of Nigeria*, Lagos and Ibadan: Macmillan Nigeria Publishers, 1981.

Isiwu, Chuks and Chinedu Offor, 'US Intelligence Report Warns Obasanjo,' *Daily Independent*, Lagos, 7 February 2006.

Iwenjora, Fred, 'Why Igbo obeyed MASSOB's call to stay home,' Interview with MASSOB leader Raph Uwazurike, *The Vanguard*, Lagos, 4 September 2004.

Leapman, Michael, 'While the Biafrans starved, the FO moaned about

hacks,' *The Independent on Sunday*, London, 3 January 1999.
Lindqvist, Sven, *'Exterminate All the Brutes'*, London: Granta Books, 1997
Madiebo, Alexander, *The Nigerian Revolution and the Biafran War*, Enugu: Fourth Dimension Publishers, 1980.
Madubuike, Ihechukwu, *The Senegalese Novel*, Washington D.C.: Three Continents, 1983.
Mahtani, Dino, 'Biafran voices of dissent grow ever louder,' *The Financial Times*, London, 5 January 2006.
Masland, Tom, 'African Duel,' *Newsweek*, New York, 30 March 1998.
Mazrui, Ali, *The Trial of Christopher Okigbo*, http://www.complete-review.com/reviews/nigeria/okigbo2.htm
Mazrui, Ali, 'Conflict Resolution and Social Justice in the Africa of Tomorrow,' *Présence Africaine*, 3rd and 4th Quarterlies, Nos. 127/128, 1983.
Mazrui, Ali, 'The Reincarnation of the African State,' *Présence Africaine*, 3rd and 4th Quarterlies, Nos. 127/128, 1983.
McCullum, Hugh, 'Biafra was the beginning,' *AfricaFiles*, http://www.africafiles.org/article.asp?ID=5549&ThisURL=./atissueforum.asp&URLName=AT+ISSUE+FORUM
Mingus, Charles, *Charles Mingus Presents Charles Mingus*, Candid CCD 79021, New York, October 1960.
Morris, Roger, *Uncertain Greatness: Henry Kissinger & American Foreign Policy*, London & New York: Quartet Books, 1977.
Morrison, Toni, *The Nobel Lecture in Literature, 1993*, London: Chatto and Windus, 1993.
Ndibe, Okey, 'MASSOB, Ohaneze, and representation,' *Nigeriaworld.com*, http://nigeriaworld.com/feature/publications/okey-ndibe/120805.html
Nduka, Otonti, 'The rationality of the rich,' in Peter Gutkind and Peter Waterman, eds., *African Social Studies: A Radical Reader*, London: Heinemann, 1977.
News24.com, 'Nigeria census stokes tensions,' http://www.news24.com/News24/Africa/News/0,,2-11-1447_1897530,00.htm
Njoku, Lawrence, 'Traders accept Biafran pounds in Enugu,' *The Guardian*, Lagos, 12 January 2006.
Njoku, O. N., 'Contributions to War Efforts,' in Falola, Toyin, ed., *Britain and Nigeria: Exploitation or Development?* London: Zed Books, 1987.
Nnamani, Tobe, 'Biafra in Retrospect: Still Counting the Losses I,' *Kwenu*, http://www.kwenu.com/publications/nnamani/biafra_retrospect1.htm

Nnoli, Okwudiba, *Ethnic Politics in Nigeria*, Enugu: Fourth Dimension Publishers, 1980.
Nnoli, Okwudiba, 'A Short History of Nigerian Underdevelopment,' in Okwudiba Nnoli, ed., *Path to Nigerian Development*, Dakar: Codesria, 1981.
Nzegwu, Femi, *Love, Motherhood and the African Heritage: The Legacy of Flora Nwapa*, Dakar: African Renaissance, 2001.
Nzimiro, Ikenna, 'The Political Implications of Multinational Corporations in Nigeria,' in Carl Widstrand, ed., *Multi-National Firms in Africa*, Dakar and Uppsala: African Institute for Economic Development and Planning/Scandinavia Institute for African Studies, 1975.
Nzimiro, Ikenna, 'Nigeria in Search of Ideology,' *Nigerian Statesman*, Owerri, 2-12 October 1982.
Obasanjo, Olusegun, *My Command*, Ibadan and London: Heinemann, 1980.
Obasanjo, Olusegun, *Nzeogwu*, Ibadan: Spectrum Books, 1987.
Obiechina, Emmanuel, *Language and Theme*, Washington, D.C: Howard University, 1990.
Obukwelu, Samuel, 'For Nigeria, Charles Taylor or the UN Security Council?' http://www.utexas.edu/conferences/africa/ads/725.html
Obumselu, Benedict, 'Ali Mazrui's submission is rubbish,' interview with James Eze, *Daily Sun*, Lagos, 21 August 2005.
Ochiama, Christian, et al, 'UNBELIEVABLE: MASSOB order cripples business in Lagos, South-East,' *Daily Sun*, Lagos, 27 August 2004.
Odogwu, Bernard, *No Place to Hide*, Enugu: Fourth Dimension Publishers, 1985.
Ojeifo, Sufuyan and Lemmy Ughegbe, 'No regrets for the Asaba massacre of Igbo – Haruna,' *The Vanguard*, Lagos, 10 October 2001.
Okigbo, Christopher, 'Lament of the Lavender List,' 1961, Web Concordance to the Poetry of Christopher Okigbo, http://echeruo.syr.edu/okigbo/19Okigbopoems.htm
Okigbo, Christopher, 'Lament of the Masks,' 1965, Web Concordance to the Poetry of Christopher Okigbo, http://echeruo.syr.edu/okigbo/19Okigbopoems.htm
Okigbo, Christopher, *Labyrinths with Path of Thunder*, New York & Ibadan: Africana Publishing and Mbari Publications, 1971.
Okonkwo, Rudolf Ogoo, 'Igbo: The final battle I,' *Kwenu*, http://ww.kwenu.com/publications/okonkwo/igbo_battle1.htm
Oliver, Roland, 'The condition of Africa,' *Times Literary Supplement*, London, 20 September 1991.
Onimode, Bade, *Imperialism and Underdevelopment in Nigeria: The Dialectics of Mass Poverty*, London: Zed Books, 1982.
Opara, Peter, 'Two Nigerians apart, naturally,' *Kwenu*,

http://www.kwenu.com/publications/opara/2006/Nigerians_apart.htl
Osinaike, Gbenga, 'Biafran pound still being spent ... at Togo, Benin

Republic,' *Sunday Punch*, Lagos, 5 June 2005.
Osinaike, Gbenga, '... It's curious – Lagos State University don recounts experience,' *Sunday Punch*, Lagos, 5 June 2005.
Osoba, Segun, 'The Nigerian Power Elite, 1952-62,' in Peter Gutkind and Peter Waterman, eds., *African Social Studies: A Radical Reader*, London: Heinemann, 1977.
Pakenham, Thomas, 'The European share-out of the spoils of Africa,' *Financial Times*, London, 15 February 1988.
Perham, Margery, *Mining, Commerce and Finance in Nigeria*, London: Faber and Faber, 1948.
Porter, A. N. and A. A. Stockwell, British *Imperial Policy and Decolonisation, 1938-51*, Basingstoke and London: Macmillan, 1987.
Reno, William, 'African Conflicts and Contemporary Intervention,' http://www.snn.flinders.edu.ac/global/afsaap/conferences/2003proceedings/reno.PDF#search='william%20reno%20on%20shadow%20state'
Rodney, Walter, *How Europe Underdeveloped Africa*, Washington, DC: Howard University, 1982.
Roth, Kenneth, 'Surrender Taylor to War Crimes Court,' *The Guardian*, Lagos, 15 August 2005.
Schurmann, Franz, 'Africa is Saving Itself,' *Choices: The Human Development Magazine*, Vol. 5, June 1996.
Shenton, Robert, *The Development of Capitalism in Northern Nigeria*, London: James Currey, 1986.
Smith, Harold, www.libertas.demon.co.uk
Solomon, Hussein and Nikki Funke, 'Revisiting Shadow States in Africa,' http://www.ac.za/academic/cips/Publications/Revisiting%20Shadow%20States%20in%20Africa.doc
Stremlau, John, *The International Politics of the Nigerian Civil War*, Princeton: Princeton University, 1977.
The Chinua Achebe Foundation Interview Series, 'Ade Ajayi in conversation with Toluwanimi Olujimi,' *Kwenu*, 12 December 2005.
'UK arming African countries,' *BBC*, http://news.bbc.co.uk/1/hi/uk_politics/699255.stm
Uneze, Amby, 'US pressure: Taylor May Leave Nigeria,' *ThisDay*, Lagos, 14 May 2005.
United Nations, *UN News Service*, New York, 1 February 2005.
Ushigiale, Joseph, et al, 'Nigeria: Biafra separatists cripple economic activities,' *ThisDay*, Lagos, 27 August 2004.
Voice of Biafra International, news analysis, 7 January 2006,

http://www.biafraland.com/NewsAnalysis2006/newsanalysis010706.htm
Whitelaw, Marjory, 'Interview with Christopher Okigbo, 1965,' *The Journal of Commonwealth Literature*, No. 9, July 1970.
Williams, Chancellor, *The Destruction of Black Civilization*, Chicago: Third World, 1987.
Wilmot, Patrick, 'Poverty amidst riches,' *West Africa*, London, 15 August 1988.
World Bank, 'Migrant Labor Remittances in Africa,' *Africa Regional Working Paper Series, No. 64*, Washington, November 2003.
Wright, Jay, *The Homecoming Singer*, New York: Corinth, 1971.

Index

Aba, 46, 88, 136, 137, 138, 140, 141, 142
  site of Igbo genocide, phase II, 88
Abacha, Sani, 17, 17n47, 92, 101, 117, 123, 127-128
  genocidist commander, Igbo genocide, northcentral Igboland/Biafra, 92
  head of state, Nigeria, 17, 92, 101
Abagana, 88
  site of Igbo genocide, phase II, 88
Abakaliki, 87, 88, 136, 137, 138, 141, 142
  site of Igbo genocide, phase II, 88
Abati, Reuben, 131n41, 138n55
Abeokuta, 62, 72, 75, 77n31, 137
  site of Igbo genocide, phase I, 75, 77n31
Abidjan, 13
Aboh, 142
Abiriba, 140
Abubakar, Abdulsalami, 16, 17, 88, 92, 101, 117, 123, 127
  genocidist commander, Igbo genocide, northcentral Igboland/Biafra, 16, 117
  head of state, Nigeria, 17, 92, 101
Abubakar, Atiku, 17n47,
Abuja, 73-74, 116n7, 137, 138, 141
Aburi, 79-86, 133
  Aburi conference and outcome, 79-86, 133
Achebe, Chinua, 4, 15n44, 34, 34n46, 93n56, 95, 98, 99, 100-101, 101n66, 103, 104, 104n75
  Chinua Achebe Foundation Interview Series, 11n35
  condemnation of Obasanjo dictatorship and murderous regime, 119
  Things Fall Apart (Achebe), 100-101
Achebe, E. C. N., 95
Adebayo, Adeyinka, 16, 84, 85
  genocidist officer, Igbo genocide, 16
Adegbenro, Dauda, 50
Adekunle, Benjamin, 6, 16, 88, 89, 91, 117, 120
  genocidist commander, Igbo genocide, south Igboland/Biafra, 6, 6n18, 16, 88, 89, 91, 117
  unapologetic, unremorseful, defiant over perpetration of Igbo genocide, 118
Adeleke, Gani, 73
Ademoyega, Adewale, 27, 27n26, 59, 59nn1, 2, 60nn3, 6, 69n23, 73
  concept of 'tripartition' in Nigerian politics, 27, 27n26,

152 Biafra Revisited

62n11, 63n13, 66n17, 69n23
Adichie, Chimamanda Ngozi, 95
Afigbo, Adiele, 95, 98, 129n40
Africa, African, African World,
2, 3, 6n18, 9, 10, 11, 12, 13,
14, 15, 16, 21, 22, 23, 24-25,
31-32, 33, 43, 45, 46, 61, 64,
73, 76, 77, 80, 83, 87, 94, 95,
97, 99, 100-101 *passim*
   arms-ban to, 12-14
   cfa currency, 137
   children and guns, 'child soldiers', 13, 118, 118n8
   'debt', 10, 122, 122n16
   dismantling genocide states of, 10-12
   east region, German genocide in, 6n18
   émigrés' financial dispatches, 11
   'failed state', critique of, 120-125
   fighting in European wars, 20-21
   foundational genocide, post conquest, 2
   genocide killing fields in, 2, 9-10, 15
   HIV/Aids, 10
   human and non human resources expropriated during World Wars I & II, 21-25
   importance of 29 May 1966, history of, 124
   losses in First World War, 21
   losses in Second World War, 21-22
   middle classes, 10
   net export-capital transfers to the West, 122, 122n16
   non-deconstructed 'inherited' state, 129-130
   officially French-speaking west and central states of, 137
   'poverty', 10
   rich continent, 10-11
   'shadow states' of 'disorder', 126-127, 128-129
   south, southern region, 6n18
   state in Africa: centralised, alienated, alienating architecture, 126
   'structural adjustment programme', 11
   total murdered in genocide states of, 10, 120, 129
   virtual destruction of economy, 11
   west region of, 32, 94
   workers' wages in occupied Nigeria, 23
Agbaani, 88, 142
   site of Igbo genocide, phase II, 88
Agbor, 134, 140, 141
Aggrey, J. E. K., 95
Aguleri, 142
Aguyi-Ironsi, Johnson, 65, 66, 67-72, 74-75, 76-79
Agyaragu, 75
   site of Igbo genocide, phase I, 75
Ahidjo, Ahmadou, 123
Ahoada, 88, 134, 140, 142
   site of Igbo genocide, phase II, 88
Aidoo, Ama Ata, 96
Ajakaye, Rafiu, 133n47
Ajanaku, Idowu, 18n1
Ajayi, Ade, 11n35
Ajayi, Sesan, 99
Ake, Claude, 35n48, 61n8
Akeze, 89, 142
   site of Igbo genocide, phase II, 88
Akinkugbe, O. I., 52

Akinola, Wale, 119n12
Akinrinade, Alani, 16, 88, 117, 120
  genocidist commander, Igbo genocide, south Igboland/Biafra, 16, 117
Akintola, Samuel, 49-50
Akpan, N. U., 98
al-Bashier, Omar Hassan, 123
Algeria, 5, 9, 98, 122n17, 125
  active involvement in Nigerian genocide against Igbo people, 5, 9, 98, 125
al-Qaeda, 116
Amadiume, Ifi, 92n54
Amasiri, 89
  site of Igbo genocide, phase II
Ameke-Item, 119
  site of Igbo genocide, phase II, 119
America, Americas, 11, 24n17, 25, 134, 140
Amichi, 4, 119-120, 131-132
Aminu, Jibril, 16, 88, 120
  genocidist operative, Igbo genocide, 16
Amnesty International South Africa, 115n3
Amoda, Moyiba, 31n37, 32n43
Ananaba, Wogu, 22n10, 23n11, 30n34, 52nn96, 97, 98, 99, 53nn100, 101, 102, 78n32
Angas, 125
  perpetrator of genocide against Igbo people, 125
Angola, 15
Anifowose, Remi, 45nn82, 83, 49nn91, 92, 93, 50nn94, 95, 56nn110, 111, 112, 113, 57nn116, 117, 118, 119, 120
Anikulapo-Kuti, Fela, 96
Ankrah, Joseph, 82, 86
An-Na'im, Abdullahi, 92n54

Anyidoho, Kofi, 96
Arab, Arab regimes, Arab World, 1, 5, 9, 43, 75, 99, 121, 122n17, 125
  active involvement in Nigerian genocide against Igbo people, 5, 9, 125
  stake in unity-in-atrocity portfolio, Igbo genocide, 133
Are, Kayode, 16, 135-136
  claims on membership strength, Movement for the Actualisation of the Sovereign State of Biafra, 135-136
  commander, notorious state security service, 135-136
  genocidist officer, Igbo genocide, phase III, 16, 135-136
Armstrong, Louis, 4, 96
Asaba, 81, 134, 140, 141, 142
  site of Igbo genocide, phase II, 81, 88, 119
Asante, Molefi Kete, 95
Asia, 11, 22, 24, 24n17, 131, 134, 140
Asu, River, 87
Atlanta, 131
Auschwitz, death camp, 2
  liberation of, 2
Austro-Hungary, 21
Awolowo, Obafemi, 4, 5, 29-30, 30n35, 31, 33-34, 44, 49-5, 63-64, 72, 89, 90-94, 111-112, 118, 119-120, 128
  Awolowoist credo on starvation as instrument of genocide against Igbo people, 4, 89, 93-94, 112,
  Awolowoist wing of Nigerian genocidist state, 93-94, 118, 119-120
  chauvinist, exclusivist and

parochial, 31, 64, 90
electoral gerrymandering, 33
genocidist strategist and
operative, Igbo genocide, 4,
89, 91-92, 112
Path to Nigerian Freedom
(Awolowo), 30
proponent, regionalisation of
Nigerian politics, 30, 30n35,
31
reactionary, racist politics of,
34
virulence of Igbophobia, 91-
92
Awoonor, Kofi, 96
Ayida, Allison, 16, 88, 91, 93,
120
genocidist official, Igbo
genocide, 16, 88, 91, 93
The Rise and Fall of Nigeria
(Ayida), 93
Ayler, Albert, 96
Ayorinde, Oluokun, 134n48,
135n49
Azikiwe, Nnamdi, 23, 25-26, 27,
34, 44, 46, 56, 65, 90-91, 95
debates on support for anti-
German World War II
alliance, 23
initiated conference of
liberation organisations
against British
occupation, 25-26
leading editor, liberation
media, 27
Zikist Movement, 29
Azumini, 88, 140
site of Igbo genocide, phase
II, 88
Azuonye, Chukwuma, 99
Azuonye, Nnamdi, 99
Azuonye, Nnorom, 99

Bâ, Mariama, 96
Babangida, Ibrahim, 16, 17, 88,
92, 101, 117, 120, 123, 127
genocidist commander, Igbo
genocide, northcentral
Igboland/Biafra, 16, 92, 117
head of state, Nigeria, 17, 92,
101
Babylon, 105
Bach, Johann Sebastian, 4
Bachama, 125
perpetrator of genocide
against Igbo people, 125
Baldwin, James, 26
Balewa, Abubakar Tafawa, 44,
53-54, 56, 58, 62, 74
Balkans, 14, 16
Banda, Kamuzu, 123
Banjo, Victor, 73
Baraka, Amiri, 95
Basie, Count, 4
Bauchi, 75
site of Igbo genocide, phase I,
75
BBC, 1n2, 10n29, 13n40, 22n7
Belgium, 15, 25, 112
genocide perpetrated by
Belgian troops in 19th
century Congo, 15
King Leopold II, 15, 87, 112
opposition to African
liberation at end of World
War II, 25
Benin, 137
Benin Republic, 56, 67, 72, 97,
137
Benson, Bobby, 4
Benue, River, 45, 97
Berg Damara, 6n18
German genocide against, 6n18
Berlin, 118
Berom, 125
perpetrator of genocide

Index 155

against Igbo people, 125
Biafra, 3-6, 12, 14, 15, 16, 17, 87, 89-90, 99, 103 *passim See also* Igbo, Igboland
   African peoples'-centred state, 125
   currency in circulation, 137
   historic task of, 125
   Movement for the Actualisation of the Sovereign State of Biafra (MASSOB), 125, 132-133, 133n47, 134-137, 139
   reactivation of Ojike Plan, transformation of Biafra/Igboland, 139-142
   repositioning of women, transformation project, 139
   source for funding of economic-industrial transformation of, 139-140
   Voice of Biafra International, 137n54
Bible, The Holy, 4
Biko, Steve, 96
Bini, 125
   perpetrator of genocide against Igbo people, 125
Birnin-Kebbi, 75
   site of Igbo genocide, phase I, 75
Bishop, Maurice, 69
Biya, Paul, 123
Blair, Tony, British prime minister, 15, 15n43, 131
Blyden, Edward Wilmot, 95
Bokassa, Jean-Bédel, 123
Boudillon, Bernard, British governor, occupied Nigeria, 24
   no restoration of independence for British-occupied Nigeria, 24-25

Brathwaite, Edward Kamau, 96
Britain, 3, 5-7, 7n22, 8-9, 10, 12, 13, 14, 15-16, 18, 19, 20, 22, 23-25, 26, 27-30, 31, 32, 33, 34, 35, 36, 37-40, 41-42, 43, 44, 48, 52, 53, 58, 59-62, 63, 66, 72, 76-79, 86-87, 94, 98, 100-101, 103, 105-106, 109-111, 120, 121, 124, 125, 126-127, 128, 131, 137, 138, 141
   active involvement in the Nigerian genocide against Igbo people, 5-9, 58, 76-79 *passim*
   Anglo-American Atlantic Charter, 23-25
   arms exporter to both sides in Congo/Great Lakes wars, 128
   backing for Igbo genocide, phase II, 87
   British banks: destination for money looted by Nigerian leaders, 128
   British Financial Services Authority, 128
   call for apology and reparation for involvement in genocide of Igbo people, 15-16
   call for withdrawal of support for Nigerian genocide-state, 15-16
   conquest and occupation of Africa, 21, 109-111
   conquest and occupation of Ireland, 109-111
   conquest and occupation of Nigeria, 18, 100-101
   construction of Nigerian state, 18n1
   creator of Northern Peoples' Congress (NPC), 18
   current arms sales to Nigeria,

12n38, 126-127
defeat of anti-German alliance, 23
entrenched economic and strategic interests in Nigeria, 37-40, 60-62
'ethical foreign policy' rhetoric, in spite of, 128
fabricated census figures favourable to north Nigeria region, 41, 121
G8 summit, Scotland, 10
leading arms exporter to, entrenched interests in militarisation of Africa, 12-13, 14, 126-127, 128
no restoration of independence for British-occupied Nigeria, Africa, 24-25
opposition to African-sponsored Aburi conference settlement, following Igbo genocide, phase I, 85-87
range of British economic and financial interests in Nigeria, 61, 61nn7, 8, 62
rigging of countrywide election in Nigeria in favour of NPC/north region of Nigeria, 42-44, 121
stake in unity-in-atrocity portfolio, Igbo genocide, 133
support for Hausa-Fulani opposition to liberation of Nigeria, 2-3, 7-8
support for Hausa-Fulani/north hegemony in Nigeria, 2-3, 7-9, 59-62, 121
'tripartitioning' of Nigeria's political process, 27-30
underdeveloping Nigerian economy, 36

war with Germany, 20, 21
Brown, James, 96
buddhism, 105
Buhari, Muhammadu, 16, 17, 88, 92, 101, 117, 120, 123, 127
genocidist commander, Igbo genocide, northcentral Igboland/Biafra, 16, 117
head of state, Nigeria, 17, 92, 101
Bukuru, 75
site of Igbo genocide, phase I, 75
Burke, Edmund, 4
Burundi, 10, 15, 117, 128
Busch, Gary K., 17n47
Bush, George, US president, 131
Bushrui, S. B., 109
Byard, Jaki, 96

Cabral, Amilcar, 96
Calabar, 28, 46, 64
Calder, Angus, 106n79
Cambridge, Cambridge University Press, 103
Cameroon, 21, 87, 97, 116n7
Campaign Against Impunity, 115
Canada, 60, 141
Caribbean, 21, 24
Carruthers, Jacob, 96
Carter, Ron, 96
Carver, George Washington, 95
Central African Republic, 15
Césaire, Aimé, 96
Chabal, P. and J-P Daloz, 126, 126n26
'disorder as political instrument', 126
Chad, 1, 5, 9, 87, 97, 98, 116n7, 125
gwodogwodo operatives: active involvement in the

Nigerian genocide against
Igbo people: 5, 9, 87, 88, 98,
125
Charles, Ray, 96
Cherry, Don, 96
'child soldiers', 118, 118n8
Chinweizu, 104n76
christianity, 105
Chukwumerije, Uche, 98
Churchill, Winston, 24
    no restoration of
independence for British-
occupied Africa, 24-25
Clapham, Christopher, 122,
122n18, 123, 123n20
    on 'failed-state' and what it is
not, 122
Clarke, John Henrik, 96
CNN, 13n41
Cobb, Jimmy, 96
Coleman, George, 96
Coleman, James, 20, 20n5,
25n19, 26, 26nn20, 21, 27,
27n24, 28nn27, 28, 29, 30,
29nn31, 32, 33, 30n36, 42n76
Coleman, Ornette, 96
Coleman, Steve, 96
Coles, Johnny, 96
Coltrane, Alice, 96
Coltrane, John, 95, 110
Conakry, 116
Congo, Democratic Republic of,
10, 13, 15, 88, 111, 117, 118,
121, 128
    arms ban to, 13
Congo, Republic of, 10, 15, 117,
118, 128
Congo/Great Lakes wars, 128
    British involvement in, 128
Cookey, S. J., 98
Cosby, Bill, 95
Côte d'Ivoire, 9, 10, 137
Crocker, Chester, 124, 124n25

African states: without
'legitimacy and authority',
124
Cronje, Suzanne, 12n37, 89n44
Crummey, Donal, 61n7
Cullen, Countee, 96
Cummings-Bruce, Francis, 77
Curson, Ted, 96, 106n81
Czech Republic, 21

Dahomey, *see* Benin Republic
Daily Comet, 26, 27
    vanguard liberation press, 26
Daily Times, 67, 67n20,
Dairo, I. K., 4
Damas, Léon-Gontran, 96
Damaturu, 75
    site of Igbo genocide, phase I,
75
Danjuma, Theophilus, 16, 81,
117, 120
    commander, death squad that
murdered General Aguyi-
Ironsi, 81
    genocidist officer, Igbo
genocide, northcentral
Igboland/Biafra, 16, 117
Danquah, J. B., 96
Dante, 105
Darazo, 75
    site of Igbo genocide, phase I,
75
Darfur, Darfuri, 1, 1nn1, 2, 3, 4,
2, 10, 121
    'final solution' in, of, 1
    genocide in, of, 1, 2,
Davidson, Basil, 123, 123n21
    state as 'curse' on African
existence, 123
Davies, Carole Boyce, 107n84
Davies, Miles, 96, 110
Davies, Ossie, 96
Davies, Richard, 96

de Gaulle, Charles, 24n17
  opposition to African liberation, end of World War II, 24n17
de St Jorre, John, 71nn26, 27, 28, 89n45
Debussy, Claude, 106
Dee, Ruby, 96
Delaney, Martin, 96
Denmark, 73-74
  'Danish cartoons' massacre of Igbo, 73
Deschambs, Hubert, 24n17
Dike, Onwuka, 95, 98
Diop, Alioune, 95, 96
Diop, David, 15, 96
Doe, Samuel, 123
Dolphy, Eric, 96, 106, 106n81, 110
Douglass, Frederick, 95
Dowden, Richard, 123-124, 124n22
  European-created states in Africa: 'scissors and paste' job, 123-124
Drechsler, Horst, 6n18
Du Bois, W. E. B., 96
Dudley, Billy, 7-8, 8n23, 31n39, 34-35, 35n47, 40n73, 42nn78, 79, 43nn80, 81, 47nn84, 85, 86, 87, 48nn88, 89, 49n90, 55nn108, 109, 57nn114, 115, 64n15, 84nn38, 39, 85n42
Duiganan, Peter, 24n17
Dunne, Louise, 116n4
Duvivier, George, 96

Ebonyi, River, 87
Éboué, Félix, African-Guyanese governor of Chad, World War II, 22
Echeruo, Kevin, 98, 99, 113-114, 114n104
Echeruo, Michael, 96, 98, 99
Economist, The, 131n42
  endorsed President Obasanjo's project to extend his second-term presidency, contrary to the clearly-stated stipulation of the Nigerian constitution, 131n42
Edet, Louis, 56
Efiong, Philip, 98
Egbema, 140
Egonu, Uzo, 95, 98
Egwu, Sam, 133
Egypt, 5, 9, 32, 98, 122n17, 125
  active involvement in Nigerian genocide against Igbo people, 5, 9, 98, 125
Eha Amufu, 88, 134, 140, 142
  site of Igbo genocide, phase II, 88
Ejoor, David, 84, 85
  genocidist officer, Igbo genocide, 84
Eke, Ifeagwu, 98
Ekundare, R. Olufemi, 37nn56, 57, 61
Ekwe-Ekwe, Herbert, 2n5, 3nn6, 7, 9, 11, 4n12, 5n15, 9nn26, 27, 28, 10n30, 11nn31, 32, 34, 36, 13n41, 19n4, 21n6, 22n8, 24n17, 31n42, 72n29, 83n37, 102n70, 119n12, 122n16, 132n45
Ekwensi, Cyprian, 98
Ekwowusi, Sonnie, 134n48
Eliot, T. S., 105
Ellington, Duke, 4, 96, 106, 110
Emeagwali, Philip, 95
Emene, 45, 47, 140
Enahoro, Anthony, 16, 88, 91
  genocidist operative, Igbo genocide, 16, 88, 91
Enekwe, Onuora, 99

Enugwu, 34, 44, 45, 47, 72, 80, 87, 88, 118, 134, 136, 137, 140, 141, 142
   site of Igbo genocide, phase II, 88
Enugwu-Ezike, 88
   site of Igbo genocide, phase II, 88
Enwonwu, Ben, 96
Equiano, Olaudah, 95
Equitorial Guinea, 141
Esua, Eyo, 57
Ethiopia, 10, 21
Europe, European World, 11, 21, 22, 23, 24, 25, 37, 73-74, 90, 121, 122, 126, 129, 132, 134
   European Union, 14, 74
Evugbo, 88, 142
   site of Igbo genocide, 88
Evugbo Road, 88, 142
   site of Igbo genocide, 88
Eyadéma, Gnassingbé, 123
Eze, James, 99n61
Eze Nri, 95
Ezekwe, Godian, 98
Ezenwa-Ohaeto, 99
Ezera, Kalu, 98

'failed state', *see* Africa
Falola, Toyin, 23n12, 61n8
Fanon, Frantz, 96
Far East, 21
Farmer, Art, 96
Fawehinmi, Gani, 96
Ferguson, C. Clyde, 5
Fido, Elaine Savory, 107n89F
Financial Times, The, 131n42
   endorsed President Obasanjo's project to extend his second-term presidency, contrary to the clearly-stated stipulation of the Nigerian constitution, 131n42
First World War, 20, 24
Fitzgerald, Ella, 95
Foreign Policy, 120n14, 121, 121n15
France, 20, 21, 24, 24n17, 128, 137, 141
   capitulation to Germany, World War II, 24n17
   continuation of supercilious disposition to African freedom, 24n17, 25
   declares war on Germany, 20
   defeat of anti-German alliance, World War II, 23
   Versailles conference, World War I, 21
Franck, César, 106
Franklin, Aretha, 96
Frazier, E. Franklin, 96
Freeman, Morgan, 95
Freetown, 115, 115n2
   United Nations court on war crimes in and around Sierra Leone, 115-116
Freud, Sigmund, 106
Freund, William, 61n7
Fund for Peace, 120n14, 121, 121n15
Funke, Nikki, 126, 126n28

Gabon, 141
Gambia, 22
Gann, L. H., 24n17
Garba, Joe, 85, 85n41
   genocidist officer, Igbo genocide, 85
Garrison, Jimmy, 96
Garvey, Marcus, 96
Gaskiya Ta Fi Kwabo (Zaria), 82, 87, 88
   lead publication and publicity advocate, Igbo genocide, 82,

87, 88
'Let's go kill the damned Igbo' jingles, 88
Gboko, 75
    site of Igbo genocide, phase I, 75
Gbulie, Ben, 60nn4, 5, 62n12, 64nn14, 16, 66n17, 67n19, 68nn21, 22, 71n25, 98
genocide, crime of, 1, 2, 3, 4-7
Germany, 2, 4, 20, 21-24, 24n17, 25, 26, 77, 98, 125, 141
    Democratic Republic of, 77; active involvement in Nigerian genocide against Igbo people, 98, 125
    Federal Republic of, 77
    invasion of Poland, 20
    loss of occupied Africa, 21
    perpetrator of genocide against Berg Damara, Herero, Nama, Vagogo peoples, 6n18
    perpetrator of genocide against Jews, Romany, others, 2, 4
Ghana, 22, 122-123, 137
Ghandi, Mahatma, 132
Gillespie, Dizzy, 96
Glover, Danny, 96
Goldie, Taubman, 61
Gombe, 75
    site of Igbo genocide, phase I, 75
Gowon, Yakubu, 2, 3, 16, 17, 71, 72, 76, 77-78, 79-92, 101, 103, 112, 117, 118, 120, 127
    British intelligence operative, Nigeria, 71, 77-78, 79
    flagrant invocation of christian religious symbols, 102
    genocidist commander, Igbo genocide, Lagos central operational headquarters, 2, 3, 16, 118
    key operative in overthrow and murder of commander-in-chief Aguyi-Ironsi, 78
    unapologetic, unremorseful, defiant over perpetration of Igbo genocide, 118
Gozney, Richard, current chief British representative in Nigeria, 14, 15
    condemnation of murder of Igbo youth by Nigerian military and police, 14-15
Graves, Anne Adams, 107n84
Greece, 21, 105
Gudi, 75
    site of Igbo genocide, phase I, 75
Guillén, Nicolás, 96
Guinea, 5, 10, 98, 116, 120, 125
    active involvement in Nigerian genocide against Igbo people, 5, 98, 125
    casualty in war in south of country as well as Sierra Leone and Liberia, 115-116, 120
Guinea-Bissau, 10
Gumi, Abubakar, 19n4
Gusau, 75
    site of Igbo genocide, phase I, 75
Gutkind, Peter, 35n49
Guyana, 22
Gwari 125, 138
    perpetrator of genocide against Igbo people, 125

Habré, Hissène, 123
Hancock, Herbie, 96
Handel, Georg Frideric, 4

Haruna, Ibrahim, 16, 88, 117, 120
  genocidist commander, Igbo genocide, northwest/central Igboland, Biafra, 16, 117
  unapologetic, unremorseful, defiant over perpetration of Igbo genocide, 118-119
Hausa-Fulani, 2-3, 18-19, 32, 36, 55, 66, 71, 72, 94 *passim See also* north Nigeria
  'Allahu akbar' exhortative signatures, Igbo genocide, 94
  'kill the damned Igbo', Igbo genocide, 94
  'kill the infidels', Igbo genocide, 94
  opposition to the liberation of Nigeria, 2-3, 7-8, 18-19, 20
  'pakistanisation' or secession, 19
  perpetrator of genocide against Igbo people, 2-3, 7, 8 *passim See also* Biafra
  perpetrator of pogrom against Igbo people, 8-9, 19-20 *passim*
  role of emirs, muslim clerics, intellectuals, military officers, politicians, public figures, in planning and execution of Igbo genocide, 2
  sabon gari, residential districts, 94, 97
  years of anti-Igbo pogroms by, 94
Hayford, Casely, 96
Haynes, Roy, 96
Henderson, Joe, 96
Herero, 6n18
  German genocide of, 6n18
Higgins, Billy, 96
Hill, Andrew, 96
hinduism, 105

Hitler, Adolf, 118
Hobbes, Thomas, 4
Holiday, Billie, 96
Hopkins, Gerald Manley, 105
Horton, James Africanus Beale, 95
Houphouët-Boigny, Félix, 9
Hughes, Langston, 96
Hurston, Zora Neale, 95

Ibadan, 4, 44, 51, 62, 71, 72, 74, 75, 76, 77n31, 93, 137
  site of Igbo genocide, phase I, 75, 77n31
  University College at,
  University of, 35, 74, 76, 93
Ibiam, Akanu, 98
Ibn Battuta, Abu Abdullah Muhammad, 2
Ibn Khaldun or Abd al-Rahman Ibn Mohammad, 2
Idi Amin Dada, 123
Idoma, 125
  perpetrator of genocide against Igbo people, 125
Ifeajuna, Emmanuel, 59, 65
Igala, 125
  perpetrator of genocide against Igbo people, 125
Igbo, Igboland, 2, 3, 4, 5, 6, 7, 8, 9, 12, 13, 13n38, 14-15, 19-20, 25, 27, 30, 31, 33, 36, 46, 66, 70-77, 77n31, 78-86, 87 *passim See also* Biafra
  Abia region of, 125, 138
  Anambra region of, 119-120, 136
  ani, 103-104
  Benue region of, 138
  call for boycott of *obusonjoist* regimes imposed on Igboland, 138
  call for British apology and

reparation for active involvement in genocide of, 15-16
call for non-cooperation with Nigerian occupation forces in Igboland, 138
call for phased evacuation of Igbo population from north Nigeria, 138
casualty in first phase of genocide of, 2, 46, 75-76, 77, 90, 97, 109, 120
casualty in second phase of genocide of, 3, 10, 12, 46, 112, 117
casualty in third phase of genocide, 13
creation of the state of Biafra at *sabon gari* death camps of north Nigeria, 124, 125
current population of, 137
'Danish cartoons' massacre of, 73-74
Delta region of, 125, 138
drastically curtail investment in Nigeria, 138
Ebonyi region of, 138
Edo region of, 138
émigrés' remittance to, 134
Enugwu region of, 138
exodus from north region and elsewhere in Nigeria, following outbreak of genocide, 76
expanding parameters of actualisation project, 138-142
extraordinary triumph of human will and tenacity, 125
first phase of genocide of, 2, 7, 8, 9, 20, 46, 66, 70-86, 94 *passim*
genocide of, 2, 3-7, 8, 9, 10, 12, 13, 14-15, 16, 20, 25, 30, 46, 58, 66, 70-86 *passim*
history of, 105
human power and economic development of, 45-46, 73
idoto, 104, 108
Igbocentric 'days of affirmation', 136-137
Imo region of, 125, 138
importance of 29 May 1966, African history, 124
irreversibility of resolve of, 124
January 12 1970: did not return to Nigeria, 124
killing fields, 10
Kogi region of, 138
'lunar eclipse' massacre of, 70
'marginalisation', 92n54, 133, 134
May 29 1966: ceased to be Nigerians forever, 124
'Miss World beauty competition' massacre of, 70
Movement for the Actualisation of the Sovereign Republic of Biafra,
    see Biafra
multidisciplinary humanpower resource, 139
Niger Delta, 12n38, 16
Nigerian occupation of, 124-125
nku-ukwa politics of opportunism, 133
Nri, 105
obusonjoists: triumvirate Ojo Maduekwe, Arthur Nzeribe, Chris Uba, 133
occupation and its termination, 124-125
ogbanje, *see* Christopher

Okigbo
ohanaeze, 133
on course: Taiwan or China or South Korea or India of Africa, 139
overwhelming boycott of Nigerian census, March 2006, 137
pogrom of, 8-9, 19-20, 27, 70, 73, 77, 94 *passim*
pro-consul politics of regimes imposed on, 133
range of professions/occupations of Igbo murdered during genocide, 96-97
reactivation of Ojike Plan, transformation of Igboland/Biafra, 139-142
rehabilitation of survivors of genocide, phase I, 80-82
repositioning of women, transformation project, 139
Rivers region of, 125
second phase of genocide of, in, 3-4, 5-7, 8, 9, 46, 86-91, 94, 95 *passim*
sites of first phase of genocide, 75
source for funding of economic/industrial transformation of, 139-140
spearhead of liberation of Nigeria, 2, 25-26
survival, triumph over forces of genocide, 98, 125
tasks for Igbo prosecutors, 131-132
third phase of Igbo genocide, 13, 119-120
total casualty of genocide of, 15, 20, 79, 120, 124, 132, 142

train with infamous cargo, Igbo genocide, phase I, 80
transformation outcome: triumph of inalienable right to freedom, 142
transformation overview, 140-142
'truce' on Nigerian campaign of Igbo genocide, 12 January 1970, 98, 120, 124, 125
trust fund transformation foundation, 139-140
unity-in-atrocity portfolio, genocide of, 133
World Igbo Congress, 133
years of anti-Igbo pogroms by Hausa-Fulani/north Nigeria, 94
Ihiala, 140
Ijo, 12n38, 72
Ike, Chukwuemeka, 98
Ikejiani, Okechukwu, 98
Ikoku, Alvan, 98
Ikpeze, Nnaemeka, 92, 92n54
Iloegbunam, Chuks, 138n56
Ilorin, 75
    site of Igbo genocide, phase I, 75
Imoudu, Michael, 29
India, 139
Innes, C. L., 124, 124n23, 129
    state in Africa: 'deeply diseased' outcome, 124, 129
International Committee of the Red Cross, 89-90
    aircraft deliberately shot down by genocidist forces, Igbo genocide, south Igboland/Biafra, 89-90
International Monetary Fund, 11
Iraq, 98, 125
    active involvement in the Nigerian genocide against

164 *Biafra Revisited*

Igbo people, 125
Irobi, Esiaba, 100
Isele-Ukwu, 88, 142
   site of Igbo genocide, phase II, 88
Ishan, 125
   perpetrator of genocide against Igbo people, 125
Isichie, Elizabeth, 7n21
Isiwu, Chuks, 131n42
islam, *see* Ali Mazrui
Israel, 5
   Six-Day War, 5
Itsekiri, 125
   perpetrator of genocide against Igbo people, 125
Iwenjora, Fred, 133n47

Jackson, Mahaila, 96
Jaja, King (Opobo), 86, 95
James, C. L. R., 96
James, George, 96
Japan, 21
Jarawa (central Nigeria), 125
   perpetrator of genocide against Igbo people, 125
Jemie, Onwuchekwa, 104n76
Jews, genocide of, 2, 5, 118
Johnson, Mobolaji, 84, 85
   genocidist officer, Igbo genocide, 84
Jones, Elvin, 96
Jones, James Earl, 96
Jordan, Clifford, 96
Jos, 8, 19, 27, 49, 50
   Igbo pogrom in, 8, 20, 27, 73
   site of Igbo genocide, phase I, 75
judaism, 105
Jukun, 125
   perpetrator of genocide against Igbo people, 125

Kaduna, 47, 54, 60n6, 69, 71, 75, 76, 77n31, 78, 79, 81, 82, 87, 88, 137
   'Let's go kill the damned Igbo' jingles, 88
   Nigerian Broadcasting Corporation radio and television Services, lead broadcaster and publicity advocate, Igbo genocide, 82, 87, 88
   site of Igbo genocide, phase I, 75, 77n31
Kafanchan, 75
   site of Igbo genocide, phase I, 75
Kainji, 47
Kalu, Ogbogu, 98
Kalu, Orji Uzor, 133
Kano, 8, 18, 19-20, 29, 45, 55, 75, 78, 79, 137, 141
   Igbo pogrom in, 8, 19-20
   site of Igbo genocide, phase I, 75
Kantagora, 75
   site of Igbo genocide, phase I, 75
Kanuri, 125
   perpetrator of genocide against Igbo people, 125
Karenga, Maulana, 96
Katsina, 65, 75, 84,
   site of Igbo genocide, phase I, 75
Katsina, Hassan, 65, 82, 84, 85, 87
   genocidist officer, Igbo genocide, 81
Kaunda, Kenneth, 9
Kaura-Namoda, 75
   site of Igbo genocide, phase I, 75

Keffi, 75
  site of Igbo genocide, phase I, 75
Kelly, Wynton, 96
Kemet ('ancient Egypt'), 105
  isis, 108-109
  'Kemet Thesis' of Igbo migratory origins, 108
Kenya, 94
Khartoum, 1, 13
King, Gbadamosi, 16, 88, 89-90, 120
  deliberately shot down International Committee of the Red Cross relief-carrying aircraft over south Igboland/Biafra, 89-90
  genocidist pilot, Igbo genocide, south Igboland/Biafra, 16
King, Martin Luther, 95, 132
Kinshasa, 121
Kogbara, Ignatius, 98
Koran, The, 2
ku-klux klan, 107

Lafia, 75
  site of Igbo genocide, phase I, 75
Lagos, 4, 18, 22, 25-26, 28, 30, 42, 44, 46, 48, 49, 55, 56, 65, 66, 71, 72, 74, 77, 77n31, 81, 137, 141
  site of Igbo genocide, phase I, 75, 77n31
  University of, 11n35, 74, 77
Lamming, George, 96
Lancet, The, 13n40
Langtang, 75
  site of Igbo genocide, phase I, 75
Largema, A., 62
Lawson, Rex, 4

Leapman, Michael, 6n17
Lee, Spike, 96
Leopold II, King, 15
  genocide perpetrated by king's Belgian troops in Congo, 15
Lewis, John, 96
Liberia, 10, 21, 115, 115n2, 116, 116n7, 117, 118, 120
  casualty in war in the country as well as Sierra Leone and southern Guinea, 115-116, 120
Libya, 122n17
Lincoln, Abbey, 96
Lindqvist, Sven, 6n18
Little, Booker, 96
London, 15, 16, 20, 24, 29, 41, 48, 66, 70, 78, 87
  University of, 35
Lugard, Frederick, British governor, occupied Nigeria, 16n45, 61
  'Lugardian contraption', 'Lugardian cage', 'Lugardian project', 16, 43, 78
  'nigger's area', Nigeria, 61
Lumumba, Patrice, 69, 111

Macauley, Herbert, 23, 29
  death of, 29
  debates on anti-German World War II alliance, 23
MacKay, Claude, 96
Mada, 75
  site of Igbo genocide, phase I, 75
Madiebo, Alexander, 7n19, 76n30
Madubuike, Ihechukwu, 95n60, 104n76
Maduekwe, Ojo, 133
  obusonjoist, 133

Mahtani, Dino, 137n51
Maiduguri, 47, 71, 79, 137
  'lunar eclipse' massacre of Igbo, 70
Makurdi, 75
  site of Igbo genocide, phase I, 75
Malcolm X, 95
Mallarmé, Stéphane, 105
Mandela, Nelson, 10, 95
Mangu, 75
  site of Igbo genocide, phase I, 75
Marley, Bob, 96
Marsalis, Wynton, 96
Maxwell, D. E., 109
Mazrui, Ali, 93, 93n55, 94, 94n57, 95, 95nn58, 59, 98-99, 99n62
  dar el harb (abode of war), 94, 99
  dar el islam (abode of islam), 94
  islam, islamic proselytising, 94-95, 99
  leading ideologue of islamic expansionism in Africa, 94
  opposition to Igbo resisitance to genocide, 95, 98-99
  The Trial of Christopher Okigbo (Mazrui), 94, 95, 99
Mbakwe, Sam, 98
Mbeki, Thabo, South Africa president, 131
McCullum, Hugh, 3nn8, 10, 5n14
McLean, Jackie, 96
McNamara, Dennis, 13
Mengistu Haile Mariam, 123
Mensah, E. T., 4
Middle East, 11, 94
Milton, John, 4, 105
Mingus, Charles, 95, 106, 106n81, 110

Charles Mingus Presents Charles Mingus (Mingus), 106
Minna, 75
  site of Igbo genocide, phase I, 75
Mitterand, François, 22, 128
  'Without Africa, France will have no history in the 21st century', 128
Mobutu Sese-Seko, 111, 127
Modebe, Anthony, 98
Mohammed, Murtala, 17, 81, 101, 117, 118-119, 123
  'butcher of Asaba', 118-119
  commander, west Niger massacres of Igbo male, 81
  genocidist officer, Igbo genocide, northwest, north, northcentral Igboland/Biafra, 81, 117
  head of state, 92, 101
Moi, Daniel arap, 123
Mojekwu, C. C., 98
Mokelu, Janet, 98
Mokwa, 75
  site of Igbo genocide, phase I, 75
Monitor, The (Kampala), 128
Monk, Thelonious, 96, 106, 110
Monrovia, 13, 115n2
Morgan, Adeyinka, 52
  Morgan Commission, 52-53
Morgan, Lee, 96
Morning Post, 67, 67n19, 68, 68nn21, 22
Morocco, 122n17
Morris, Roger, 5n16
Morrison, Toni, 96
Mozart, Wolfgang Amadeus, 4
Mubi, 75
  site of Igbo genocide, phase I, 75

Mugabe, Robert, 123
Munonye, John, 98
Murray, David, 96
Murray, Sunny, 96
Museveni, Yoweri, 123

Nairobi, 13
Nama, 6n18
    German genocide against, 6n18
Namibia, 6n18, 21, 128
    German genocide in, 6n18
Ndem, Okoko, 98
Ndibe, Okey, 134n48
Ndu, Pol, 98, 99
Nduka, Otonti, 36n53
Nduka, Uche, 100
Neto, Agostinho, 96
New Nigeria (Kaduna), 82, 87, 88
    lead publication and publicity advocate, Igbo genocide, 82, 87, 88
    'Let's go kill the damned Igbo' jingles, 88
Ngugi wa Thiong'o, 96
Nguru, 75
    site of Igbo genocide, phase I, 75
Nichols, Herbie, 96
Niger, Republic of, 87, 97
Niger, River, 81, 119, 141
    west of, site of Igbo genocide, phase II, 81
Nigeria, 2-10, 12, 13, 14-15, 16-17, 18 *passim*
    Action Group, 18, 19, 20, 30-31, 32, 33-34, 40-51, 54, 55
    agbada, 4
    air force, 5
    alimajiri, 'area boys', 4
    all-Nigeria project, *see* Igbo, National Council of Nigeria and Cameroon
    Anglo-Swiss banks' destinations of looted funds by leaders of, 127-128
    arms ban to, 13
    aso oke, 4
    babariga, 4
    breathtakingly obscene: bid for UN security council, 116-117
    British entrenched economic and strategic interests in, 37-40
    British fabrication of census figures favourable to north region of, 41
    British rigging of countrywide election in favour of NPC/north region of, 42-44
    cascaded into degenerative slump, 125
    catastrophic precedence, 118
    census figures rigged and aftermath, 47-48
    commendation for US reported opposition to 'bid' for seat on UN security council by, 116-117
    coup d'état, 58, 59-60, 60nn3, 6, 62-70
    current British arms sales to, 13, 126-127
    dan doka, 67
    'Danish cartoons' massacre of Igbo, 73-74
    east region of, 2, 19, 34, 35, 40-51, 72, 74 *passim*
    effect of 1945 countrywide workers' strike on quest for freedom, 26-27
    essential collapse of state of, 125
    failure to accomplish final goal of Igbo genocide, 98,

125
fraudulent elections, 55-58
genocide-state, 5-11, 12, 14-15, 16 *passim*
genocidist officials, generals, 16, 17
head of state: flagrant invocation of christian religious symbols, 102
January 12 1970: 'truce' on campaign of Igbo genocide, 98, 120, 124, 125
Justice Oputa Commission on Nigerian state's violation of human rights, 119
kleptocracy, kteptocratic state, 17, 17n47
'Lugardian contraption', *see* Frederick Lugard
'lunar eclipse' massacre of Igbo, 70
Macpherson Constitution, 33
midbelt province of north region, 45, 54, 62
midwest region of, 55
'Miss World beauty competition' massacre of, 70
murders the Igbo, 16
National Council of Nigeria and Cameroon (NCNC), freedom party, 18, 19, 20, 23, 25-27, 28-34, 39, 40-51, 53-54, 55, 63, 73, 91
National Union of Nigerian Students, 67
neo-Royal Nigeria Company estate, 128
Niger Delta, 12n38, 16, 134, 140
Nigeria, Charles Taylor and genocide, 115-118
Nigerian National Alliance, 51, 55-57, 62-63, 64, 67, 69, 70, 78
Nigerian National Democratic Party, 51, 57, 62
Nigerian Youth Movement, 28, 29-30
'nigger's area', *see* Frederick Lugard
no restoration of independence after British victory in World War II, 24-25
north region of, 2, 7, 18-20, 32-33, 34, 35, 40-51, 55, 58, 59, 60, 60n6, 61, 62, 63, 65-66, 67, 70 *passim*
Northern Elements Progressive Union, 33, 45, 55
Northern Peoples' Congress (NPC), islamo-aristocratic party of Hausa-Fulani interests, 18-19, 20, 31-33, 34, 40-51, 53-54, 55, 57, 58, 59, 62-63, 64, 67, 69, 78, 111 *See also* Hausa-Fulani
'northernisation' policy, 32, 76-77
'obnoxious ordinances', 28-30
occupation of Biafra/Igboland and its termination, 124-125
perpetrator of Igbo genocide, 2, 3-10 *passim See also* Biafra
perpetrator of Igbo pogroms since 1945, 8-9, 19-20, 27, 70, 73, 77
perpetrators of Igbo genocide: unapologetic, unremorseful, defiant, 118ff
plateau province, north region, 55
police craving to be deployed to Igboland, 138-139
poorly-run state, indices of,

135-136
  pressure from United States to handover ex-President Taylor of Liberia to UN special court on Sierra Leone, 116-117, 120
  reestablishment of independence of, 18
  regionalisation, education, economy, 35-37
  Richards Constitution, *see* Arthur Richards
  south region of, 7, 19, 59-60, 60nn3, 6, 65, 66
  train with infamous cargo, Igbo genocide, phase I, 80
  Transparency International on, 128
  'tripartitioning' of political landscape, 27-30, 33
  troops who fought in World War II, 21
  union of students, 25
  United Labour Congress, 51, 52n96
  United Middle Belt Congress, 33, 45, 54
  United Peoples Party, 50
  United Progressive Grand Alliance, 51, 55-5-57
  war-time hardship, 22-25
  west region of, 19, 30-31, 34-35, 40-51, 58, 62, 67, 73, 90 *passim*
  'work of Allah' victory, 57
  workers' strike for freedom of country (1945), 26-27
  workers' strike on country's deteriorating social and political situation (1964), 53-54
  workers' wages during occupation, 23
Nile, River, 97

Ningi, 75
  site of Igbo genocide, phase I, 75
Njoku, Eni, 95, 98
Njoku, Lawrence, 137n51
Njoku, O. N., 23nn12, 15, 24n17
Nkalagu, 45, 47, 88
  site of Igbo genocide, phase II, 88
Nnamani, Chimaroke, 133
Nnewi, 140
Nnobi, 142
Nnoli, Okwudiba, 8n25, 19nn2, 3, 27n25, 31, 31nn37, 38, 40, 41, 34n45, 37n62, 38nn63, 64, 65, 66, 67, 68, 90, 90n52, 91n53
Nsukka, 35, 74, 77, 87, 88, 137, 140, 141, 142
  jettison anachronistic name: University of Nigeria, 142
  site of Igbo genocide, phase II, 88
  University of, first fully-fledged university in Nigeria, southeast west Africa, 35, 74, 77
Numan, 75
  site of Igbo genocide, phase I, 75
Nwankwo, Chimalum, 99
Nwankwo, Nkem, 98
Nwapa, Flora, 96, 98
  Efuru (Nwapa), 100
Nwoga, Donatus, 95, 98
Nwokedi, Alex, 98
Nwokedi, C. O., 52
Nwokocha, John, 119n12
Nwokolo, Chukwuedo, 98
Nwosu, Maik, 100
Nyerere, Julius, 9, 96
Nzegwu, Okwuonicha Femi, 36n53, 100, 100nn64, 65,

139n57
Love, Motherhood and the African Heritage (Nzegwu), 100
Nzegwu, Theophilus Enwezor, 96
Nzekwu, Onuora, 98
Nzeogwu, Chukwuma, 59, 62-63, 66, 67, 69, 71, 75
Nzeribe, Arthur, 133
  obusonjoist, 133
Nzimiro, Ikenna, 32n44, 61nn8, 9, 62, 62n10

Obasanjo, Olusegun, 4, 7, 7n19, 13n38, 15, 16, 17, 17n47, 66n17, 72, 72n29, 82n34, 84n40, 88, 89, 89nn46, 47, 48, 49, 90, 90nn50, 51, 92-93, 101, 102, 115, 115n2, 116, 116n7, 117, 120, 123, 125, 127, 130, 131n42, 132, 132n45, 133, 136
  call for restrictions on travel and sequestration of assets of, 132
  endorsement from *The Economist* (London) and *The Financial Times* (London) for plans to extend second-term presidency, contrary to Nigerian constitutional provisions, 131n42
  flagrant invocation of christian religious symbols, 102
  fleecing treasury to extend presidential term, 131
  genocidist commander, Igbo genocide, south Igboland/Biafra, 4, 7, 16, 17, 72, 89-90, 92-93
  head of state, Nigeria, 4, 7, 13n38, 17, 72, 92-93, 101, 102
  'kitchen cabinet', 136
  obusonjoist(s), 133, 136, 139
  'travelling supremo', 102
  unapologetic, unremorseful, defiant over perpetration of Igbo genocide, 119-120, 130-131
  virulence of Igbophobia, 92-93
Obenga, Théophile, 96
Obi, Chike, 96
Obiechina, Emmanuel, 96, 98, 101, 101n69
Obiigbo, 88
  site of Igbo genocide, phase II, 88
Obollo Afo, 88, 134
  site of Igbo genocide, phase II, 88
Obollo Eke, 88
  site of Igbo genocide, phase II, 88
Obote, Milton, 123
Observer, The, 12n38
Obukwelu, Samuel, 116n6
Obumselu, Benedict, 98, 99n61
Ochiama, Christian, 134n48
Odili, Peter, 133
Odogwu, Bernard, 82nn35, 36, 85n43
Odumegwu-Ojukwu, Chukwuemeka, 25, 79-87, 95, 98, 133
  blunt censure of former colleagues' involvement in Igbo genocide, 83-87
Offor, Chinedu, 131n42
Oguibe, Olu, 99-100
Ogwashi-Ukwu, 88, 134
  site of Igbo genocide, phase II, 88
Ogwu, 88

site of Igbo genocide, phase II, 88
Ohadike, Don, 96
Ojeifo, Sufuyan, 119n11
Ojike, Mbonu, 45, 96,
   Ojike Transformation Plan, reactivation of, 45-46, 139-142
Oka, 88, 137, 140, 141
   site of Igbo genocide, phase II, 88
Okadigbo, Chuba, 98
Okara, Gabriel, 98
Okeke, Uche, 96, 98
Okigbo, Christopher, 4, 94, 95, 98-99, 99n61, 100-101, 101nn66, 67, 102, 102n72, 103, 103n74, 104, 104n77, 105, 105n78, 106, 106nn80, 82, 107, 107nn83, 85, 86, 87, 88, 90, 108, 108nn91, 92, 93, 94, 95 109, 109nn96, 97, 110-111, 111nn98, 99, 100, 112, 112nn101, 102, 113n103, 114
   Africa's most celebrated poet and influences, 99-100
   call for: Christopher Okigbo University, 142
   Distances (Okigbo), 107
   'fireseed' of conquest, 109ff
   Heavensgate (Okigbo), 100, 102, 104, 106, 107, 108
      influences on, 105-106
   Labyrinths (Okigbo), 104, 111
   'Lament of the Lavender Mist', 106
   'Lament of the Masks', 109
   Limits (Okigbo), 101, 107, 108
   ogbanje, 114
   Okigboan humanism, 99-114
   Path of Thunder (Okigbo),
104, 109, 111, 112
   primacy of African spirituality and religiocultural system, 99ff
   Silences (Okigbo), 111
Okigbo, Pius, 95, 98
Okigwe, 88, 136, 140
   site of Igbo genocide, phase II, 88
Oko, Akomaya, 99
Okonkwo, Rudolf Ogoo, 8n24
Okonta, Eddie, 4
Okpaku, Joseph, 31n37
Okpanku, Agwu, 98
Okpara, Michael, 98
Okposi, 140
Okwu, Celestine, 98
Olaiya, Victor, 4
Oliver, Roland, 123, 123n19
   'first world' standards, 123
Olujimi, Toluwanimi, 11n35
Onicha, 45, 88, 134, 136, 137, 138, 140, 141, 142
   site of Igbo genocide, phase II, 88
Onimode, Bade, 37nn55, 58, 59, 60
Onwuatuegwu, Tim, 98
Onwuejiogwu, Angulu, 95
Onyango-Obbo, Charles, 128
   British arms sales to both sides in Congo/Great Lakes wars, 128
Onyia, Zeal, 4
Opara, Peter, 78, 78n33
Opi, 88
   site of Igbo genocide, phase II, 88
Opobo, 89, 134, 140, 141, 142
   site of Igbo genocide, phase II, 89
Oragwu, Felix, 98
Organisation of African Unity, 3,

80
  indifference to Igbo genocide, 3
Orizu, Nwafor, 65
Orlu, 136, 140
Osadebe, Dennis, 98
Osadebe, Osita, 4, 98
Osinaike, Gbenga, 137nn52, 53
Osoba, Segun, 35nn49, 50, 51, 52, 53, 39nn69, 70, 71, 72
Osogbo, 75
  site of Igbo genocide, phase I, 75
Osundare, Niyi, 100
Otukpo, 75
  site of Igbo genocide, phase I, 75
Ovid, 105
Owere, 88, 119, 136, 137, 138, 141
  site of Igbo genocide, phase II, 88
Oyo, 75
  site of Igbo genocide, phase I, 75
p'Bitek, Okot, 96
Pacific, The, 24n17
Paine, Thomas, 4
Pakenham, Thomas, 124, 124n24
  'craziness' of these cartographical stetches, 124
Pakistan, 19, 32
  'pakistanisation' or secession, 19 *See also* Hausa-Fulani
Paris, 24
Parker, Charlie, 96, 106, 110
Perham, Margery, 30, 61n8
  ideologue of British occupation regime, Nigeria, 10
Peters, Karl, 6n18
Pettiford, Oscar, 95
Poitier, Sydney, 96

Poland, 20, 21, 125
  active involvement in the Nigerian genocide against Igbo people, 125
  invaded by Germany, 20
Porter, A. N., 24nn16, 17
Pound, Ezra, 105
Powell, Bud, 96, 110
Présence Africaine (Paris), 95
Pretoria, 21, 131

Ransome-Kuti, Funmilayo, 96
Ravel, Joseph-Maurice, 106
Rawlings, Jerry, 123
Renfrew, Kim, 116n4
Reno, William, 126, 126n27
  'state shadow' concept, 126
Ribadu, Nuhu, 16-17
Richards, Arthur, British governor, occupied Nigeria, 25, 28
  British governor, occupied Jamaica, 25
  Richards Constitution, 28-30, 33, 34
Richmond, Danny, 99, 106n81
Rivers, Sam, 96
Roach, Max, 96
Robertson, James, British governor, occupied Nigeria, 43, 121
  subversion of electoral process, 43, 121
Rodney, Walter, 22n9, 95
Rollins, Sonny, 96
Roth, Kenneth, 115n1
Rotimi, Oluwole, 16, 117, 120
  genocidist commander, Igbo genocide, south Igboland/Biafra, 16, 117
Rousseau, Jean-Jacques, 4
Russell, George, 95
Rwanda, 10, 15, 88, 117, 118,

128
Salem, Kam, 84, 85
   genocidist officer, Igbo genocide, 84
Saminaka, 75
   site of Igbo genocide, phase I, 75
Sanders, Pharoah, 96
Sandhurst, military academy, 79
São Tomé and Principe, 141
Saudi Arabia, 5, 32, 98, 125
   active involvement in Nigerian genocide against Igbo people, 5, 98, 125
Schurmann, Franz, 102, 102n71, 129
Schwarz, Walter, 84
Scott, Robert, 89
   Nigerian military rampage in Igboland/Biafra: 'best defoliant agent known', 89
Seacole, Mary, 95
Second World War, 20, 23-25, 118, 125
   aftermath of war on African liberation, 23-25
Sembene, Ousmanne, 96
Senegal, Senegalese, 15
Senghor, Léopold Sédar, 96
Shagari, Shehu, 92
   genocidist official, Igbo genocide, 92
Shakespeare, William, 2, 4
Shaw, Woody, 96
Shendam, 75
   site of Igbo genocide, phase I, 75
Shenton, Robert, 61n8
Shonekan, Ernest, 92
   genocidist official, Igbo genocide, 92
Shorter, Wayne, 96

Sierra Leone, 10, 22, 88, 115, 115n3, 116, 118, 120
   casualty in long war of 1980s-1990s, 115, 116, 120
Silver, Horace, 96
Simone, Nina, 95
Slovakia, 21
Smith, Harold, 7n22, 18, 18n1, 41, 41nn74, 75, 42n77
Smithers, Peter, 18n1
   British construction of Nigerian state, 18n1
Sojourner Truth, 95
Sokei, Chudi, 98
Sokoto, 65, 75, 79
   site of Igbo genocide, phase I
Solanke, Ladipo, 96
Solomon, Hussein, 126, 126n28
Somalia, 10, 121
South Africa, 10, 21, 32, 61, 78, 121, 131, 132, 141
   National Party, 32
South America, 24
South Korea, 139
Southern World, 25
Soviet Union, 5, 9, 77, 125, 126, 133
   active involvement in Nigerian genocide against Igbo people, 5, 9, 125
   stake in unity-in-atrocity portfolio, Igbo genocide, 133
Soyinka, Wole, 73, 99
Stiglitz, Joseph, 128
Stockwell, A. A., 24nn16 17
Strayhorn, Billy, 96
Stremlau, John, 6n18
Sudan, The, 1, 5, 9, 10, 13, 32, 43, 117, 121, 122, 125
   arms ban to, 13
   active involvement in Nigerian genocide against Igbo people, 5, 9, 125

perpetrator of genocide in Darfur, 1 *See also*, Darfur
Sun Ra, 95
Sura, 125
   perpetrator of genocide against Igbo people, 125
Sutherland, Efua, 96
Switzerland, 128
   Swiss banks: destination for money looted by Nigerian leaders, 128
Syria, 5, 32, 125
   active involvement in Nigerian genocide against Igbo people, 5, 125

Taiwan, 139
Takum, 75,
   site of Igbo genocide, phase I, 75
Tanglawaja, 75
   site of Igbo genocide, phase I, 75
Tanzania, 9, 21
Tatum, Art, 96
Taylor, Cecil, 96
Taylor, Charles, 115, 115n2, 116, 116n7 117-118, 120, 123, 127
   charges of crimes against humanity, 115-117, 120
Terry, Clark, 95
The Hague, 16, 120, 131
   International Criminal Court, 16, 88, 92, 120, 131
ThisWeek (Lagos), 118
Tiv, Tivland, 13n38, 45, 54, 72, 125
   perpetrator of genocide against Igbo people, 125
Togo, 21, 137
Tosh, Peter, 96
Touré, Ahmed Sékou, 123

Transition, 108, 111
Transparency International, 128
   on Nigeria: 128
Tubman, Harriet, 96
Tunisia, 122n17
Tutsi, 10
Tyner, McCoy, 96

U Thant, 3
Uba, Chris, 133, 136
   obusonjoist, 133, 136
Uburu, 140
Udechukwu, Obiora, 99
Udenwa, Achike, 133
Udi, 88, 140
   site of Igbo genocide, phase II, 88
Uganda, 10, 117, 128
Ughegbe, Lemmy, 119n11
Ugwuocha/Port Harcourt, 45, 88, 134, 136, 137, 138, 140, 141, 142
   site of Igbo genocide, phase II, 88
Ugwuta, 89, 140, 141
   site of Igbo genocide, phase II, 89
Ukehe, 88
   site of Igbo genocide, phase II, 88
Ukwu, Celestine, 4
Umu Ubani/Bonny, 89, 134, 140, 142
   site of Igbo genocide, phase II, 89
Umuahia, 88, 137, 138
   site of Igbo genocide, phase II, 88
Umuebelengwu, 140
Umunede, 88
   site of Igbo genocide, phase II, 88
Uneze, Amby, 116n6

United Nations, 1, 1n1, 1nn3, 4, 2, 5, 9, 10, 80, 94, 115
general assembly commemoratory session, Auschwitz liberation, 2
indifference to Igbo genocide, 3, 5
investigating commission report on Darfur, 1
secretary-general, 10
security council, 116
United States, 14, 21, 77, 116, 116n7, 117, 120, 127, 137, 141 commendation for US reported opposition to Nigeria's 'bid' for seat on UN security council, 116-117, 132
pressure on Nigeria to handover ex-President Taylor of Liberia to UN special court on Sierra Leone, 116-117, 120
unity-in-atrocity portfolio, Igbo genocide, 133
Urhobo, 72, 125
perpetrator of genocide against Igbo people, 125
Ushigiale, Joseph, 134n48
Usman, Baba, 71, 72
Uwazurike, Ralph, 95, 133n47
Uzuakoli, 89
site of Igbo genocide, phase II, 89

Vagogo, 6n18
German genocide against, 6n18
van Beethoven, Ludwig, 4
Van Sertima, Ivan, 96
Virgil, 105
von Trotha, Lother, 6n18

Wase, 75
site of Igbo genocide, phase I, 75
Washington, 116, 116n7
Washington, Denzel, 96
Waterman, Peter, 35n49
West African Pilot (Lagos), 23, 26, 27
vanguard liberation press, 26
West, Western World, 10, 11, 13, *passim*
ban arms to Africa, 13-14
creation of 'shadow states' of 'disorder' in Africa, 126-127, 128-129
G7, G8, Davos world economic forum, 10, 13, 14
Wey, J. E., 84, 85
genocidist officer, Igbo genocide, 84
Whitelaw, Marjory, 103n73
Widstrand, Carl, 61n8
Williams, Chancellor, 96, 129, 129n39
African blood and tragedy in history, 129
Williams, Tony, 96
Wilmot, Patrick, 70, 70n24
Wilson, Harold, British prime minister, 5, 14, 89
support for Nigerian genocide against Igbo people, 5-6, 89
Winfrey, Oprah, 96
Wonder, Stevie, 96
Wonodi, Okogbule, 99
World Bank, 11, 11n33
Wright, Jay, 96, 100, 100n63
The Homecoming Singer (Wright), 100
Wukari, 75
site of Igbo genocide, phase I, 75

Yar'Adua, Shehu, 117
genocidist officer, Igbo

genocide, 117
Yeats, William Butler, 105, 109
Yergam, 125
    perpetrator of genocide against Igbo people, 125
Yola, 75
    site of Igbo genocide, phase I, 75
Yoruba/Oduduwa, 4, 18, 30-31, 33-34, 36, 63, 64, 72-73, 81, 89 *passim*
    Action Group (AG), regionalist party of, 18
    obas (kings), north region tour of 'thanks' for Yoruba protection during Igbo genocide, phase I, 90
    Oodua People's Congress and its violence, 133
    perpetrator of genocide against Igbo people, 4 *passim*
Yugoslavia, 126
Yusufu, T. M., 52-53, 72

Zambia, 9, 15
Zaria, 66, 71, 75, 76, 77, 79
    Ahmadu Bello University: planning, logistics and execution of genocide against Igbo people, phase I, 66, 75, 76
    site of Igbo genocide, phase I, 75, 77n31
Zimbabwe, 128
Zungeru, 75
    site of Igbo genocide, phase I, 75

www.ingramcontent.com/pod-product-compliance
Lightning Source LLC
Chambersburg PA
CBHW070641300426
44111CB00013B/2198